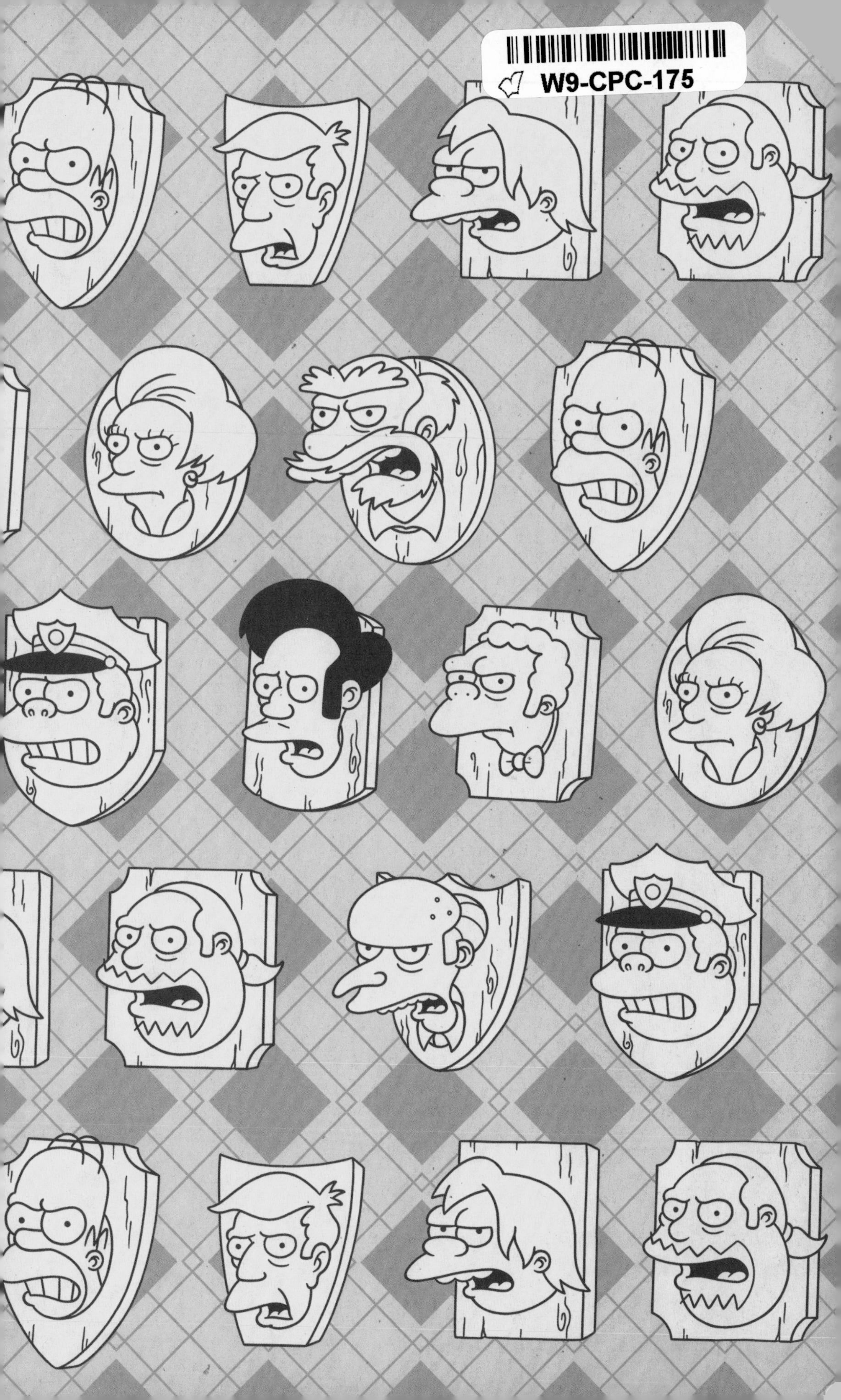

BIG BEASTLY BOOK OF
BART SIMPSON

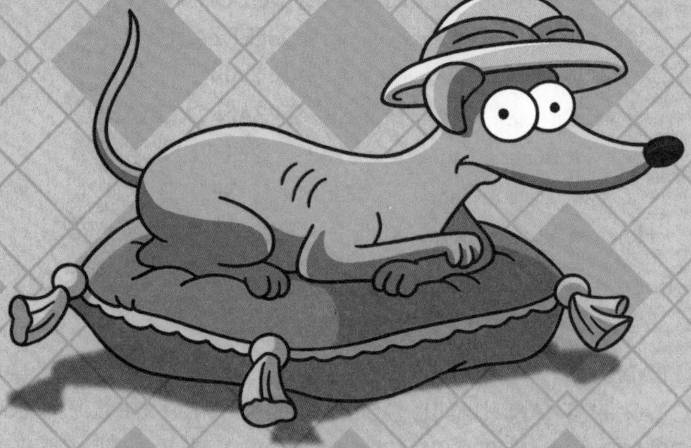

BONGO COMICS GROUP

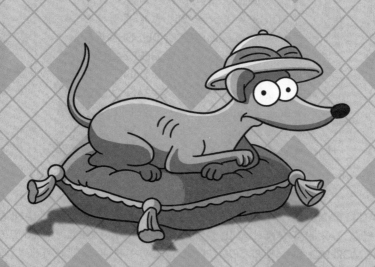

BIG BEASTLY BOOK OF BART SIMPSON

Copyright © 2004, 2005 & 2007 by
Bongo Entertainment, Inc. All rights reserved.
No part of this book may be used or reproduced in any manner whatsoever
without written permission except in the case of brief quotations
embodied in critical articles and reviews. For information address
Bongo Comics Group
P.O. Box 1963, Santa Monica, CA 90406-1963

Bongo Comics Group books may be purchased for educational, business,
or sales promotional use. For information, please call or write
P.O. Box 1963, Santa Monica, CA 90406-1963

FIRST EDITION

ISBN-10: 1-892849-19-4
ISBN-13: 978-1-892849-19-9

07 08 09 00 11 QWM 10 9 8 7 6 5 4 3 2 1

Publisher: MATT GROENING
Creative Director: BILL MORRISON
Managing Editor: TERRY DELEGEANE
Director of Operations: ROBERT ZAUGH
Art Director: NATHAN KANE
Art Director Special Projects: SERBAN CRISTESCU
Production Manager: CHRISTOPHER UNGAR
Legal Guardian: SUSAN A. GRODE
HarperCollins Editors: HOPE INNELLI, JEREMY CESAREC

Trade Paperback Concepts and Design: SERBAN CRISTESCU

Contributing Artists:
KAREN BATES, JOHN COSTANZA, SERBAN CRISTESCU, JOHN DELANEY,
LUIS ESCOBAR, NATHAN HAMILL, JASON HO, NATHAN KANE, JAMES LLOYD,
JEANETTE MORENO, BILL MORRISON, PHYLLIS NOVIN, PHIL ORTIZ, PATRICK OWSLEY,
ANDREW PEPOY, MIKE ROTE, HOWARD SHUM, ART VILLANUEVA, CHRIS UNGAR

Contributing Writers:
JAMES W. BATES, TONY DIGEROLAMO, TOM PEYER, ERIC ROGERS

PRINTED IN CANADA

TABLE OF CONTENTS

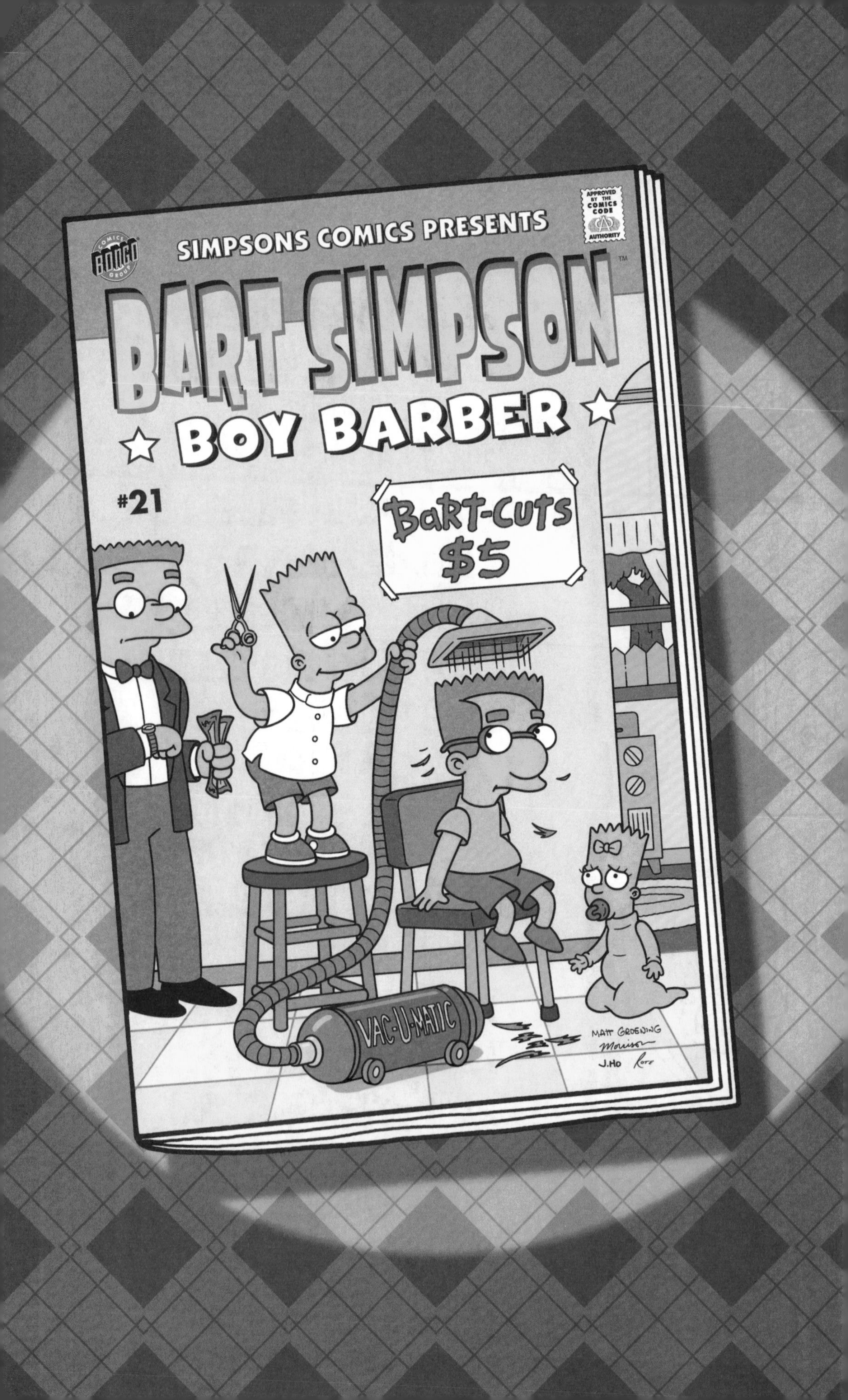
SIMPSONS COMICS PRESENTS
BART SIMPSON
BOY BARBER
#21
APPROVED BY THE COMICS CODE AUTHORITY
Bart-Cuts $5
VAC-U-MATIC
MATT GROENING

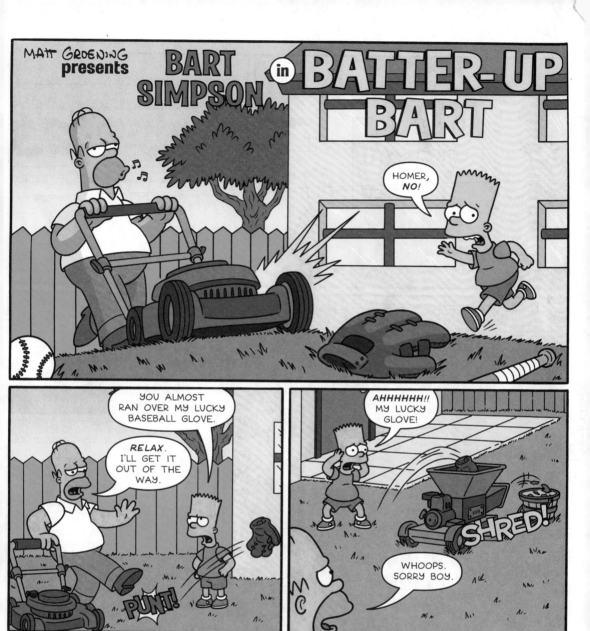

MATT GROENING **presents** BART SIMPSON **in** BATTER-UP BART

HOMER, *NO!*

YOU ALMOST RAN OVER MY LUCKY BASEBALL GLOVE.

RELAX. I'LL GET IT OUT OF THE WAY.

PUNT!

AHHHHHH!! MY LUCKY GLOVE!

SHRED!

WHOOPS. SORRY BOY.

DAD! I HAVE A GAME ON SATURDAY! YOU GOTTA BUY ME A NEW GLOVE!

WHAT FOR?

SORRY, NO CAN DO. I SPENT MY WHOLE PAY CHECK RENTING THIS WOOD-CHIPPER.

I WAS GETTING TIRED OF THOSE LITTLE JARS OF SALSA! THEY NEVER GIVE YOU ENOUGH.

SEE THAT? NOW THAT'S A *MAN-SIZED* QUANTITY FOR *MAN-SIZED* DIPPING!

SHRED! SHRED! SHRED!

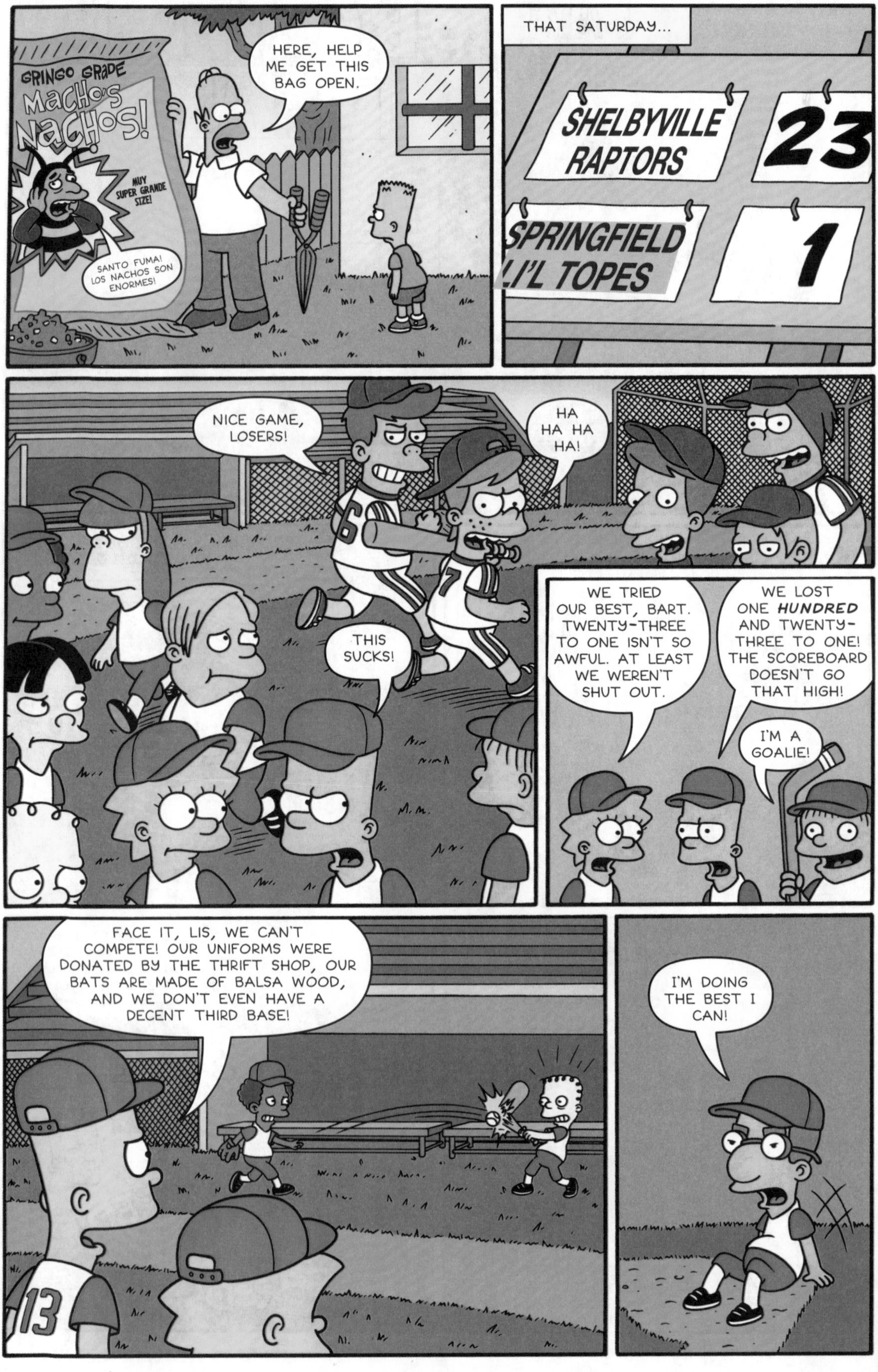
GRINGO GRADE
MACHO'S NACHOS!
MUY SUPER GRANDE SIZE!
SANTO FUMA! LOS NACHOS SON ENORMES!
HERE, HELP ME GET THIS BAG OPEN.
THAT SATURDAY...
SHELBYVILLE RAPTORS
23
SPRINGFIELD LI'L TOPES
1
NICE GAME, LOSERS!
HA HA HA HA!
THIS SUCKS!
WE TRIED OUR BEST, BART. TWENTY-THREE TO ONE ISN'T SO AWFUL. AT LEAST WE WEREN'T SHUT OUT.
WE LOST ONE **HUNDRED** AND TWENTY-THREE TO ONE! THE SCOREBOARD DOESN'T GO THAT HIGH!
I'M A GOALIE!
FACE IT, LIS, WE CAN'T COMPETE! OUR UNIFORMS WERE DONATED BY THE THRIFT SHOP, OUR BATS ARE MADE OF BALSA WOOD, AND WE DON'T EVEN HAVE A DECENT THIRD BASE!
I'M DOING THE BEST I CAN!

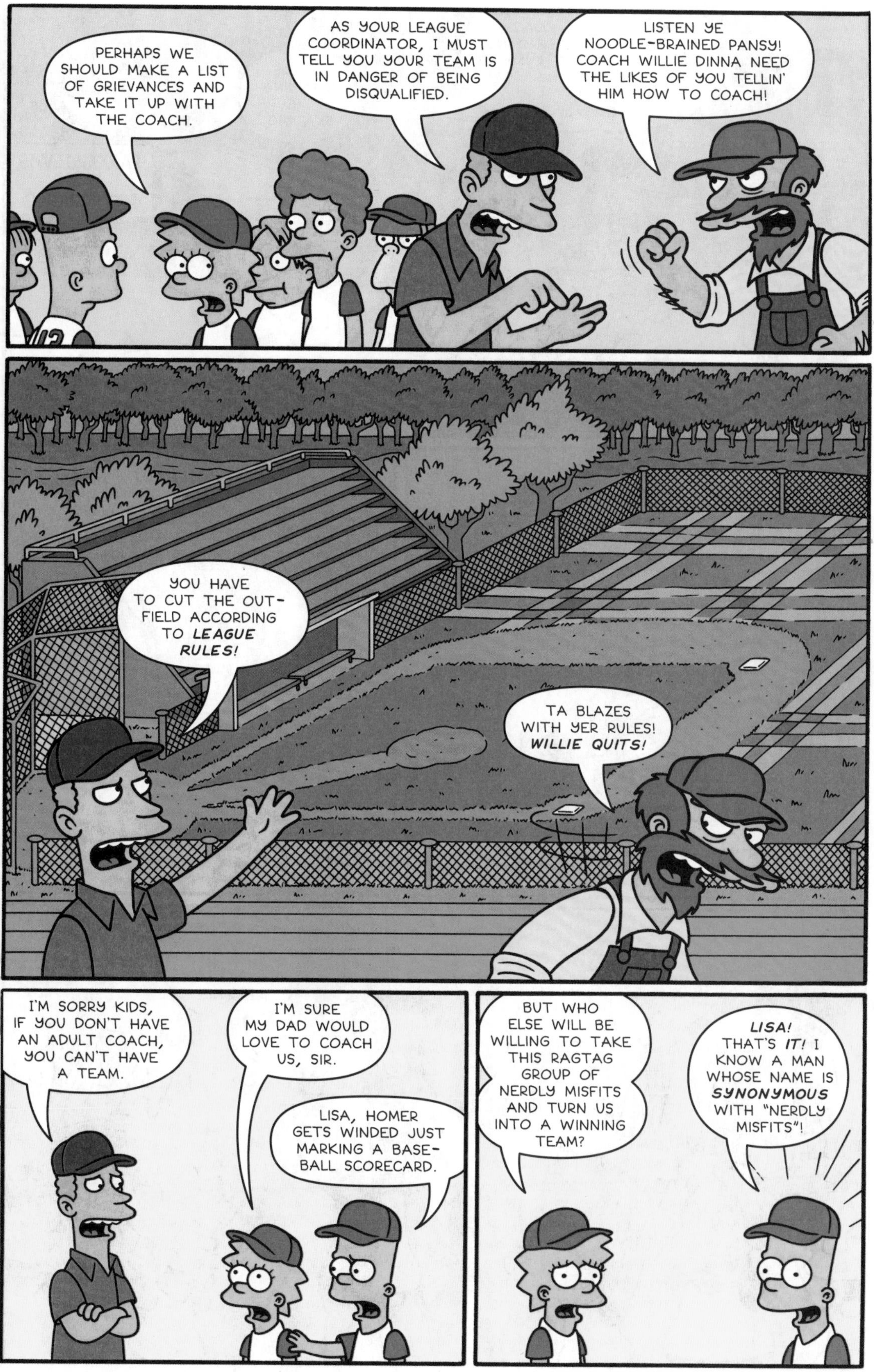
PERHAPS WE SHOULD MAKE A LIST OF GRIEVANCES AND TAKE IT UP WITH THE COACH.
AS YOUR LEAGUE COORDINATOR, I MUST TELL YOU YOUR TEAM IS IN DANGER OF BEING DISQUALIFIED.
LISTEN YE NOODLE-BRAINED PANSY! COACH WILLIE DINNA NEED THE LIKES OF YOU TELLIN' HIM HOW TO COACH!
YOU HAVE TO CUT THE OUT-FIELD ACCORDING TO LEAGUE RULES!
TA BLAZES WITH YER RULES! WILLIE QUITS!
I'M SORRY KIDS, IF YOU DON'T HAVE AN ADULT COACH, YOU CAN'T HAVE A TEAM.
I'M SURE MY DAD WOULD LOVE TO COACH US, SIR.
LISA, HOMER GETS WINDED JUST MARKING A BASE-BALL SCORECARD.
BUT WHO ELSE WILL BE WILLING TO TAKE THIS RAGTAG GROUP OF NERDLY MISFITS AND TURN US INTO A WINNING TEAM?
LISA! THAT'S IT! I KNOW A MAN WHOSE NAME IS SYNONYMOUS WITH "NERDLY MISFITS"!

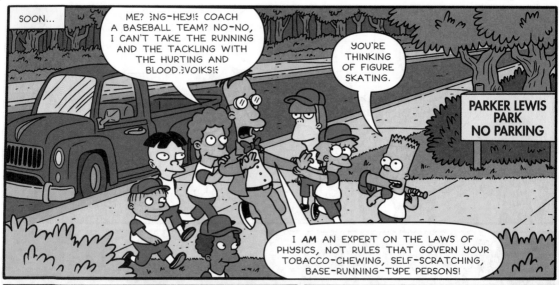

SOON...

ME? ⦂NG-HEY!⦂ COACH A BASEBALL TEAM? NO-NO, I CAN'T TAKE THE RUNNING AND THE TACKLING WITH THE HURTING AND BLOOD.⦂VOIKS!⦂

YOU'RE THINKING OF FIGURE SKATING.

PARKER LEWIS PARK NO PARKING

I **AM** AN EXPERT ON THE LAWS OF PHYSICS, NOT RULES THAT GOVERN YOUR TOBACCO-CHEWING, SELF-SCRATCHING, BASE-RUNNING-TYPE PERSONS!

PROFESSOR, WE ALREADY *KNOW* HOW TO PLAY BASEBALL. WE JUST NEED A TOKEN ADULT AND BETTER EQUIPMENT.

I KNOW! WHY DON'T WE CORK THE BATS?

RIDICULOUS! I COULD REBUILD ALL YOUR EQUIPMENT IN MY LAB FOR PENNIES. ⦂GA-HOY!⦂ BUT AS ALBERT EINSTEIN ONCE SAID, "YOU WILL LEARN ABOUT RELATIVITY FASTER THAN I LEARN ABOUT BASEBALL."

WELL, I SUPPOSE YOU'RE RIGHT. I JUST THOUGHT A *BRILLIANT* MIND LIKE YOURS COULD *IMPROVE* ON AMERICA'S FAVORITE PASTIME, BUT I GUESS YOU'RE NOT UP TO THE TASK.

NOW SEE HERE, YOUNG BART, IF I CAN OPERATE A SUPER COLLIDER WHILE COMPUTING QUANTUM MECHANICS, I CAN CERTAINLY COACH A BASEBALL TEAM!

NOW SHOW ME YOUR TEAM'S ICE RINK!

YAAAAAY!

YAAAY!

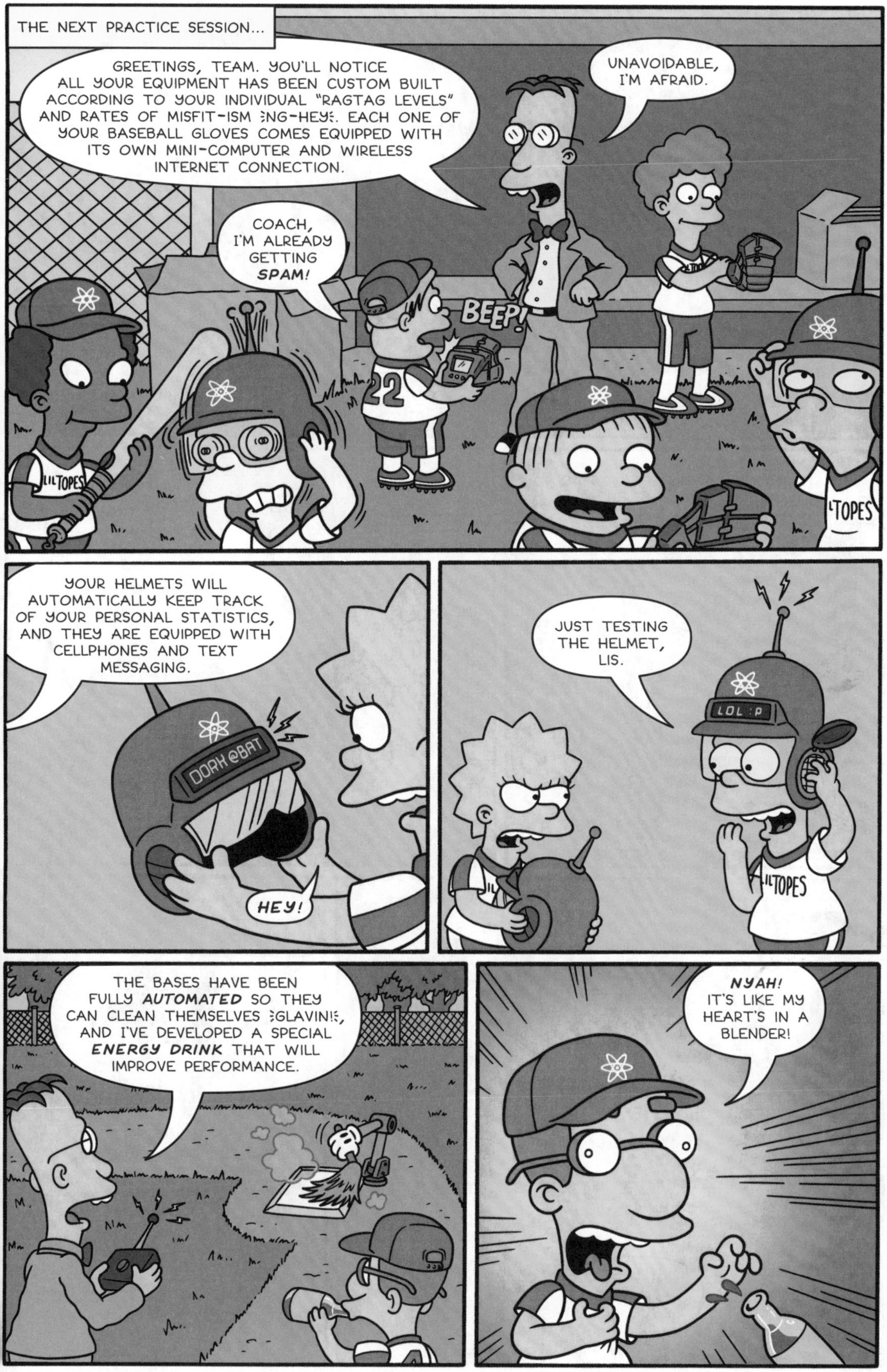
THE NEXT PRACTICE SESSION...
GREETINGS, TEAM. YOU'LL NOTICE ALL YOUR EQUIPMENT HAS BEEN CUSTOM BUILT ACCORDING TO YOUR INDIVIDUAL "RAGTAG LEVELS" AND RATES OF MISFIT-ISM ƎNG-HEYƐ. EACH ONE OF YOUR BASEBALL GLOVES COMES EQUIPPED WITH ITS OWN MINI-COMPUTER AND WIRELESS INTERNET CONNECTION.
UNAVOIDABLE, I'M AFRAID.
COACH, I'M ALREADY GETTING *SPAM!*
BEEP!
L'IL TOPES
L'TOPES
YOUR HELMETS WILL AUTOMATICALLY KEEP TRACK OF YOUR PERSONAL STATISTICS, AND THEY ARE EQUIPPED WITH CELLPHONES AND TEXT MESSAGING.
DORK @BAT
HEY!
JUST TESTING THE HELMET, LIS.
LOL :P
L'IL TOPES
THE BASES HAVE BEEN FULLY *AUTOMATED* SO THEY CAN CLEAN THEMSELVES ƎGLAVINƐ, AND I'VE DEVELOPED A SPECIAL *ENERGY DRINK* THAT WILL IMPROVE PERFORMANCE.
NYAH! IT'S LIKE MY HEART'S IN A BLENDER!

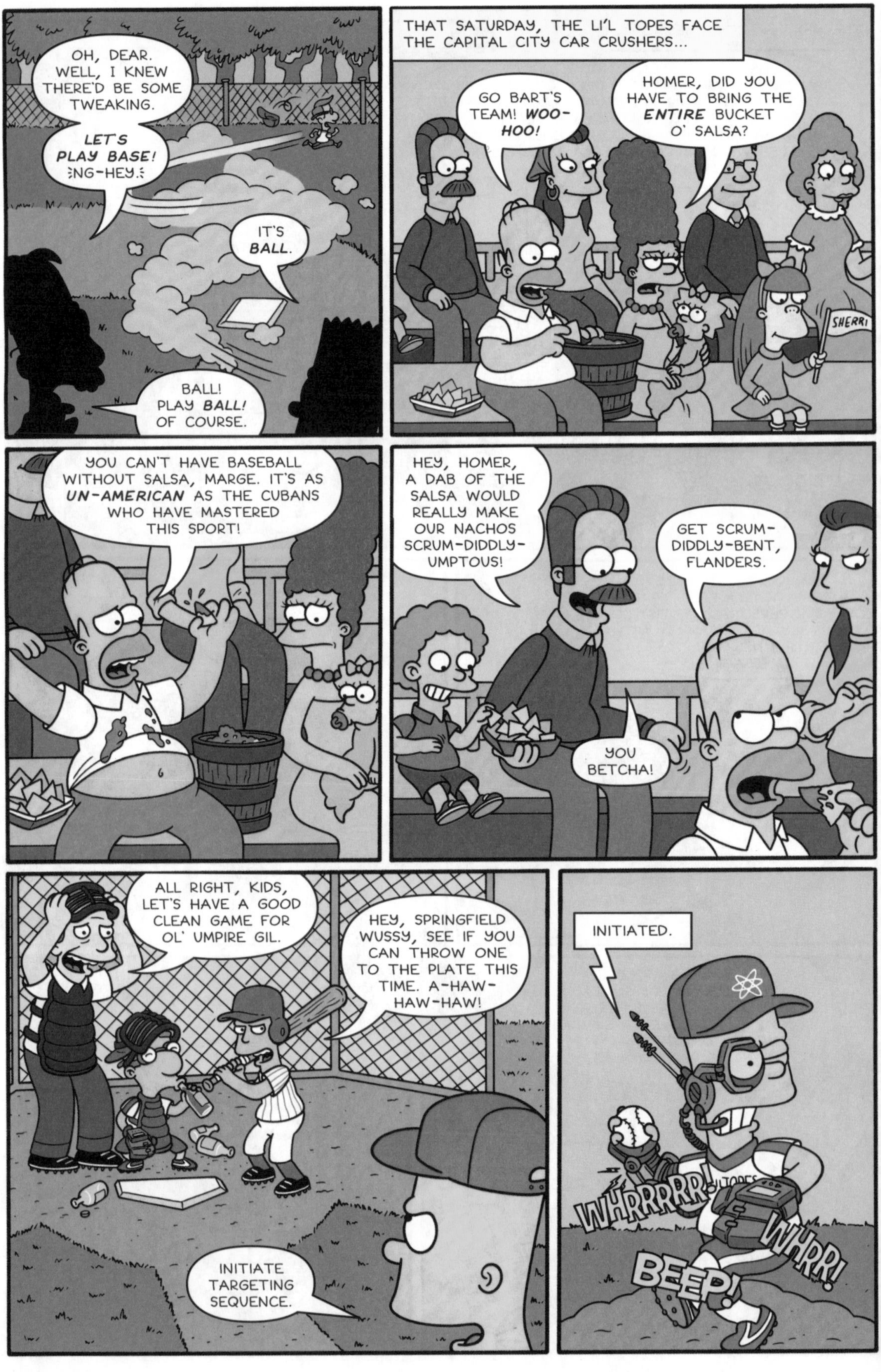
OH, DEAR. WELL, I KNEW THERE'D BE SOME TWEAKING.
LET'S PLAY BASE! NG-HEY.
IT'S BALL.
BALL! PLAY BALL! OF COURSE.
THAT SATURDAY, THE LI'L TOPES FACE THE CAPITAL CITY CAR CRUSHERS...
GO BART'S TEAM! WOO-HOO!
HOMER, DID YOU HAVE TO BRING THE ENTIRE BUCKET O' SALSA?
SHERRI
YOU CAN'T HAVE BASEBALL WITHOUT SALSA, MARGE. IT'S AS UN-AMERICAN AS THE CUBANS WHO HAVE MASTERED THIS SPORT!
HEY, HOMER, A DAB OF THE SALSA WOULD REALLY MAKE OUR NACHOS SCRUM-DIDDLY-UMPTOUS!
GET SCRUM-DIDDLY-BENT, FLANDERS.
YOU BETCHA!
ALL RIGHT, KIDS, LET'S HAVE A GOOD CLEAN GAME FOR OL' UMPIRE GIL.
HEY, SPRINGFIELD WUSSY, SEE IF YOU CAN THROW ONE TO THE PLATE THIS TIME. A-HAW-HAW-HAW!
INITIATE TARGETING SEQUENCE.
INITIATED.
WHRRRRR!
WHRR!
BEEP!

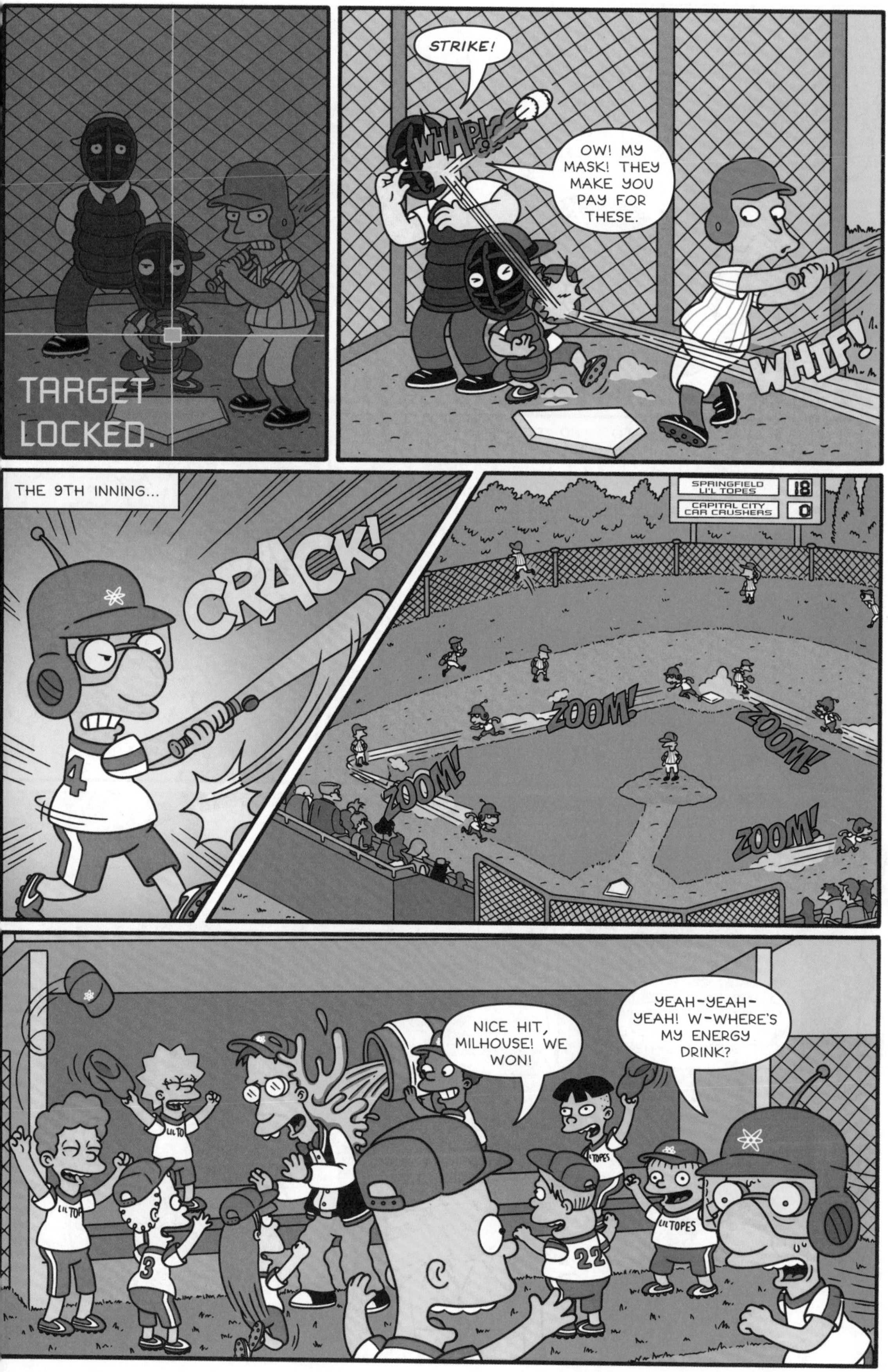
TARGET LOCKED.
STRIKE!
WHAP!
OW! MY MASK! THEY MAKE YOU PAY FOR THESE.
WHIF!
THE 9TH INNING...
CRACK!
SPRINGFIELD LI'L TOPES 18
CAPITAL CITY CAR CRUSHERS 0
ZOOM!
ZOOM!
ZOOM!
ZOOM!
NICE HIT, MILHOUSE! WE WON!
YEAH-YEAH-YEAH! W-WHERE'S MY ENERGY DRINK?

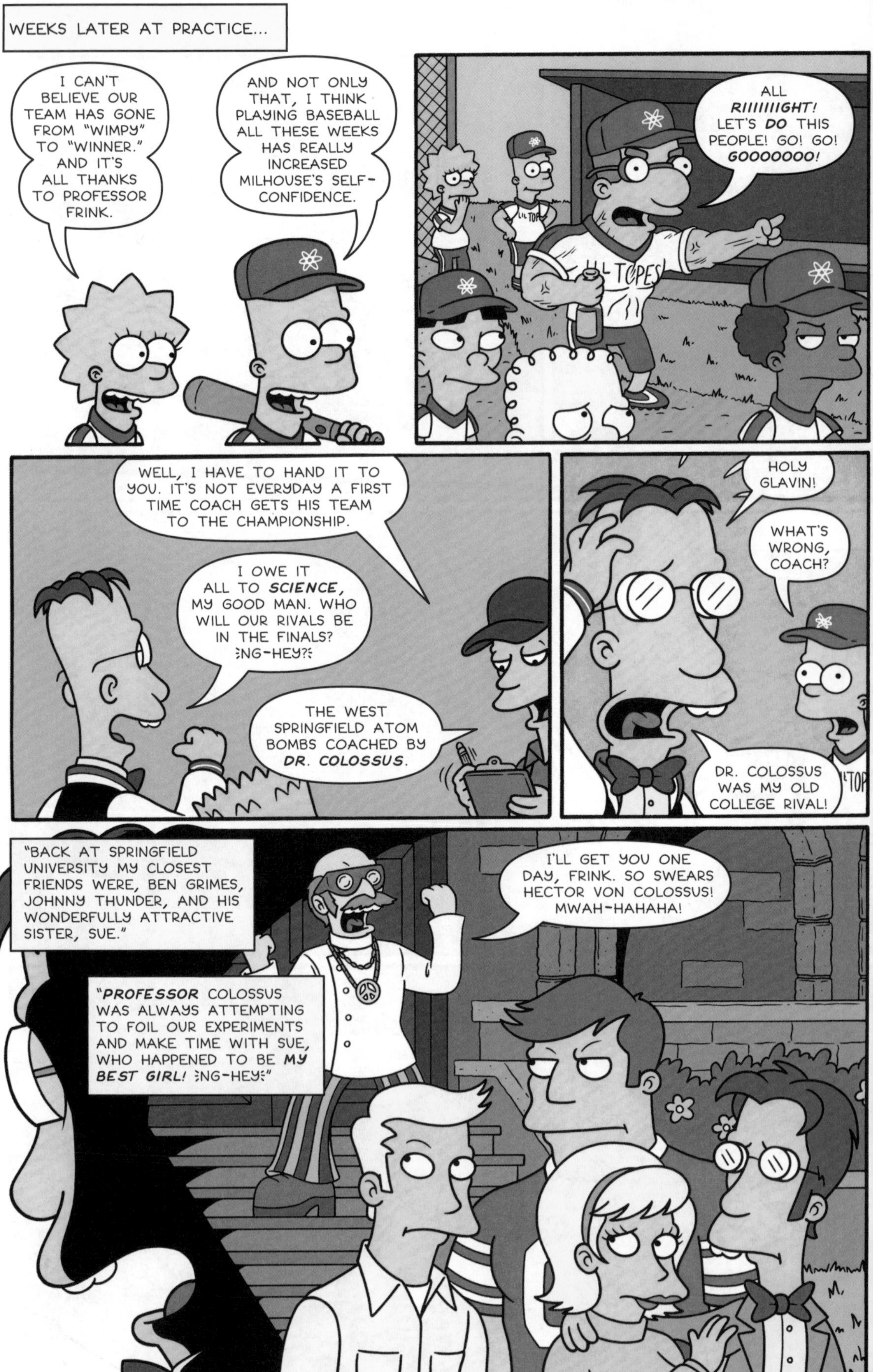
WEEKS LATER AT PRACTICE...
I CAN'T BELIEVE OUR TEAM HAS GONE FROM "WIMPY" TO "WINNER." AND IT'S ALL THANKS TO PROFESSOR FRINK.
AND NOT ONLY THAT, I THINK PLAYING BASEBALL ALL THESE WEEKS HAS REALLY INCREASED MILHOUSE'S SELF-CONFIDENCE.
ALL RIIIIIIGHT! LET'S DO THIS PEOPLE! GO! GO! GOOOOOOO!
L'IL TOPES
WELL, I HAVE TO HAND IT TO YOU. IT'S NOT EVERYDAY A FIRST TIME COACH GETS HIS TEAM TO THE CHAMPIONSHIP.
I OWE IT ALL TO SCIENCE, MY GOOD MAN. WHO WILL OUR RIVALS BE IN THE FINALS? NG-HEY?
THE WEST SPRINGFIELD ATOM BOMBS COACHED BY DR. COLOSSUS.
HOLY GLAVIN!
WHAT'S WRONG, COACH?
DR. COLOSSUS WAS MY OLD COLLEGE RIVAL!
"BACK AT SPRINGFIELD UNIVERSITY MY CLOSEST FRIENDS WERE, BEN GRIMES, JOHNNY THUNDER, AND HIS WONDERFULLY ATTRACTIVE SISTER, SUE."
I'LL GET YOU ONE DAY, FRINK. SO SWEARS HECTOR VON COLOSSUS! MWAH-HAHAHA!
"PROFESSOR COLOSSUS WAS ALWAYS ATTEMPTING TO FOIL OUR EXPERIMENTS AND MAKE TIME WITH SUE, WHO HAPPENED TO BE MY BEST GIRL! NG-HEY!"

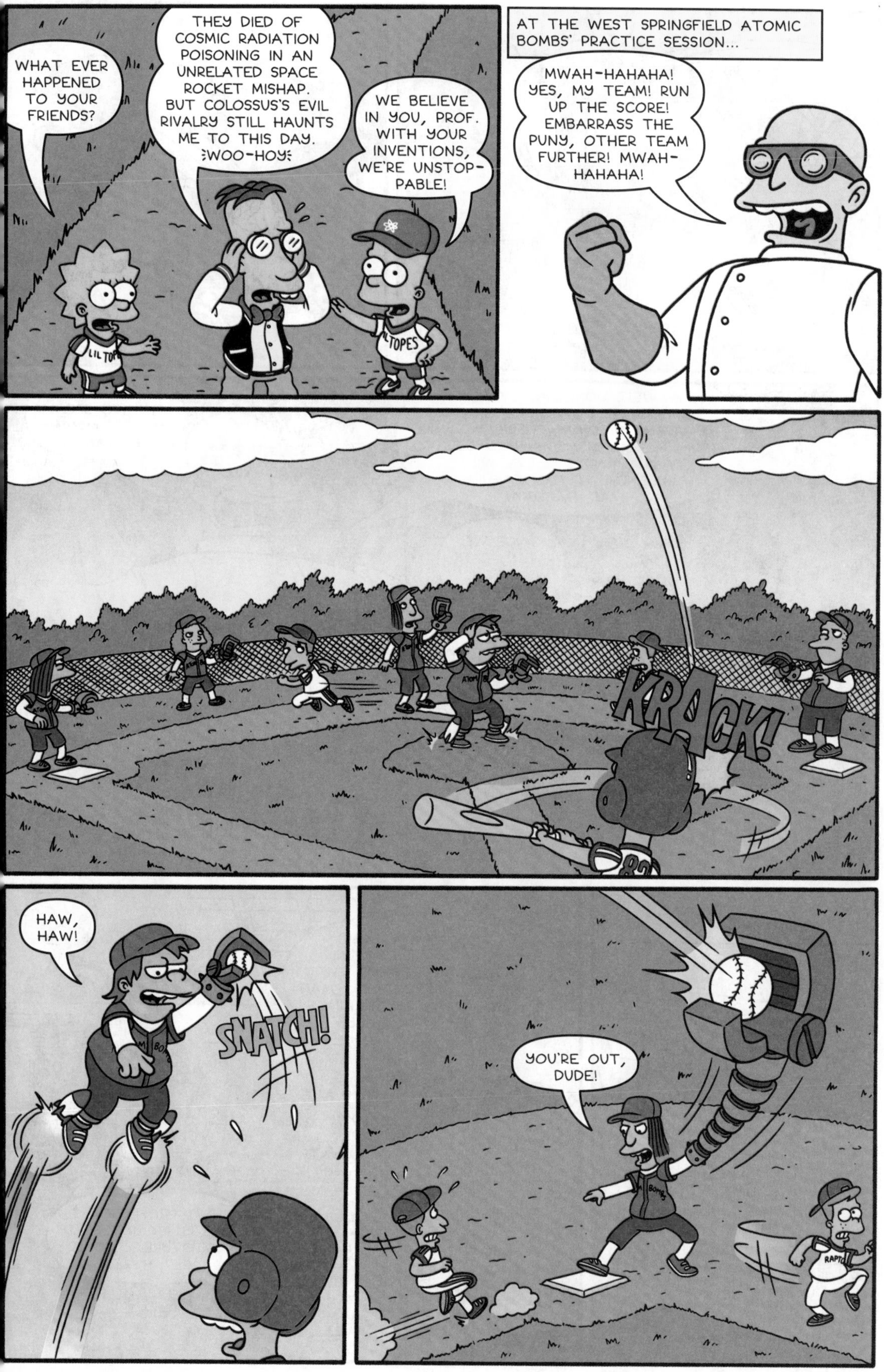
WHAT EVER HAPPENED TO YOUR FRIENDS?
THEY DIED OF COSMIC RADIATION POISONING IN AN UNRELATED SPACE ROCKET MISHAP. BUT COLOSSUS'S EVIL RIVALRY STILL HAUNTS ME TO THIS DAY. WOO-HOY
WE BELIEVE IN YOU, PROF. WITH YOUR INVENTIONS, WE'RE UNSTOPPABLE!
AT THE WEST SPRINGFIELD ATOMIC BOMBS' PRACTICE SESSION...
MWAH-HAHAHA! YES, MY TEAM! RUN UP THE SCORE! EMBARRASS THE PUNY, OTHER TEAM FURTHER! MWAH-HAHAHA!
KRACK!
HAW, HAW!
SNATCH!
YOU'RE OUT, DUDE!

WHAT THE--?

TRIPLE PLAY, LOSER!

SMACK!

WELL DONE, MY EVIL MINIONS! WE NOW MOVE ON TO *THE CHAMPIONSHIP!* THERE, WE WILL CRUSH MY OLD NEMESIS, *PROFESSOR FRINK,* AND OUR EVIL WILL RULE THE LITTLE LEAGUE! *MWAH-HAHAHA!*

SINCE WE WON, CAN WE GET ICE CREAM?

YES! TO THE ICE CREAM PARLOR! *MWAH-HAHAHA!*

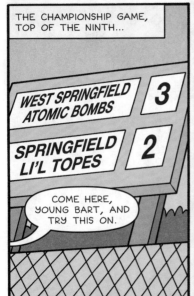

THE CHAMPIONSHIP GAME, TOP OF THE NINTH...

| WEST SPRINGFIELD ATOMIC BOMBS | 3 |
| SPRINGFIELD LI'L TOPES | 2 |

COME HERE, YOUNG BART, AND TRY THIS ON.

THIS AERODYNAMIC BASEBALL HELMET WILL HAVE YOU ROUNDING THIRD BEFORE THE FIRST BASEMAN CAN FINISH SCRATCHING HIMSELF. ¿NG-HEY?

BUT PROFESSOR, THIS IS AN UNTESTED PROTOTYPE. I COULD GET HURT.

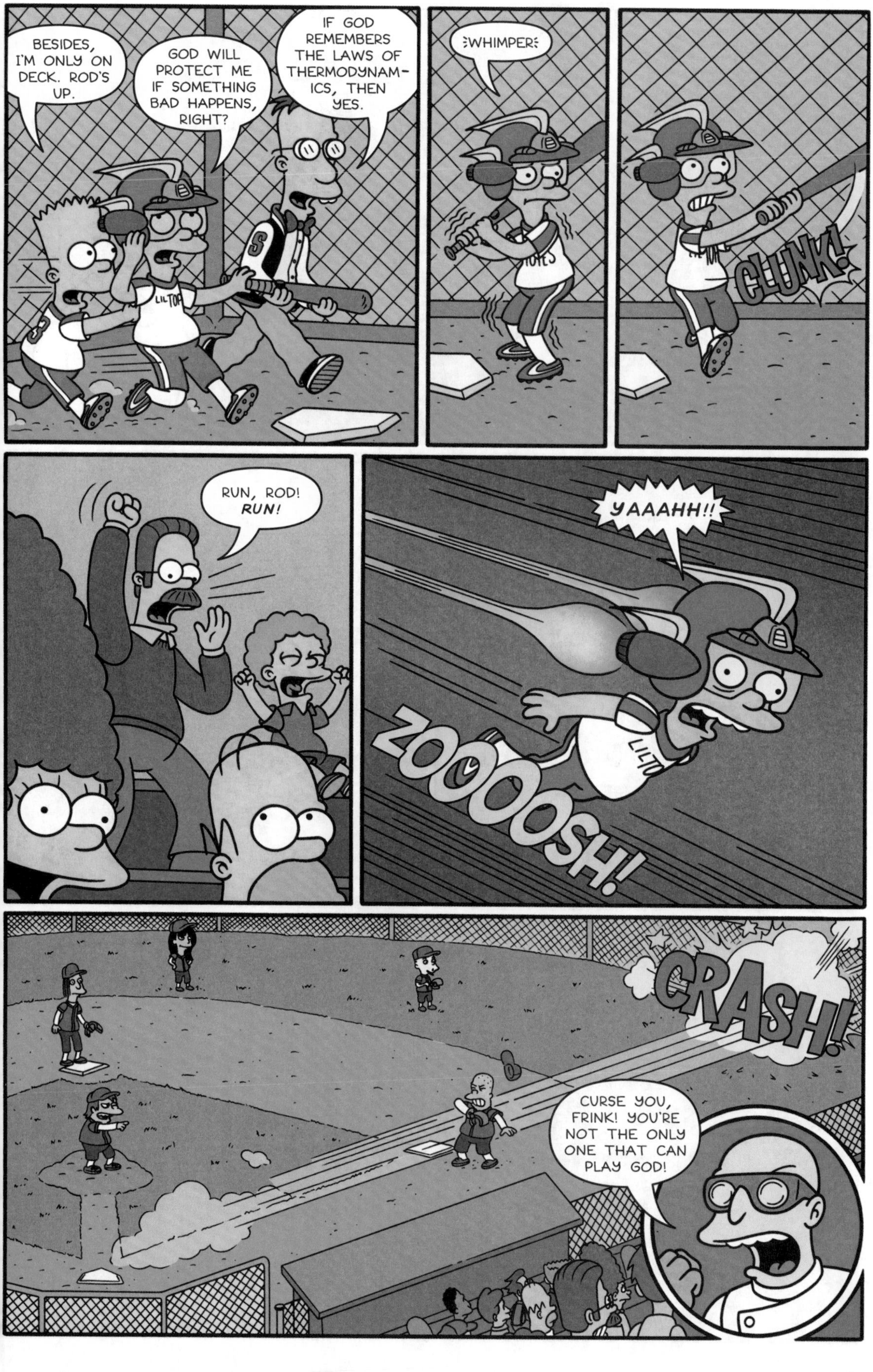
BESIDES, I'M ONLY ON DECK. ROD'S UP.
GOD WILL PROTECT ME IF SOMETHING BAD HAPPENS, RIGHT?
IF GOD REMEMBERS THE LAWS OF THERMODYNAMICS, THEN YES.
WHIMPER
CLUNK!
RUN, ROD! RUN!
YAAAHH!!
ZOOOOOSH!
CRASH!
CURSE YOU, FRINK! YOU'RE NOT THE ONLY ONE THAT CAN PLAY GOD!

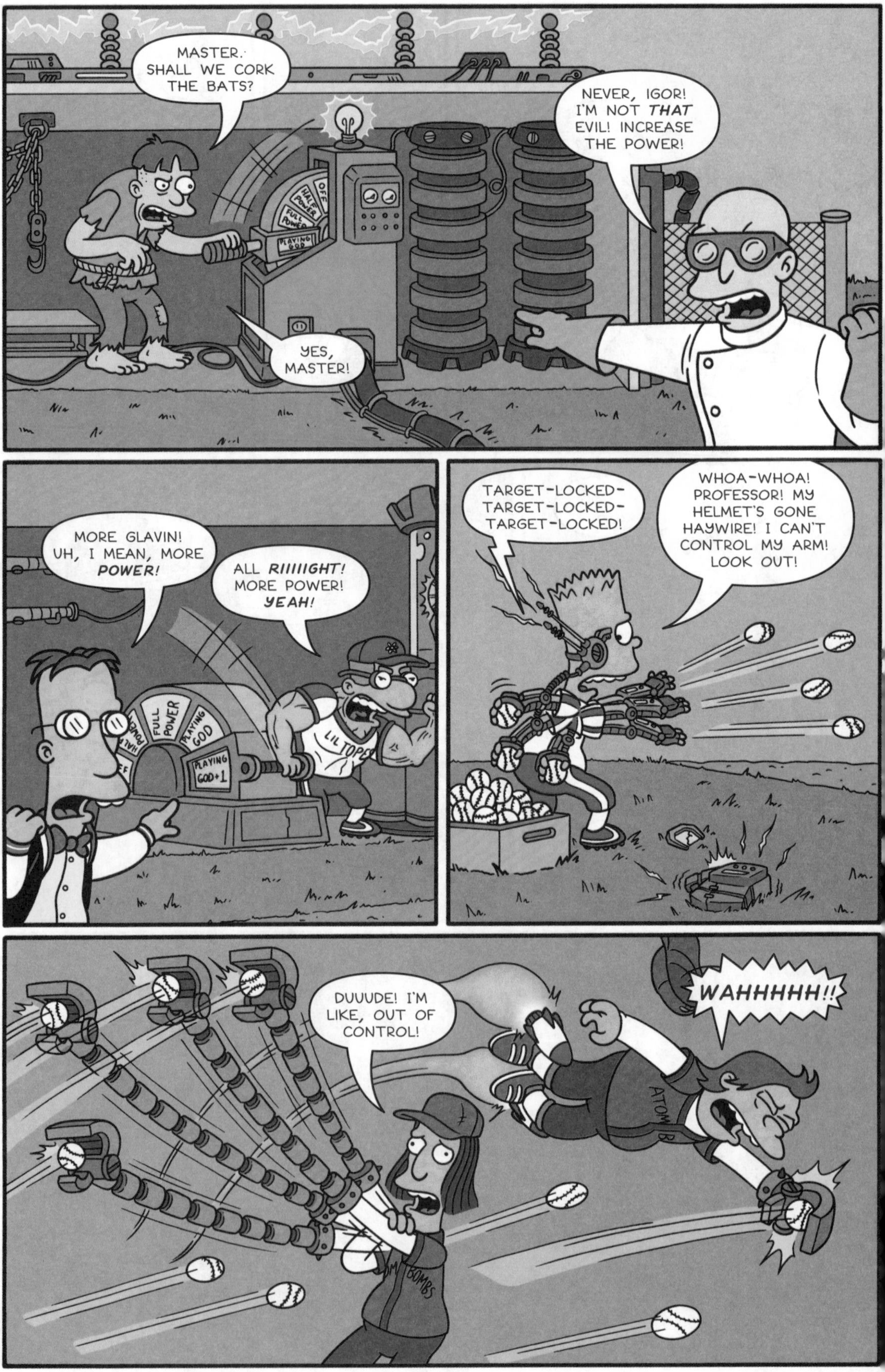
MASTER. SHALL WE CORK THE BATS?
NEVER, IGOR! I'M NOT *THAT* EVIL! INCREASE THE POWER!
OFF
HALF POWER
FULL POWER
PLAYING GOD
YES, MASTER!
MORE GLAVIN! UH, I MEAN, MORE *POWER*!
ALL *RIIIIIGHT*! MORE POWER! *YEAH*!
FULL POWER
PLAYING GOD
PLAYING GOD+1
TARGET-LOCKED-
TARGET-LOCKED-
TARGET-LOCKED!
WHOA-WHOA! PROFESSOR! MY HELMET'S GONE HAYWIRE! I CAN'T CONTROL MY ARM! LOOK OUT!
DUUUDE! I'M LIKE, OUT OF CONTROL!
WAHHHHH!!

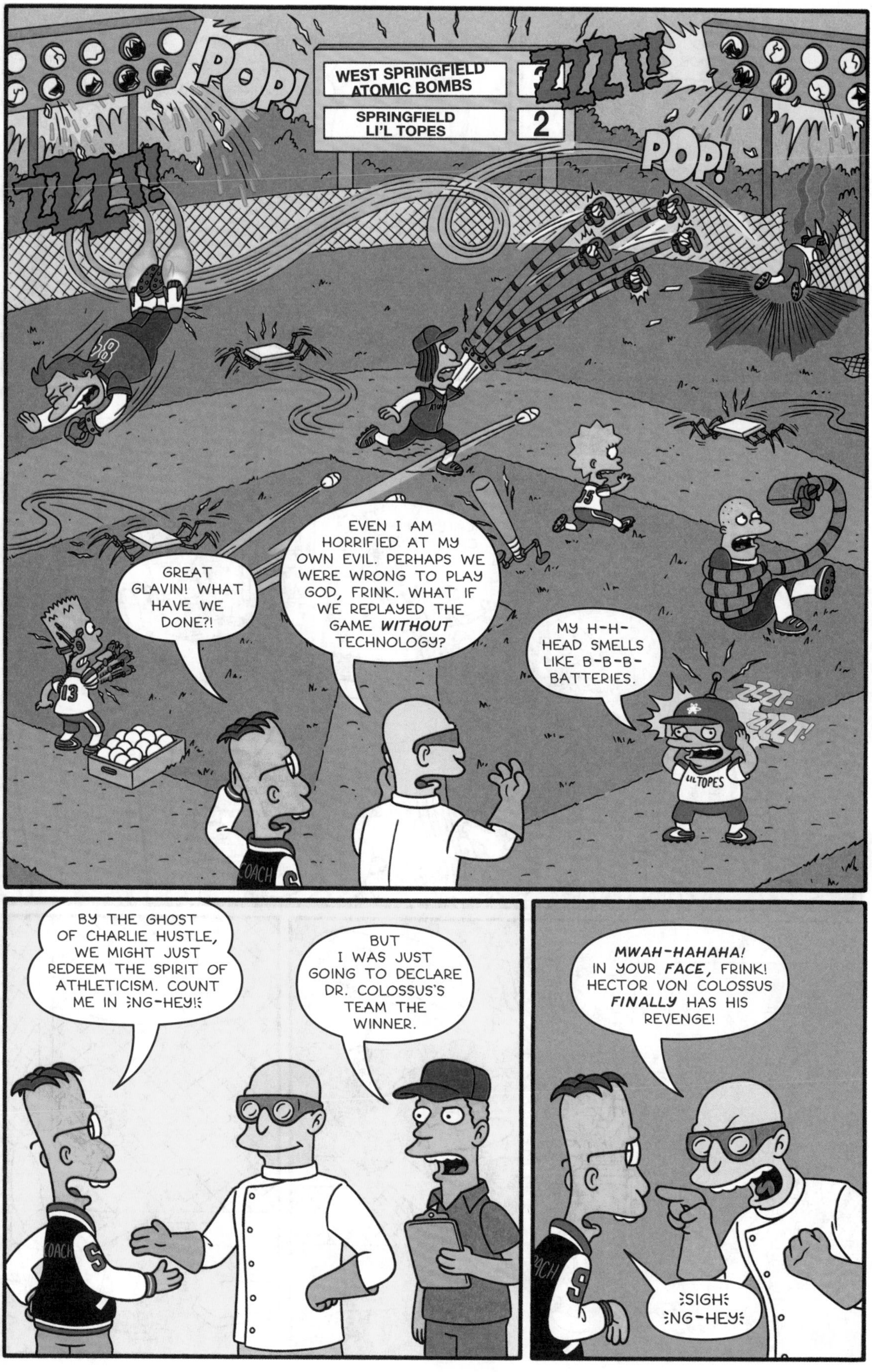
POP!
WEST SPRINGFIELD ATOMIC BOMBS
SPRINGFIELD LI'L TOPES 2
ZZZT!
ZZZT!
POP!
GREAT GLAVIN! WHAT HAVE WE DONE?!
EVEN I AM HORRIFIED AT MY OWN EVIL. PERHAPS WE WERE WRONG TO PLAY GOD, FRINK. WHAT IF WE REPLAYED THE GAME *WITHOUT* TECHNOLOGY?
MY H-H-HEAD SMELLS LIKE B-B-B-BATTERIES.
ZZZT-ZZZZT!
LIL TOPES
COACH
BY THE GHOST OF CHARLIE HUSTLE, WE MIGHT JUST REDEEM THE SPIRIT OF ATHLETICISM. COUNT ME IN ⁝NG-HEY!⁝
BUT I WAS JUST GOING TO DECLARE DR. COLOSSUS'S TEAM THE WINNER.
MWAH-HAHAHA! IN YOUR ***FACE,*** FRINK! HECTOR VON COLOSSUS ***FINALLY*** HAS HIS REVENGE!
⁝SIGH⁝ ⁝NG-HEY⁝

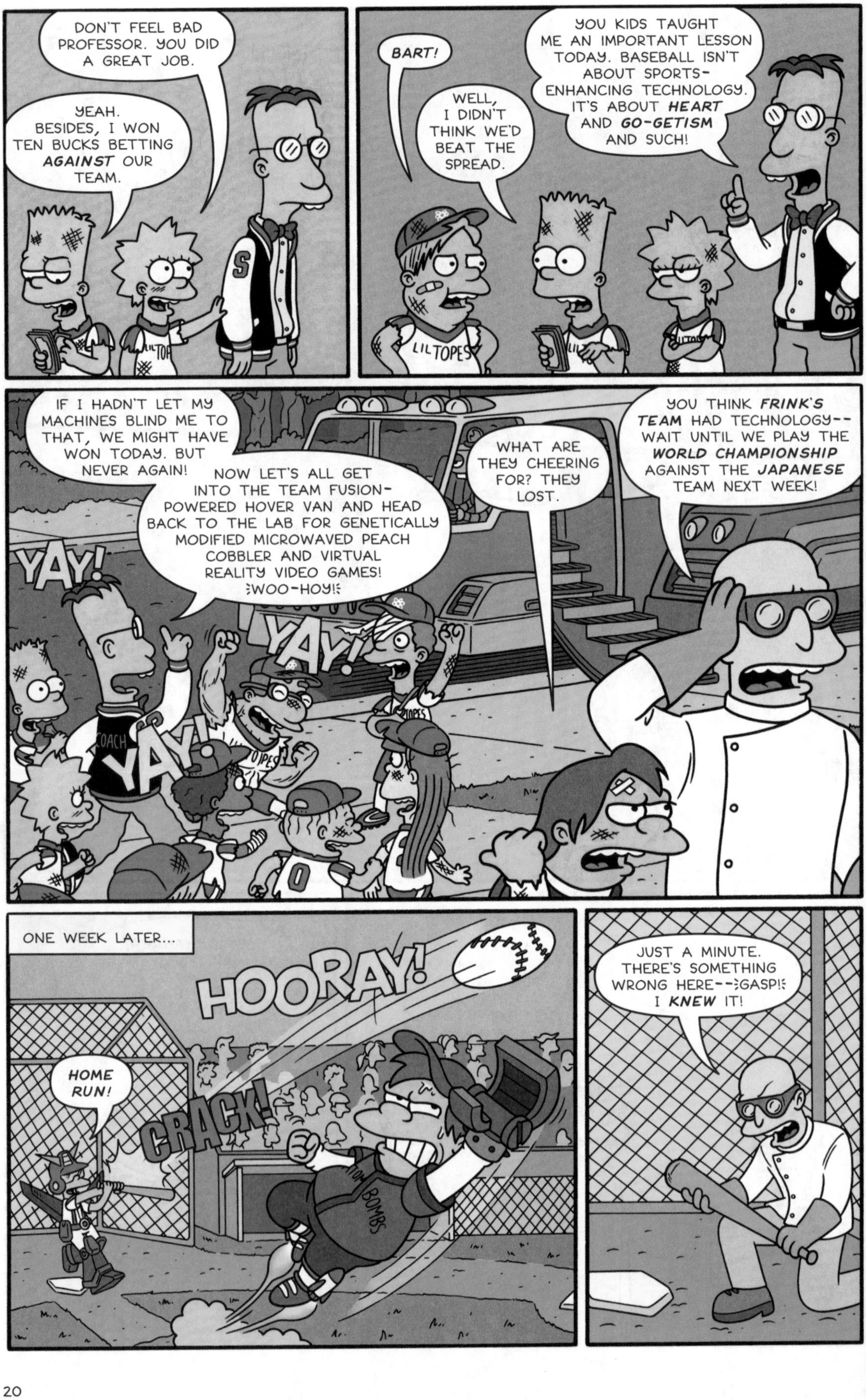
DON'T FEEL BAD PROFESSOR. YOU DID A GREAT JOB.
YEAH. BESIDES, I WON TEN BUCKS BETTING AGAINST OUR TEAM.
S
LIL TOP
BART!
WELL, I DIDN'T THINK WE'D BEAT THE SPREAD.
YOU KIDS TAUGHT ME AN IMPORTANT LESSON TODAY. BASEBALL ISN'T ABOUT SPORTS-ENHANCING TECHNOLOGY. IT'S ABOUT HEART AND GO-GETISM AND SUCH!
LIL TOPES
IF I HADN'T LET MY MACHINES BLIND ME TO THAT, WE MIGHT HAVE WON TODAY. BUT NEVER AGAIN!
NOW LET'S ALL GET INTO THE TEAM FUSION-POWERED HOVER VAN AND HEAD BACK TO THE LAB FOR GENETICALLY MODIFIED MICROWAVED PEACH COBBLER AND VIRTUAL REALITY VIDEO GAMES! WOO-HOY!
WHAT ARE THEY CHEERING FOR? THEY LOST.
YOU THINK FRINK'S TEAM HAD TECHNOLOGY-- WAIT UNTIL WE PLAY THE WORLD CHAMPIONSHIP AGAINST THE JAPANESE TEAM NEXT WEEK!
YAY!
YAY!
YAY!
COACH
ONE WEEK LATER...
HOORAY!
HOME RUN!
CRACK!
BOMBS
JUST A MINUTE. THERE'S SOMETHING WRONG HERE--GASP! I KNEW IT!

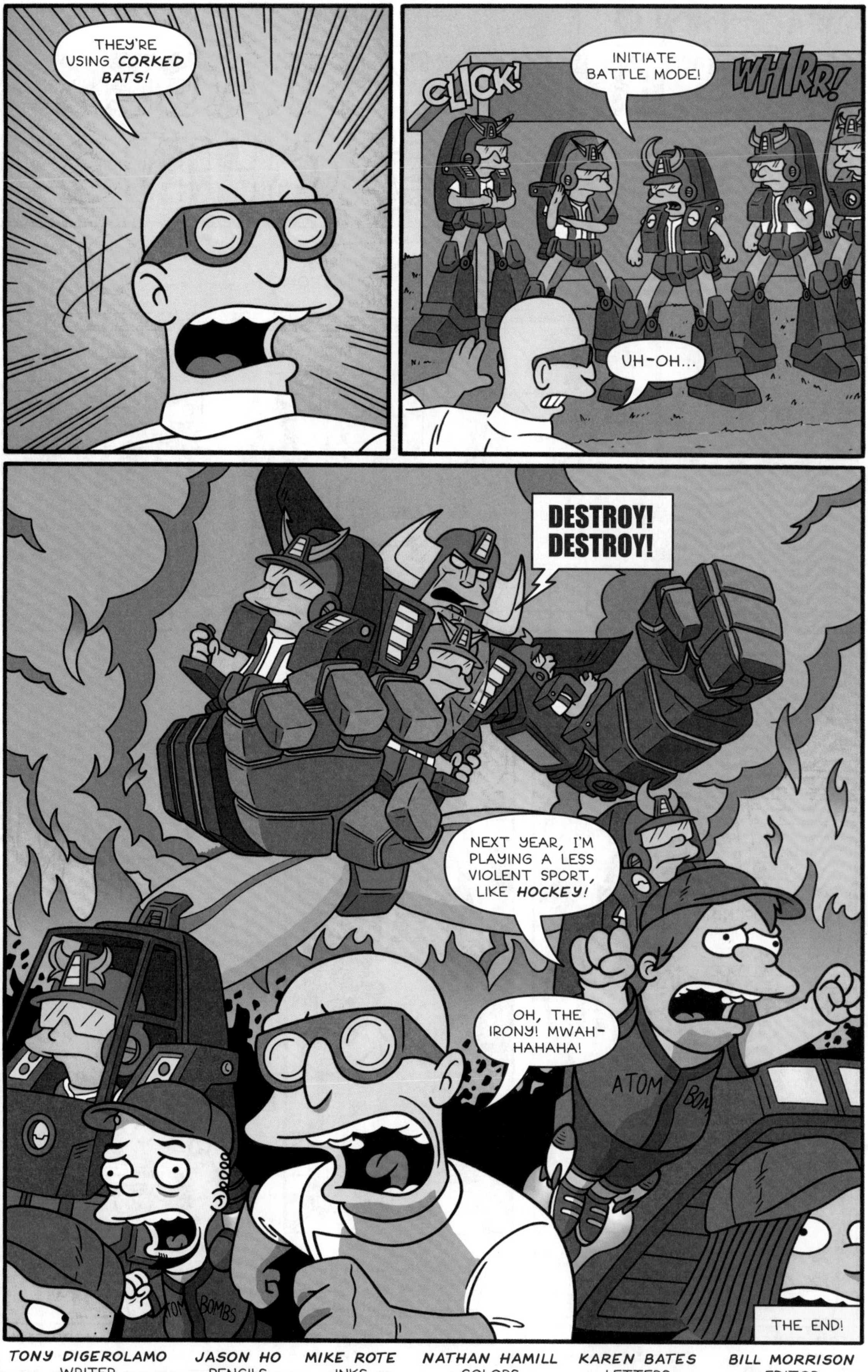
THEY'RE USING CORKED BATS!
CLICK!
INITIATE BATTLE MODE!
WHIRR!
UH-OH...
DESTROY! DESTROY!
NEXT YEAR, I'M PLAYING A LESS VIOLENT SPORT, LIKE HOCKEY!
OH, THE IRONY! MWAH-HAHAHA!
ATOM BOM
ATOM BOMBS
THE END!

TONY DIGEROLAMO WRITER | JASON HO PENCILS | MIKE ROTE INKS | NATHAN HAMILL COLORS | KAREN BATES LETTERS | BILL MORRISON EDITOR

LISA SIMPSON IN
THE THREE STAGES OF TEACHING
ALL RIGHT, CLASS, THE BELL DOESN'T RING FOR ANOTHER 20 MINUTES, SO...UH...
...LET'S TAKE TURNS READING OUT LOUD FROM THIS TV GUIDE.
MISS HOOVER?
TEACHING DOESN'T SEEM TO EXCITE YOU VERY MUCH.
DON'T YOU LIKE OPENING YOUNG MINDS TO THE WORLD OF KNOWLEDGE?
HA! I SUPPOSE YOU CAN DO BETTER?
WAIT, I DIDN'T MEAN--
THE CLASS IS YOURS, LISA! TEACH THEM WHATEVER YOU WANT!
BUT--!
SLAM!

TOM PEYER	*JOHN DELANEY*	*HOWARD SHUM*	*ART VILLANUEVA*	*CHRIS UNGAR*	*BILL MORRISON*
WRITER	PENCILS	INKS	COLORS	LETTERS	EDITOR

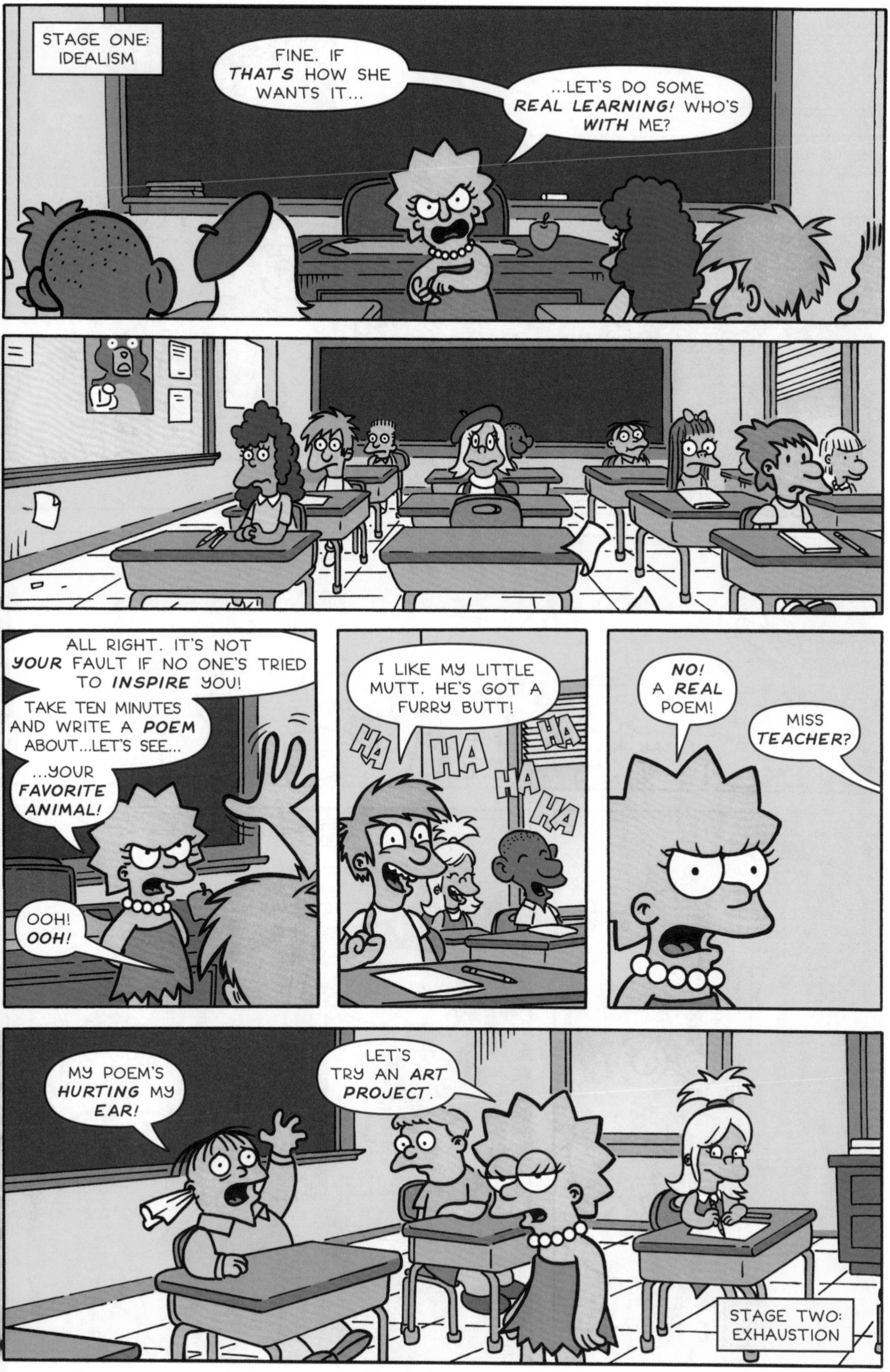
STAGE ONE: IDEALISM
FINE. IF THAT'S HOW SHE WANTS IT...
...LET'S DO SOME REAL LEARNING! WHO'S WITH ME?
ALL RIGHT. IT'S NOT YOUR FAULT IF NO ONE'S TRIED TO INSPIRE YOU!
TAKE TEN MINUTES AND WRITE A POEM ABOUT...LET'S SEE...
...YOUR FAVORITE ANIMAL!
OOH! OOH!
I LIKE MY LITTLE MUTT. HE'S GOT A FURRY BUTT!
HA HA HA HA HA
NO! A REAL POEM!
MISS TEACHER?
MY POEM'S HURTING MY EAR!
LET'S TRY AN ART PROJECT.
STAGE TWO: EXHAUSTION

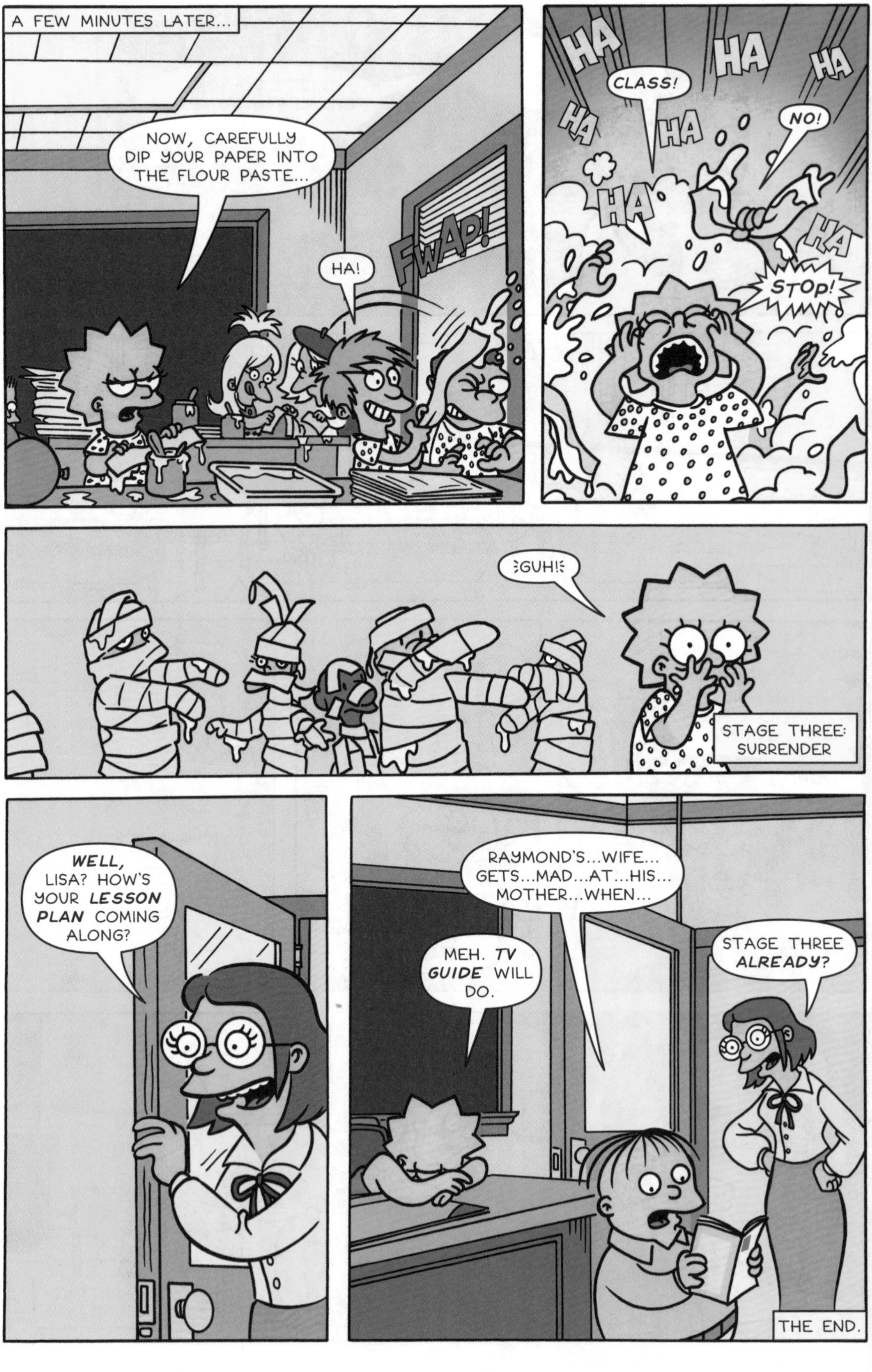
A FEW MINUTES LATER...
NOW, CAREFULLY DIP YOUR PAPER INTO THE FLOUR PASTE...
HA!
FWAP!
HA
HA
HA
CLASS!
HA
NO!
HA
HA
HA
STOP!
GUH!
STAGE THREE: SURRENDER
WELL, LISA? HOW'S YOUR LESSON PLAN COMING ALONG?
RAYMOND'S...WIFE... GETS...MAD...AT...HIS... MOTHER...WHEN...
MEH. TV GUIDE WILL DO.
STAGE THREE ALREADY?
THE END.

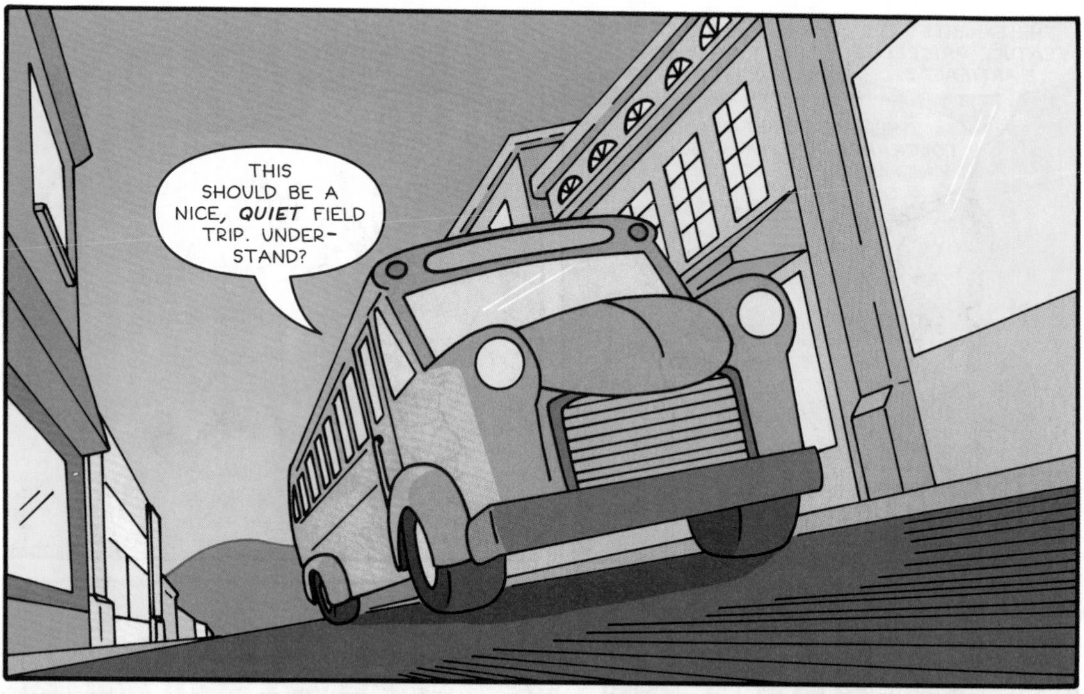
THIS SHOULD BE A NICE, QUIET FIELD TRIP. UNDER-STAND?

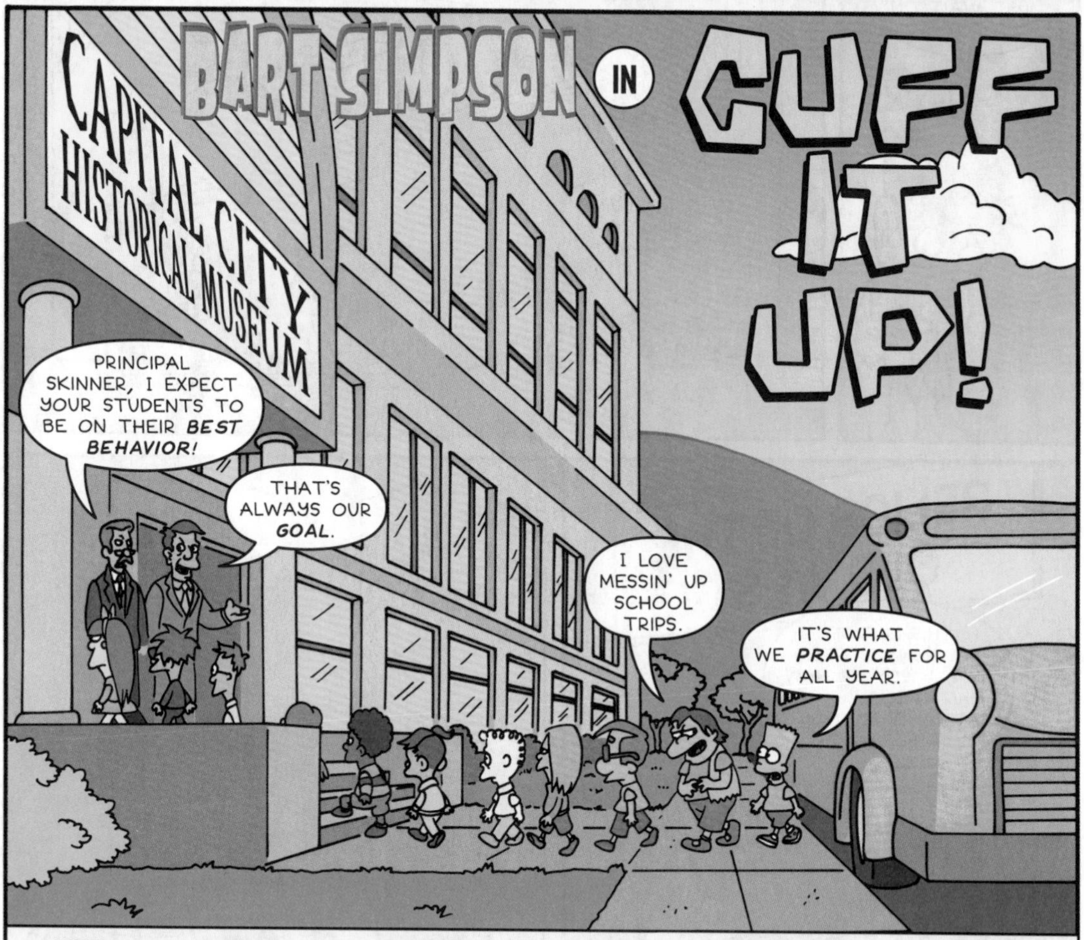
CAPITAL CITY HISTORICAL MUSEUM
BART SIMPSON IN CUFF IT UP!
PRINCIPAL SKINNER, I EXPECT YOUR STUDENTS TO BE ON THEIR BEST BEHAVIOR!
THAT'S ALWAYS OUR GOAL.
I LOVE MESSIN' UP SCHOOL TRIPS.
IT'S WHAT WE PRACTICE FOR ALL YEAR.

JAMES BATES WRITER	LUIS ESCOBAR PENCILS	PATRICK OWSLEY INKS	NATHAN HAMILL COLORS	KAREN BATES LETTERS	BILL MORRISON EDITOR

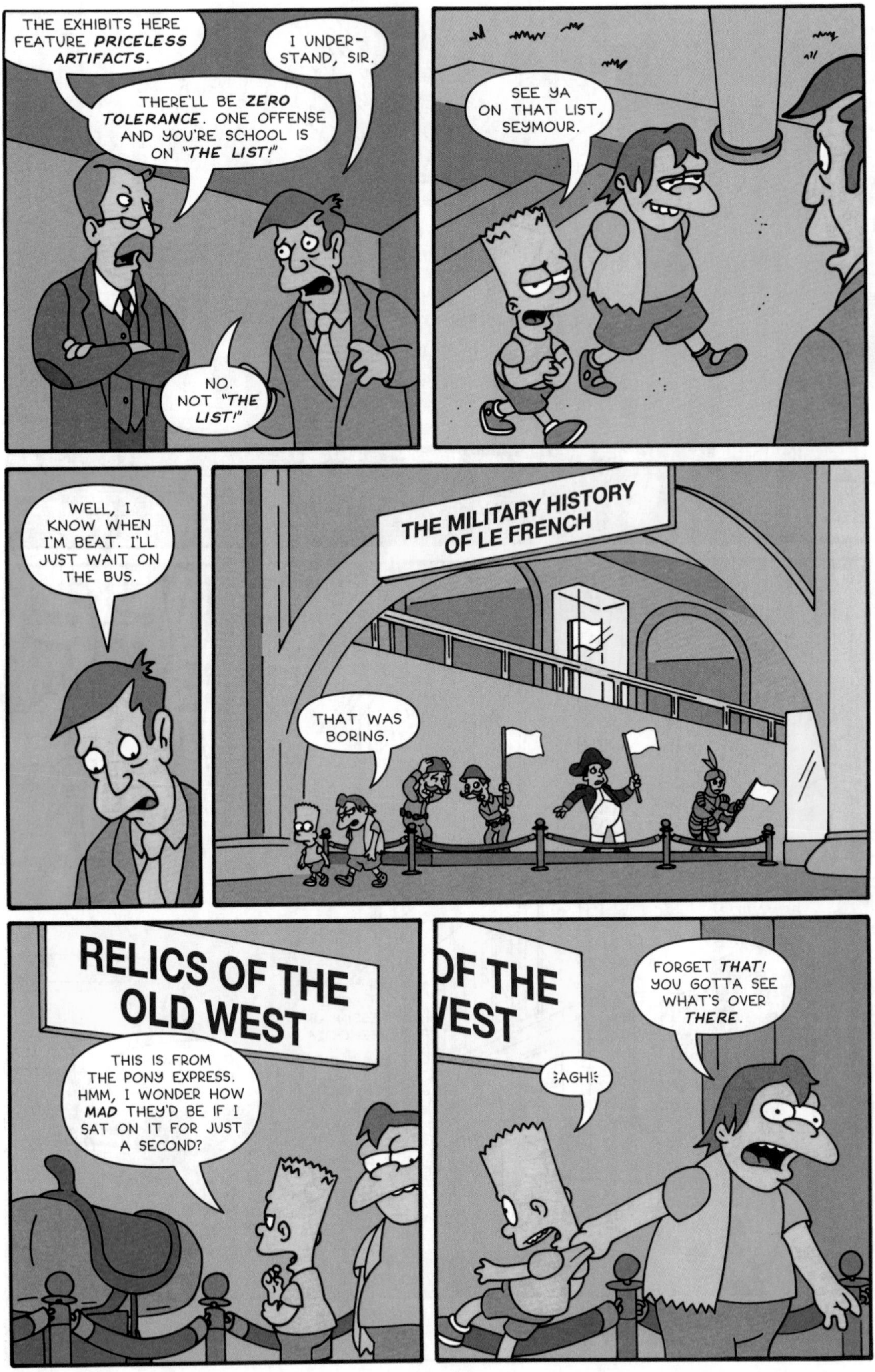
THE EXHIBITS HERE FEATURE PRICELESS ARTIFACTS.
I UNDER-STAND, SIR.
THERE'LL BE ZERO TOLERANCE. ONE OFFENSE AND YOU'RE SCHOOL IS ON "THE LIST!"
NO. NOT "THE LIST!"
SEE YA ON THAT LIST, SEYMOUR.
WELL, I KNOW WHEN I'M BEAT. I'LL JUST WAIT ON THE BUS.
THE MILITARY HISTORY OF LE FRENCH
THAT WAS BORING.
RELICS OF THE OLD WEST
THIS IS FROM THE PONY EXPRESS. HMM, I WONDER HOW MAD THEY'D BE IF I SAT ON IT FOR JUST A SECOND?
OF THE
WEST
FORGET THAT! YOU GOTTA SEE WHAT'S OVER THERE.
AGH!

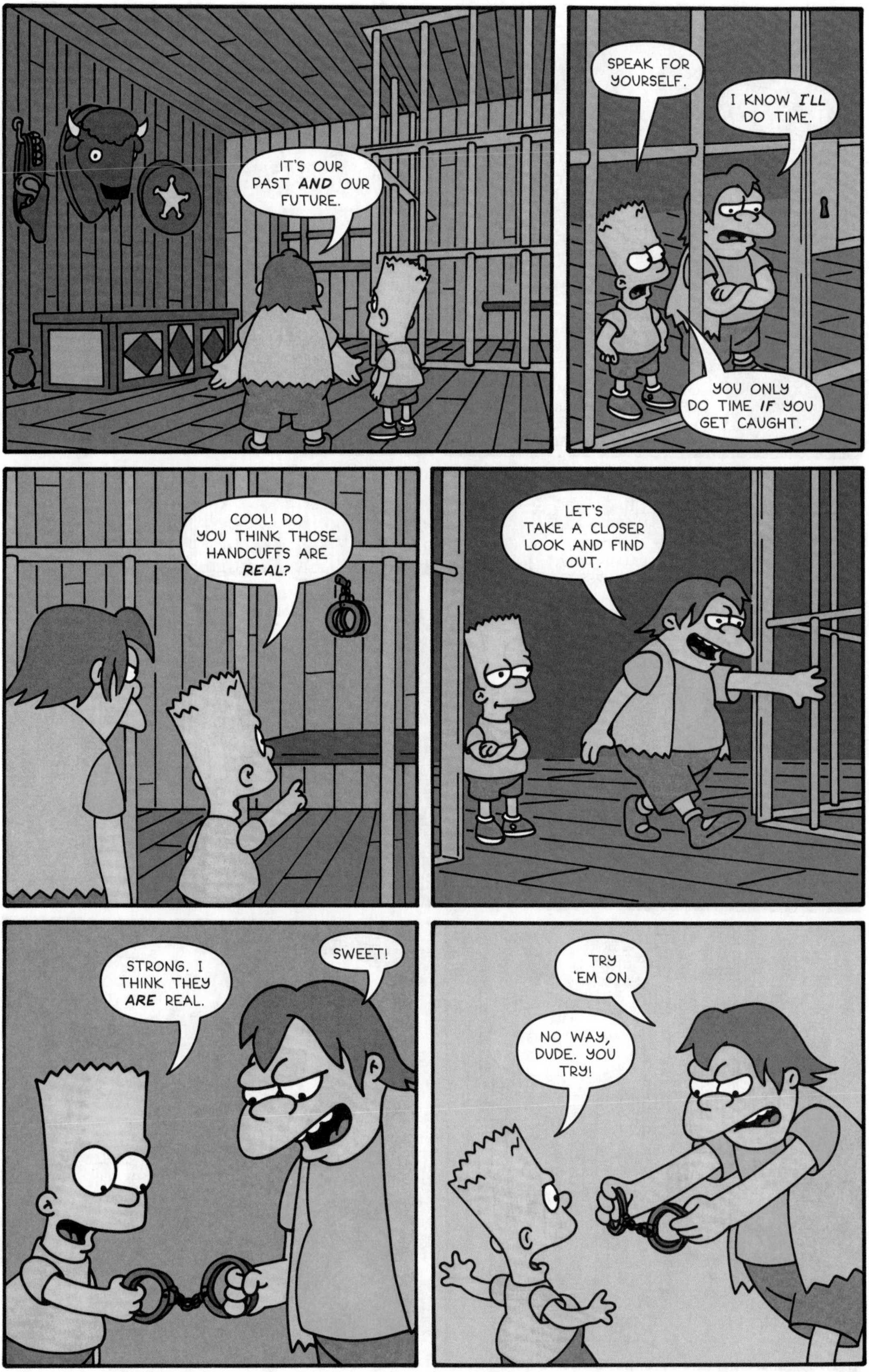
IT'S OUR PAST AND OUR FUTURE.
SPEAK FOR YOURSELF.
I KNOW I'LL DO TIME.
YOU ONLY DO TIME IF YOU GET CAUGHT.
COOL! DO YOU THINK THOSE HANDCUFFS ARE REAL?
LET'S TAKE A CLOSER LOOK AND FIND OUT.
STRONG. I THINK THEY ARE REAL.
SWEET!
TRY 'EM ON.
NO WAY, DUDE. YOU TRY!

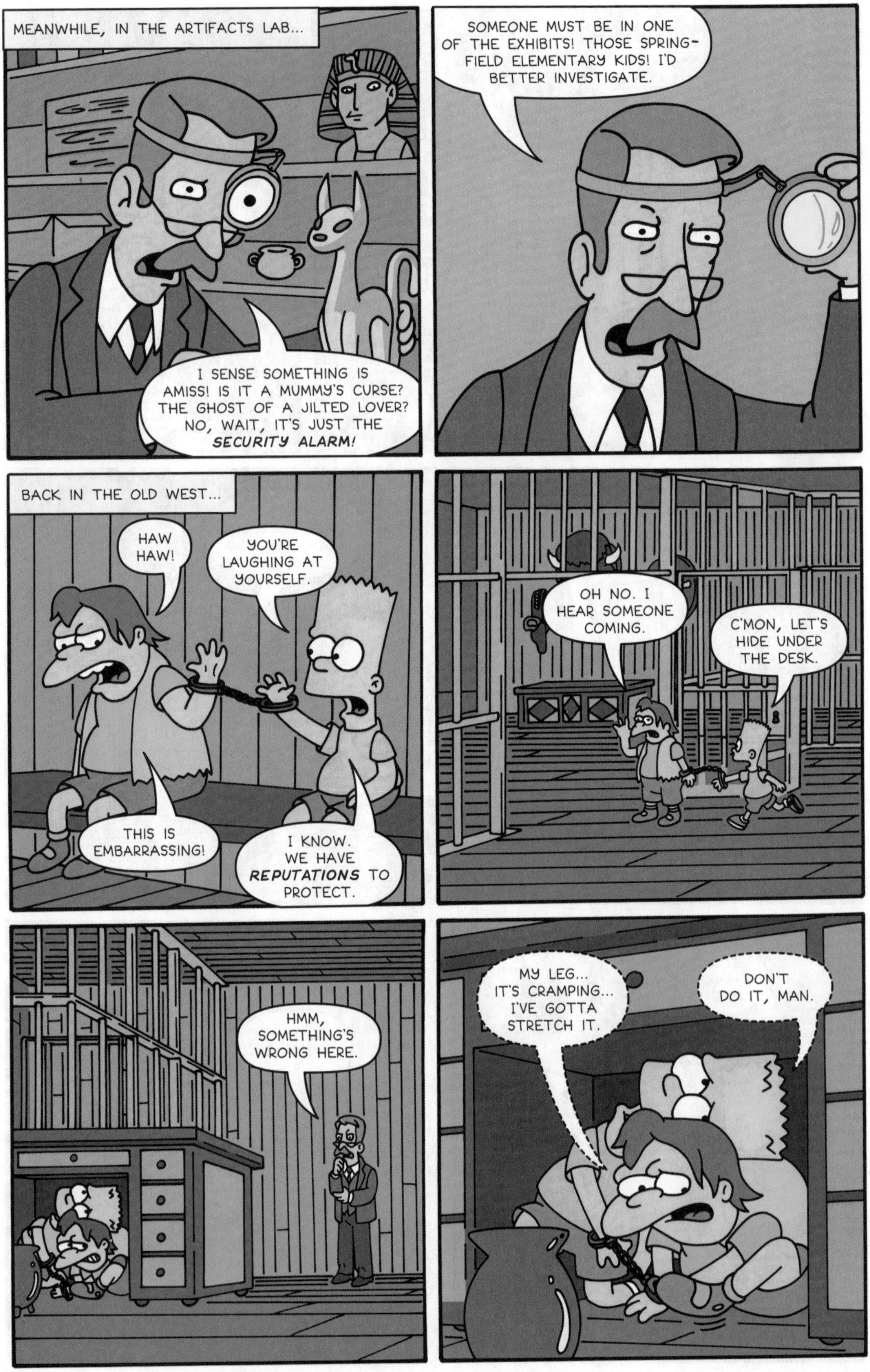
MEANWHILE, IN THE ARTIFACTS LAB...
I SENSE SOMETHING IS AMISS! IS IT A MUMMY'S CURSE? THE GHOST OF A JILTED LOVER? NO, WAIT, IT'S JUST THE SECURITY ALARM!
SOMEONE MUST BE IN ONE OF THE EXHIBITS! THOSE SPRING-FIELD ELEMENTARY KIDS! I'D BETTER INVESTIGATE.
BACK IN THE OLD WEST...
HAW HAW!
YOU'RE LAUGHING AT YOURSELF.
THIS IS EMBARRASSING!
I KNOW. WE HAVE REPUTATIONS TO PROTECT.
OH NO. I HEAR SOMEONE COMING.
C'MON, LET'S HIDE UNDER THE DESK.
HMM, SOMETHING'S WRONG HERE.
MY LEG... IT'S CRAMPING... I'VE GOTTA STRETCH IT.
DON'T DO IT, MAN.

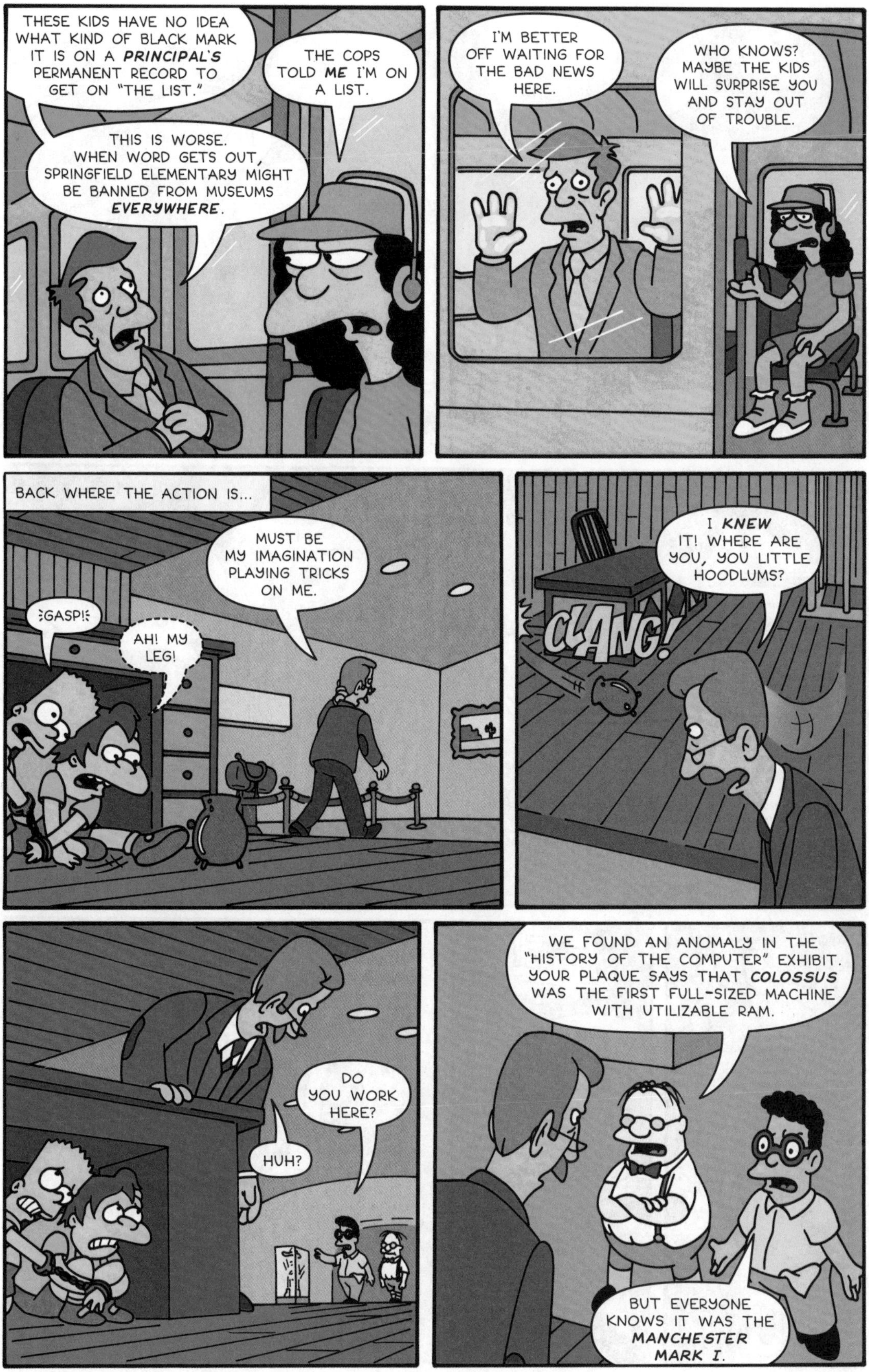
THESE KIDS HAVE NO IDEA WHAT KIND OF BLACK MARK IT IS ON A PRINCIPAL'S PERMANENT RECORD TO GET ON "THE LIST."
THE COPS TOLD ME I'M ON A LIST.
THIS IS WORSE. WHEN WORD GETS OUT, SPRINGFIELD ELEMENTARY MIGHT BE BANNED FROM MUSEUMS EVERYWHERE.
I'M BETTER OFF WAITING FOR THE BAD NEWS HERE.
WHO KNOWS? MAYBE THE KIDS WILL SURPRISE YOU AND STAY OUT OF TROUBLE.
BACK WHERE THE ACTION IS...
MUST BE MY IMAGINATION PLAYING TRICKS ON ME.
GASP!
AH! MY LEG!
CLANG!
I KNEW IT! WHERE ARE YOU, YOU LITTLE HOODLUMS?
DO YOU WORK HERE?
HUH?
WE FOUND AN ANOMALY IN THE "HISTORY OF THE COMPUTER" EXHIBIT. YOUR PLAQUE SAYS THAT COLOSSUS WAS THE FIRST FULL-SIZED MACHINE WITH UTILIZABLE RAM.
BUT EVERYONE KNOWS IT WAS THE MANCHESTER MARK I.

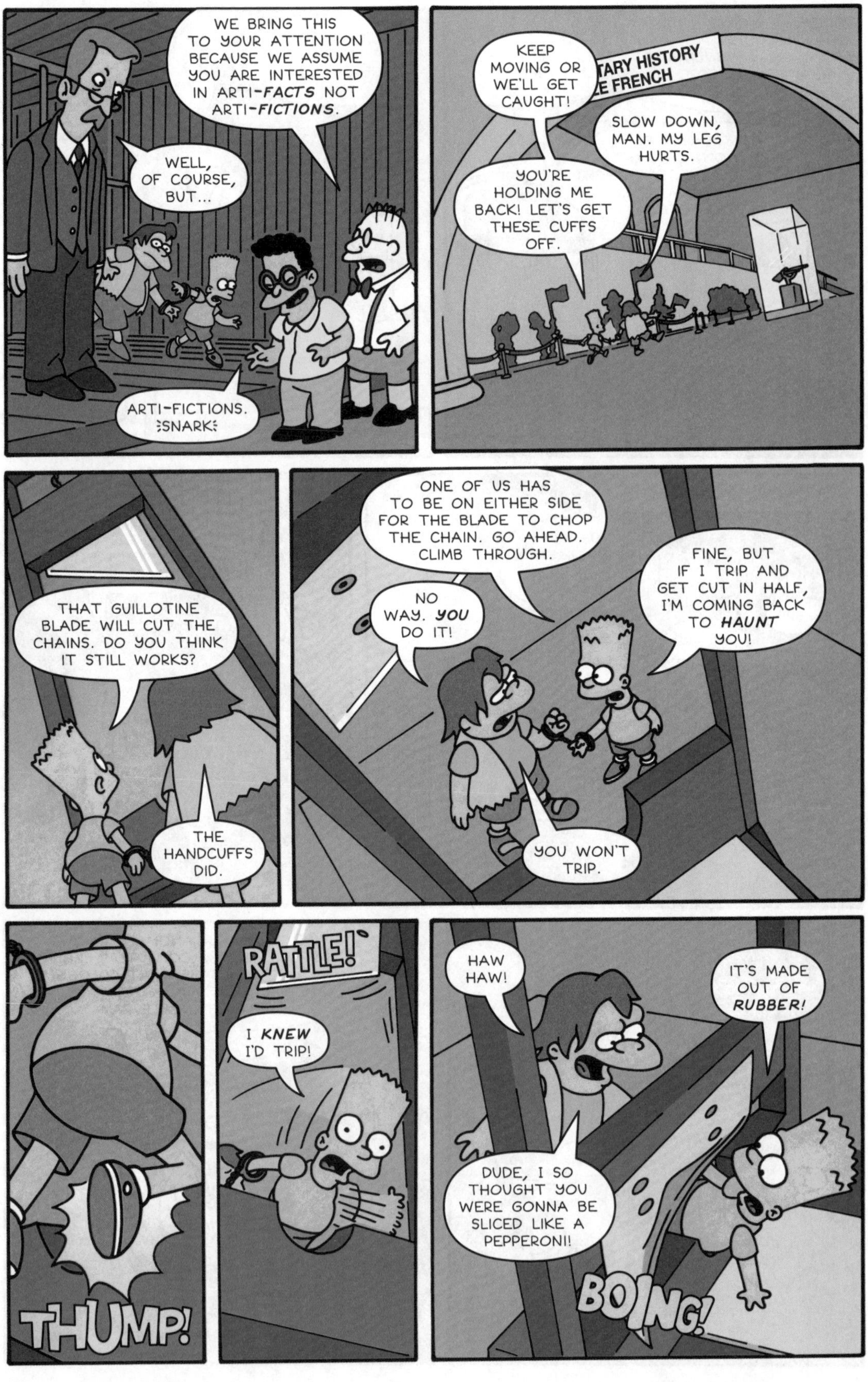

WE BRING THIS TO YOUR ATTENTION BECAUSE WE ASSUME YOU ARE INTERESTED IN ARTI-*FACTS* NOT ARTI-*FICTIONS*.
WELL, OF COURSE, BUT...
ARTI-FICTIONS. SNARK
KEEP MOVING OR WE'LL GET CAUGHT!
TARY HISTORY
E FRENCH
SLOW DOWN, MAN. MY LEG HURTS.
YOU'RE HOLDING ME BACK! LET'S GET THESE CUFFS OFF.
THAT GUILLOTINE BLADE WILL CUT THE CHAINS. DO YOU THINK IT STILL WORKS?
THE HANDCUFFS DID.
ONE OF US HAS TO BE ON EITHER SIDE FOR THE BLADE TO CHOP THE CHAIN. GO AHEAD. CLIMB THROUGH.
NO WAY. *YOU* DO IT!
FINE, BUT IF I TRIP AND GET CUT IN HALF, I'M COMING BACK TO *HAUNT* YOU!
YOU WON'T TRIP.
THUMP!
RATTLE!
I *KNEW* I'D TRIP!
HAW HAW!
IT'S MADE OUT OF *RUBBER*!
DUDE, I SO THOUGHT YOU WERE GONNA BE SLICED LIKE A PEPPERONI!
BOING!

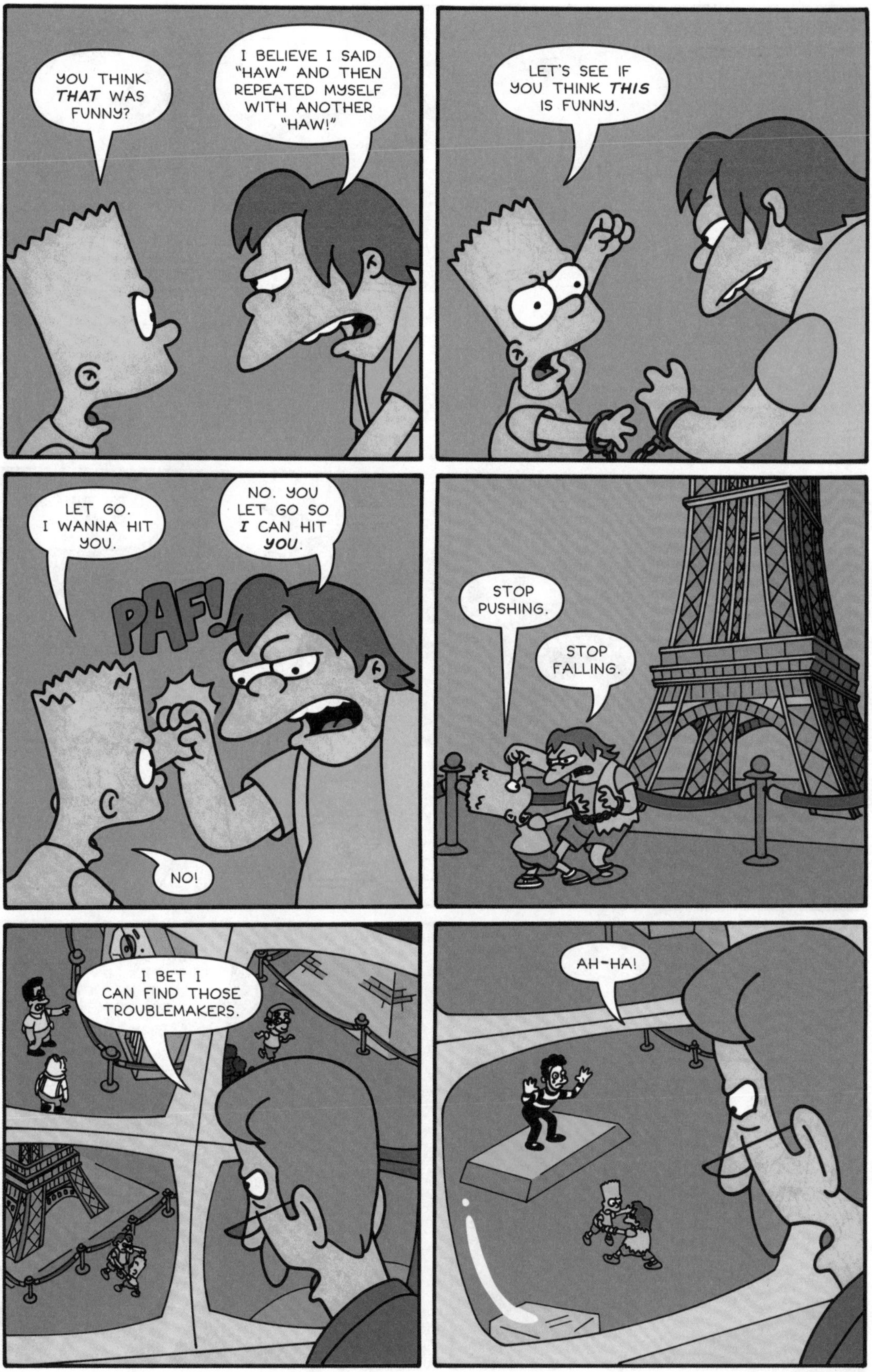
YOU THINK THAT WAS FUNNY?
I BELIEVE I SAID "HAW" AND THEN REPEATED MYSELF WITH ANOTHER "HAW!"
LET'S SEE IF YOU THINK THIS IS FUNNY.
LET GO. I WANNA HIT YOU.
NO. YOU LET GO SO I CAN HIT YOU.
PAF!
NO!
STOP PUSHING.
STOP FALLING.
I BET I CAN FIND THOSE TROUBLEMAKERS.
AH-HA!

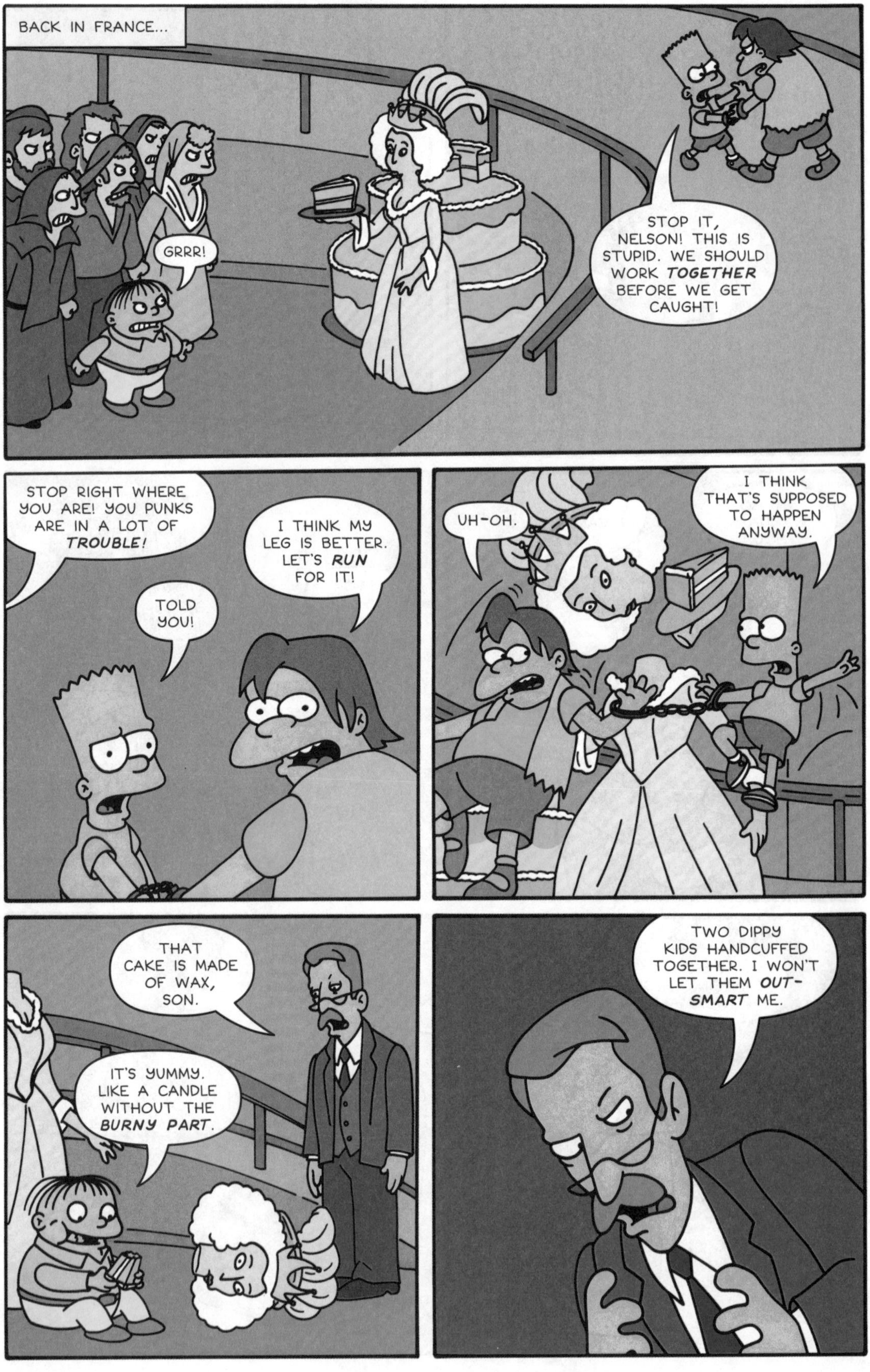
BACK IN FRANCE...
GRRR!
STOP IT, NELSON! THIS IS STUPID. WE SHOULD WORK TOGETHER BEFORE WE GET CAUGHT!
STOP RIGHT WHERE YOU ARE! YOU PUNKS ARE IN A LOT OF TROUBLE!
TOLD YOU!
I THINK MY LEG IS BETTER. LET'S RUN FOR IT!
UH-OH.
I THINK THAT'S SUPPOSED TO HAPPEN ANYWAY.
THAT CAKE IS MADE OF WAX, SON.
IT'S YUMMY. LIKE A CANDLE WITHOUT THE BURNY PART.
TWO DIPPY KIDS HANDCUFFED TOGETHER. I WON'T LET THEM OUT-SMART ME.

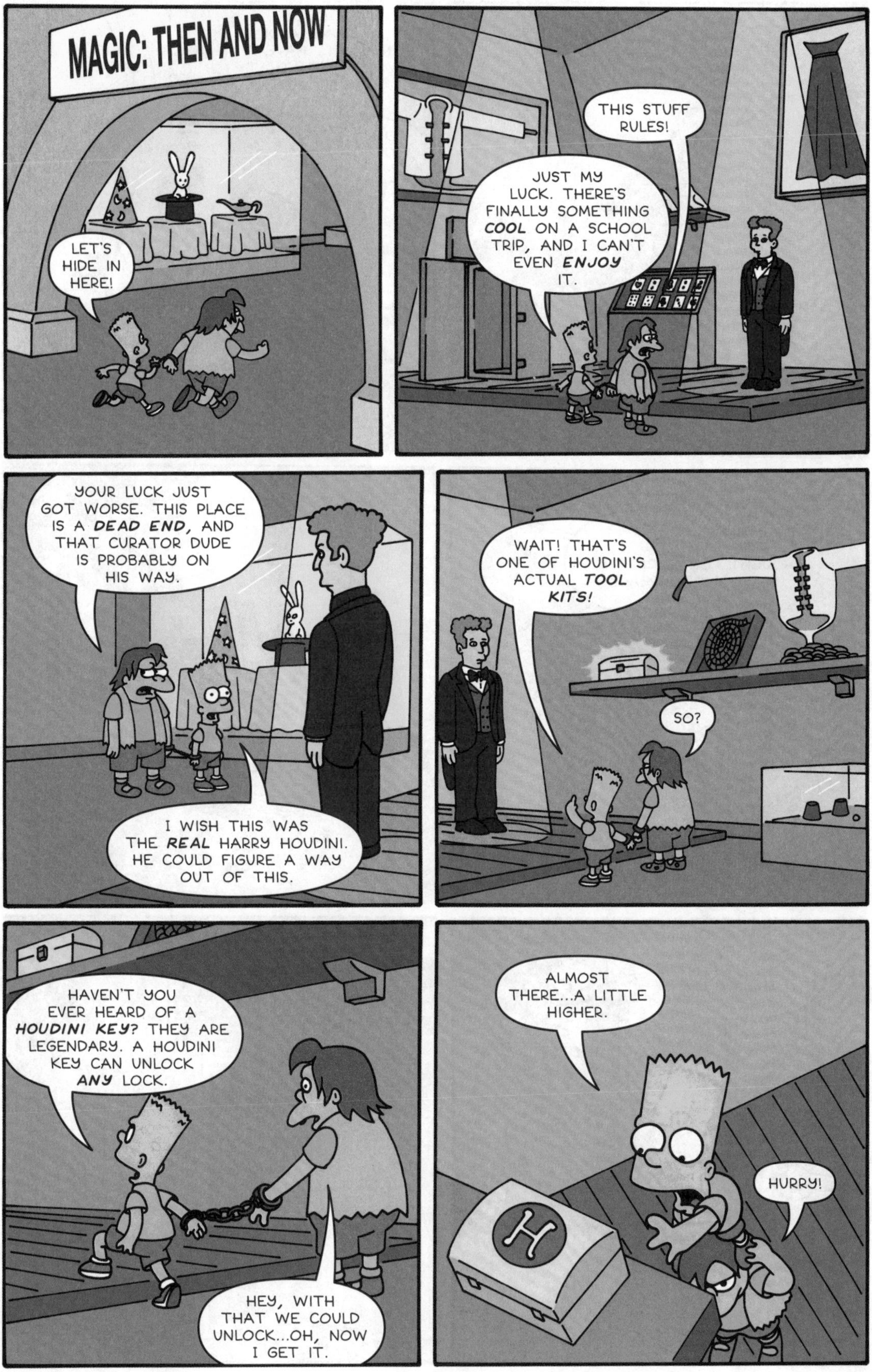
MAGIC: THEN AND NOW
LET'S HIDE IN HERE!
THIS STUFF RULES!
JUST MY LUCK. THERE'S FINALLY SOMETHING COOL ON A SCHOOL TRIP, AND I CAN'T EVEN ENJOY IT.
YOUR LUCK JUST GOT WORSE. THIS PLACE IS A DEAD END, AND THAT CURATOR DUDE IS PROBABLY ON HIS WAY.
I WISH THIS WAS THE REAL HARRY HOUDINI. HE COULD FIGURE A WAY OUT OF THIS.
WAIT! THAT'S ONE OF HOUDINI'S ACTUAL TOOL KITS!
SO?
HAVEN'T YOU EVER HEARD OF A HOUDINI KEY? THEY ARE LEGENDARY. A HOUDINI KEY CAN UNLOCK ANY LOCK.
HEY, WITH THAT WE COULD UNLOCK...OH, NOW I GET IT.
ALMOST THERE...A LITTLE HIGHER.
HURRY!

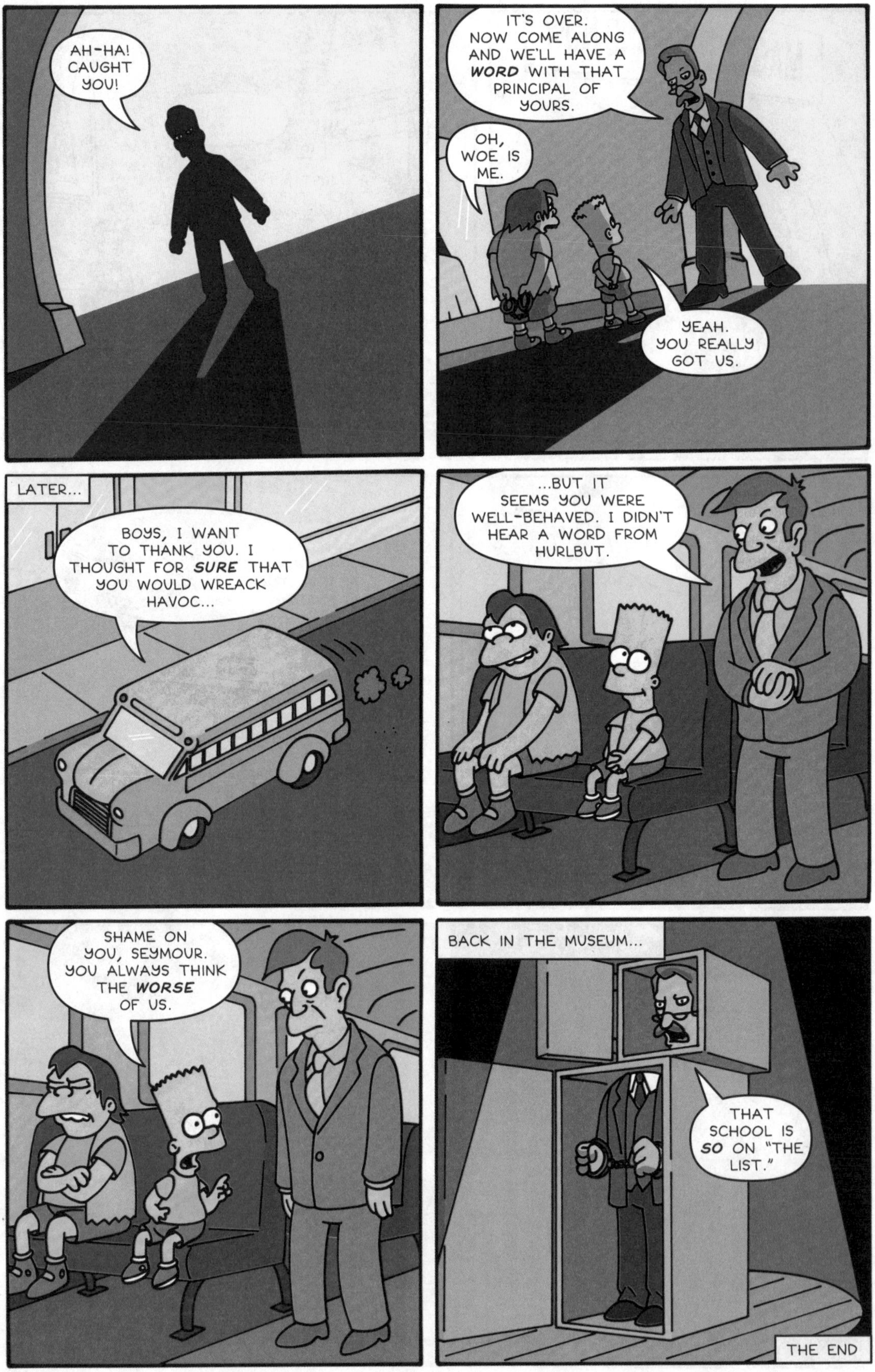
AH-HA! CAUGHT YOU!
IT'S OVER. NOW COME ALONG AND WE'LL HAVE A **WORD** WITH THAT PRINCIPAL OF YOURS.
OH, WOE IS ME.
YEAH. YOU REALLY GOT US.
LATER...
BOYS, I WANT TO THANK YOU. I THOUGHT FOR **SURE** THAT YOU WOULD WREACK HAVOC...
...BUT IT SEEMS YOU WERE WELL-BEHAVED. I DIDN'T HEAR A WORD FROM HURLBUT.
SHAME ON YOU, SEYMOUR. YOU ALWAYS THINK THE **WORSE** OF US.
BACK IN THE MUSEUM...
THAT SCHOOL IS **SO** ON "THE LIST."
THE END

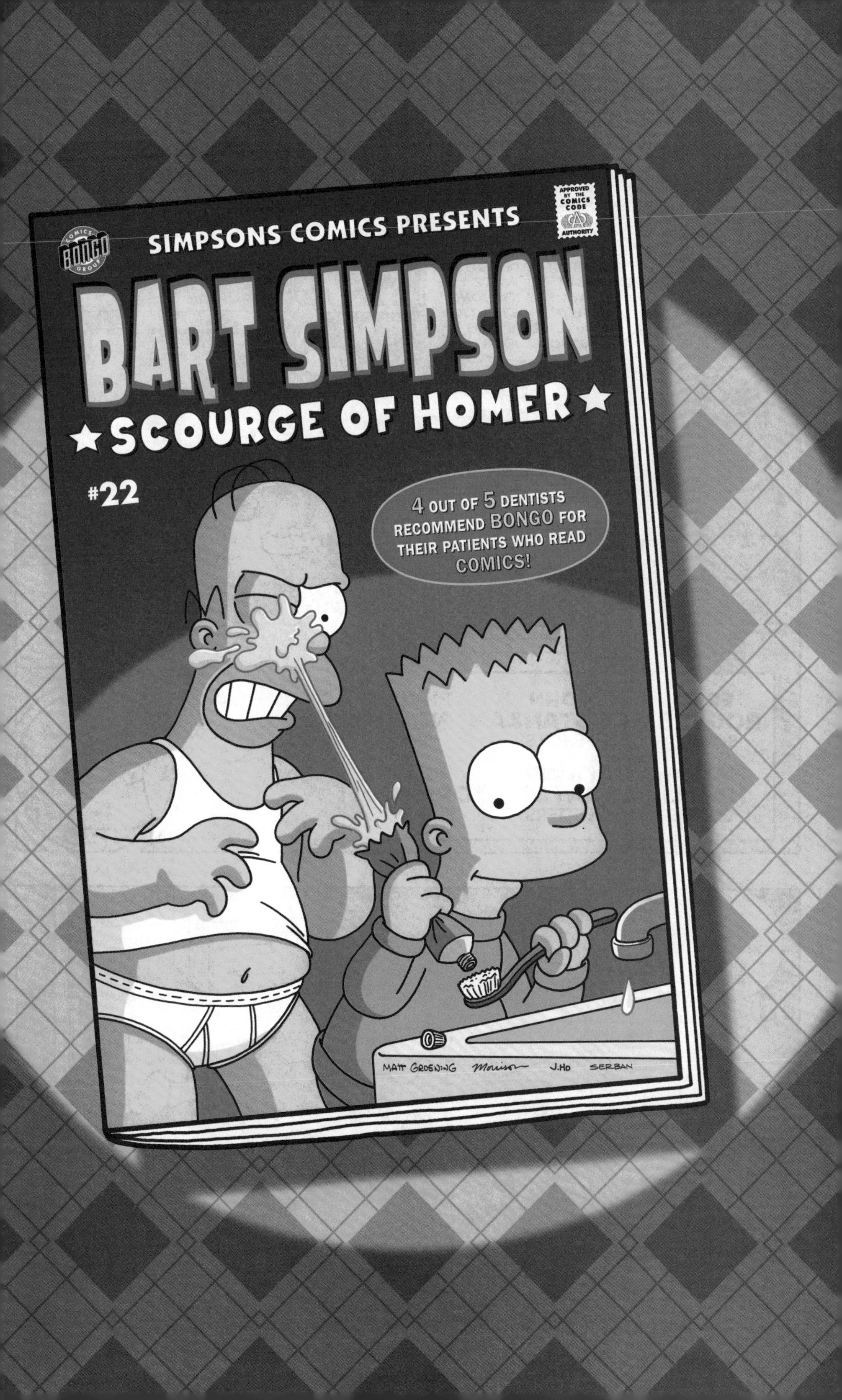

COMICS BONGO GROUP
SIMPSONS COMICS PRESENTS
APPROVED BY THE COMICS CODE AUTHORITY
BART SIMPSON
★SCOURGE OF HOMER★
#22
4 OUT OF 5 DENTISTS RECOMMEND BONGO FOR THEIR PATIENTS WHO READ COMICS!
MATT GROENING
J.HO
SERBAN

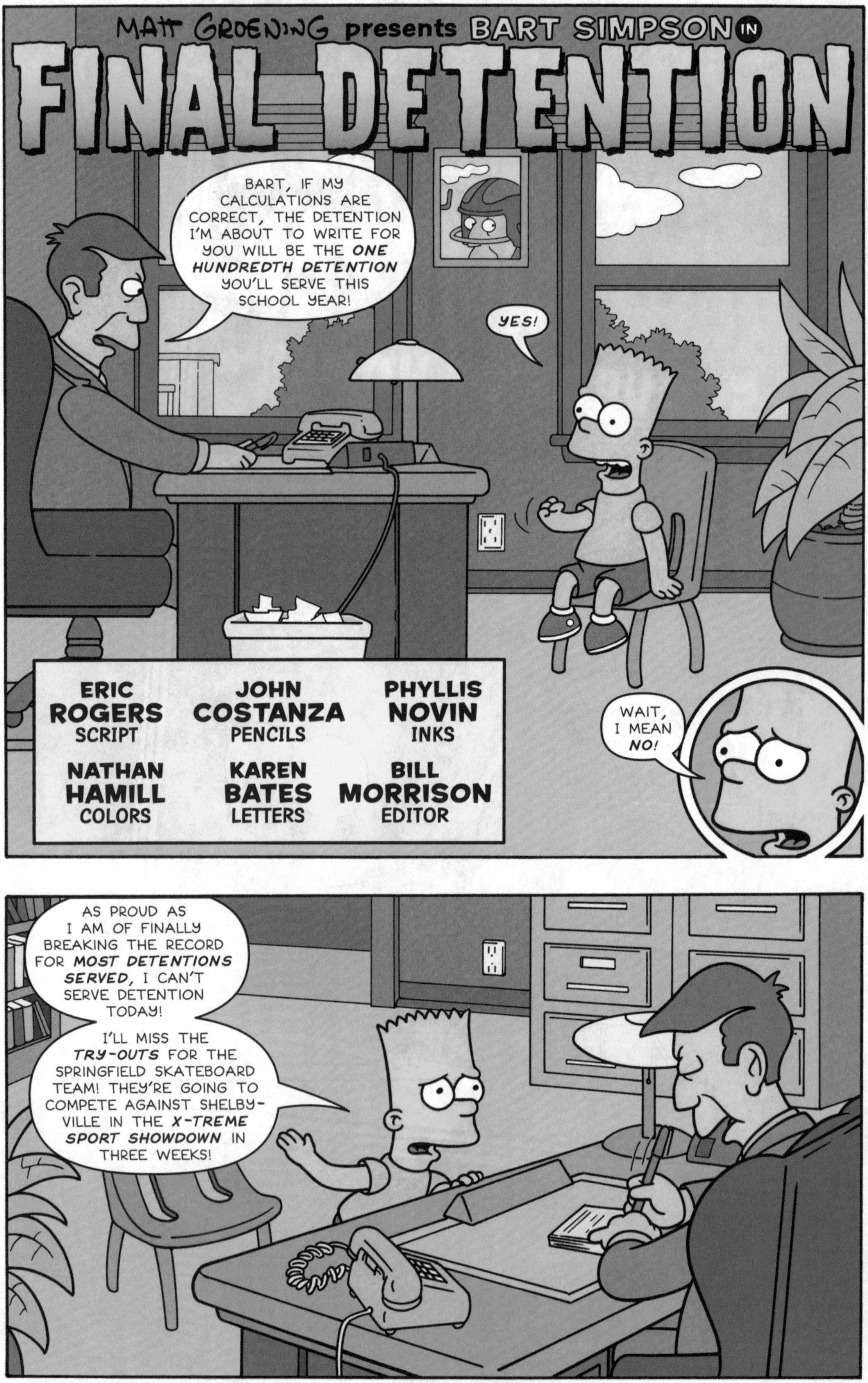
MATT GROENING presents BART SIMPSON IN
FINAL DETENTION
BART, IF MY CALCULATIONS ARE CORRECT, THE DETENTION I'M ABOUT TO WRITE FOR YOU WILL BE THE ONE HUNDREDTH DETENTION YOU'LL SERVE THIS SCHOOL YEAR!
YES!
ERIC ROGERS SCRIPT
JOHN COSTANZA PENCILS
PHYLLIS NOVIN INKS
NATHAN HAMILL COLORS
KAREN BATES LETTERS
BILL MORRISON EDITOR
WAIT, I MEAN NO!
AS PROUD AS I AM OF FINALLY BREAKING THE RECORD FOR MOST DETENTIONS SERVED, I CAN'T SERVE DETENTION TODAY!
I'LL MISS THE TRY-OUTS FOR THE SPRINGFIELD SKATEBOARD TEAM! THEY'RE GOING TO COMPETE AGAINST SHELBY-VILLE IN THE X-TREME SPORT SHOWDOWN IN THREE WEEKS!

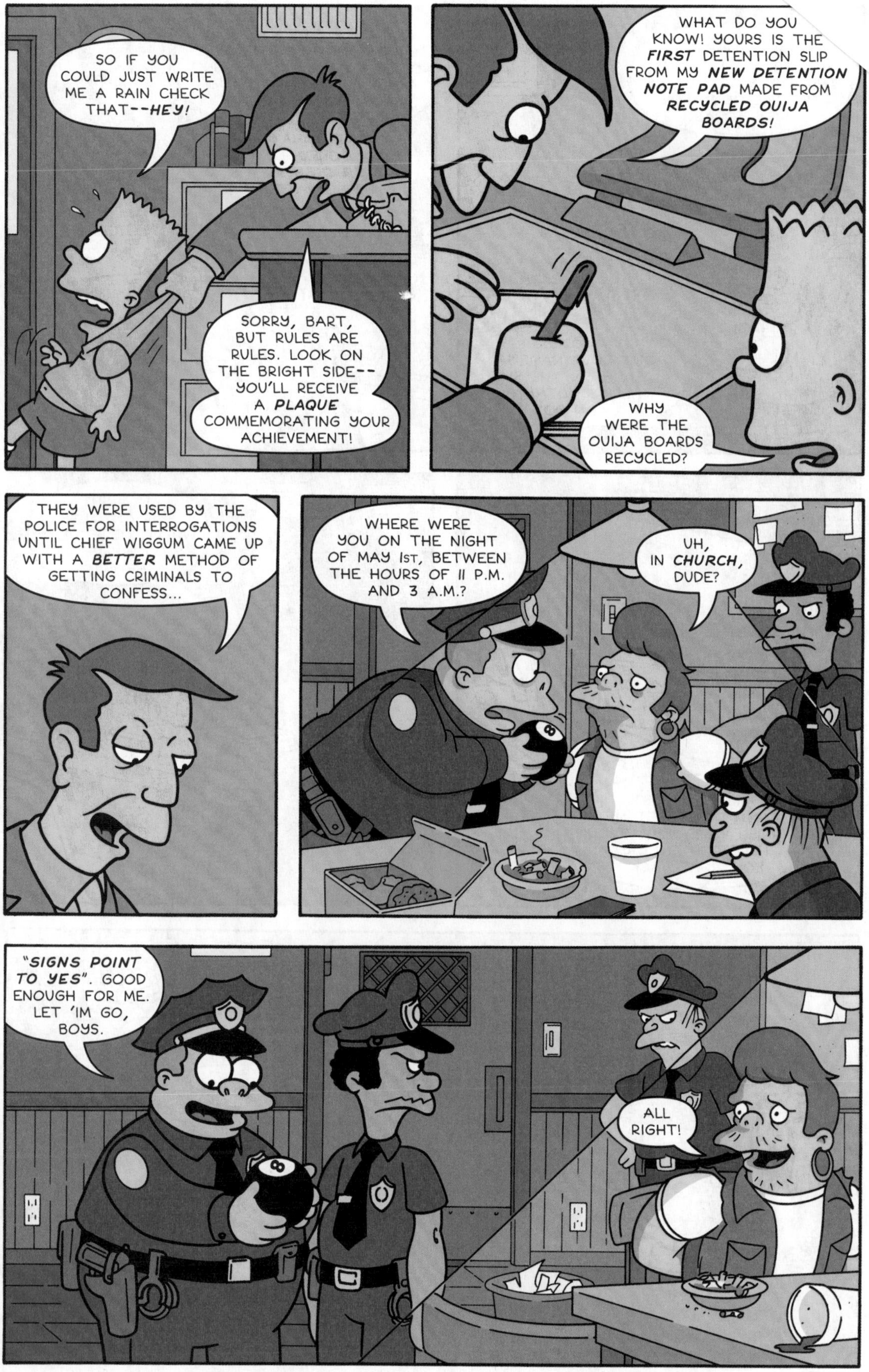
SO IF YOU COULD JUST WRITE ME A RAIN CHECK THAT--HEY!
SORRY, BART, BUT RULES ARE RULES. LOOK ON THE BRIGHT SIDE-- YOU'LL RECEIVE A PLAQUE COMMEMORATING YOUR ACHIEVEMENT!
WHAT DO YOU KNOW! YOURS IS THE FIRST DETENTION SLIP FROM MY NEW DETENTION NOTE PAD MADE FROM RECYCLED OUIJA BOARDS!
WHY WERE THE OUIJA BOARDS RECYCLED?
THEY WERE USED BY THE POLICE FOR INTERROGATIONS UNTIL CHIEF WIGGUM CAME UP WITH A BETTER METHOD OF GETTING CRIMINALS TO CONFESS...
WHERE WERE YOU ON THE NIGHT OF MAY 1st, BETWEEN THE HOURS OF 11 P.M. AND 3 A.M.?
UH, IN CHURCH, DUDE?
"SIGNS POINT TO YES". GOOD ENOUGH FOR ME. LET 'IM GO, BOYS.
ALL RIGHT!

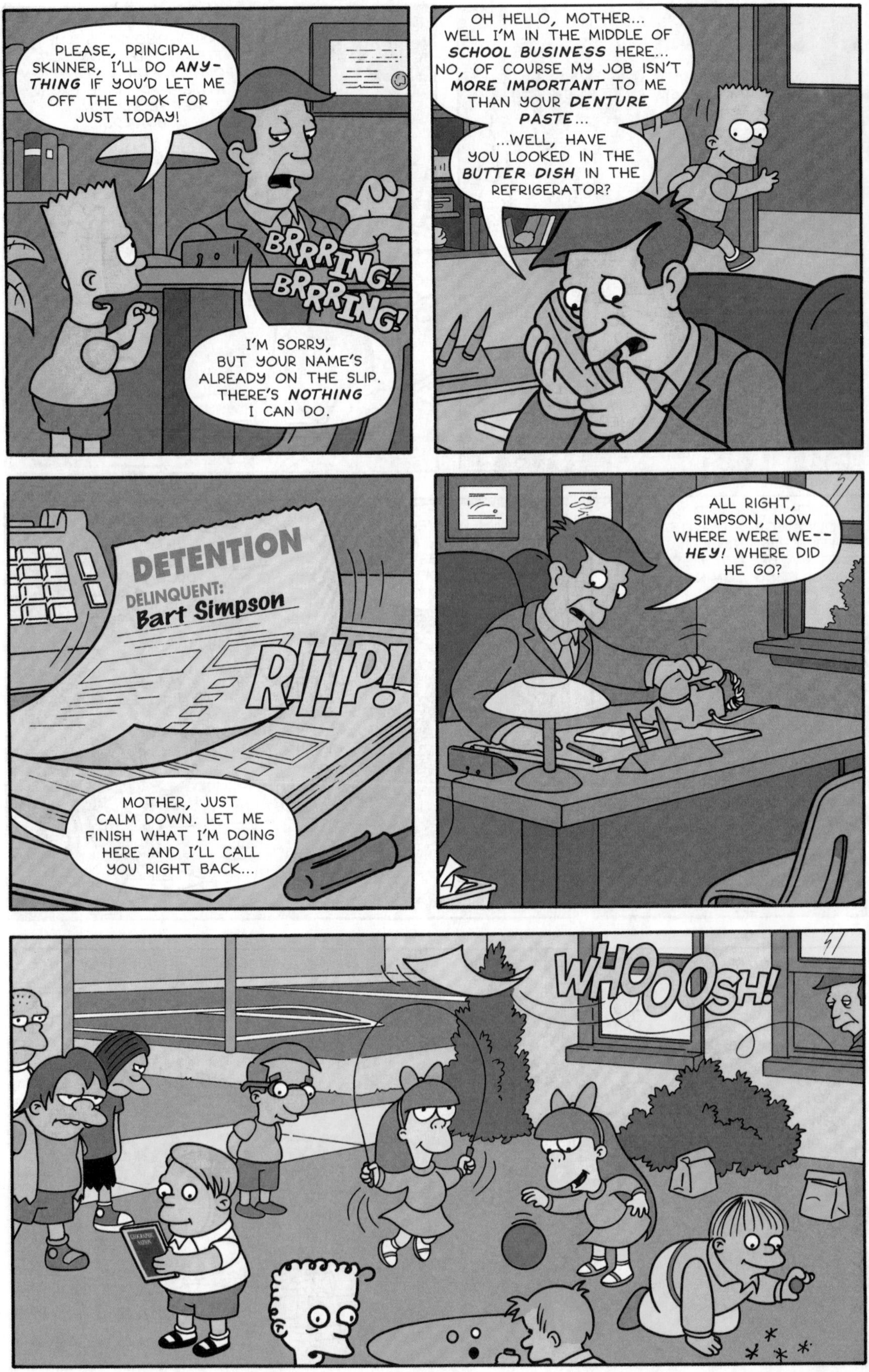
PLEASE, PRINCIPAL SKINNER, I'LL DO ANY-THING IF YOU'D LET ME OFF THE HOOK FOR JUST TODAY!
BRRRING! BRRRING!
I'M SORRY, BUT YOUR NAME'S ALREADY ON THE SLIP. THERE'S NOTHING I CAN DO.
OH HELLO, MOTHER... WELL I'M IN THE MIDDLE OF SCHOOL BUSINESS HERE... NO, OF COURSE MY JOB ISN'T MORE IMPORTANT TO ME THAN YOUR DENTURE PASTE...
...WELL, HAVE YOU LOOKED IN THE BUTTER DISH IN THE REFRIGERATOR?
DETENTION
DELINQUENT:
Bart Simpson
RIIIP!
MOTHER, JUST CALM DOWN. LET ME FINISH WHAT I'M DOING HERE AND I'LL CALL YOU RIGHT BACK...
ALL RIGHT, SIMPSON, NOW WHERE WERE WE-- HEY! WHERE DID HE GO?
WHOOOSH!

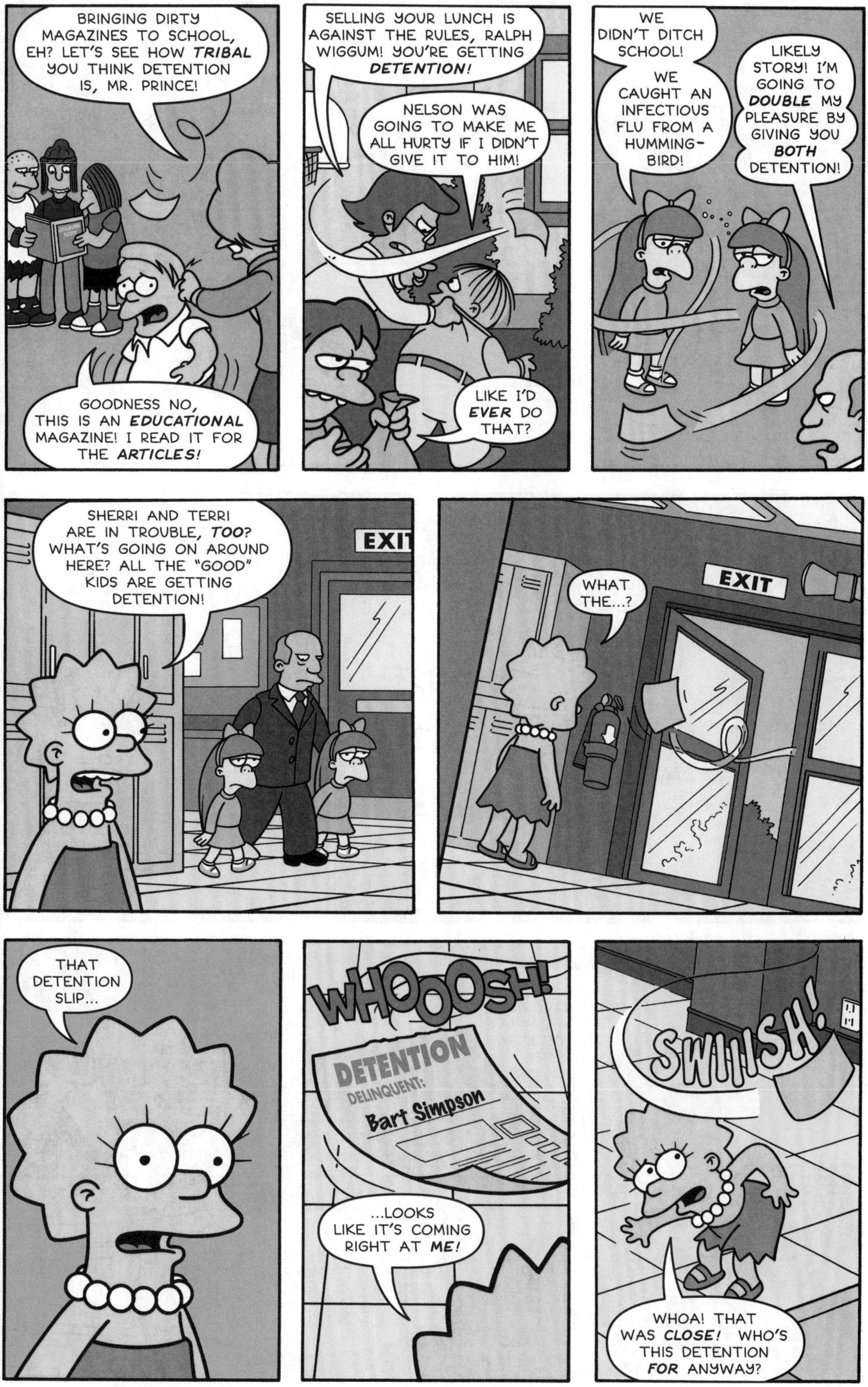
BRINGING DIRTY MAGAZINES TO SCHOOL, EH? LET'S SEE HOW TRIBAL YOU THINK DETENTION IS, MR. PRINCE!
GEOGRAPHIC NATION
GOODNESS NO, THIS IS AN EDUCATIONAL MAGAZINE! I READ IT FOR THE ARTICLES!
SELLING YOUR LUNCH IS AGAINST THE RULES, RALPH WIGGUM! YOU'RE GETTING DETENTION!
NELSON WAS GOING TO MAKE ME ALL HURTY IF I DIDN'T GIVE IT TO HIM!
LIKE I'D EVER DO THAT?
WE DIDN'T DITCH SCHOOL!
WE CAUGHT AN INFECTIOUS FLU FROM A HUMMING-BIRD!
LIKELY STORY! I'M GOING TO DOUBLE MY PLEASURE BY GIVING YOU BOTH DETENTION!
SHERRI AND TERRI ARE IN TROUBLE, TOO? WHAT'S GOING ON AROUND HERE? ALL THE "GOOD" KIDS ARE GETTING DETENTION!
EXIT
WHAT THE...?
EXIT
THAT DETENTION SLIP...
WHOOOSH!
DETENTION
DELINQUENT:
Bart Simpson
...LOOKS LIKE IT'S COMING RIGHT AT ME!
SWIIISH!
WHOA! THAT WAS CLOSE! WHO'S THIS DETENTION FOR ANYWAY?

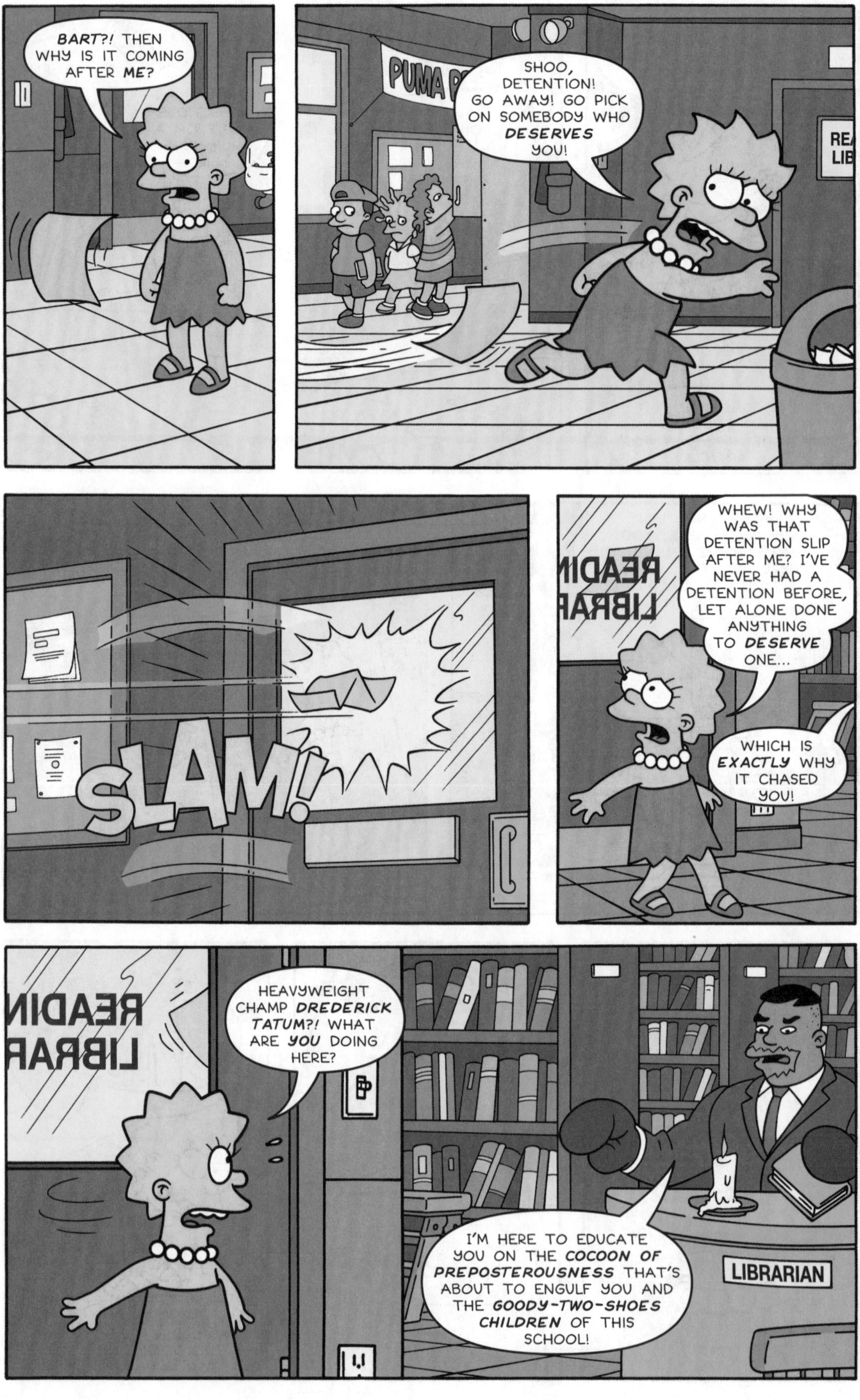
BART?! THEN WHY IS IT COMING AFTER ME?
PUMA P
SHOO, DETENTION! GO AWAY! GO PICK ON SOMEBODY WHO DESERVES YOU!
REA LIB
SLAM!
READIN LIBRAR
WHEW! WHY WAS THAT DETENTION SLIP AFTER ME? I'VE NEVER HAD A DETENTION BEFORE, LET ALONE DONE ANYTHING TO DESERVE ONE...
WHICH IS EXACTLY WHY IT CHASED YOU!
READIN LIBRAR
HEAVYWEIGHT CHAMP DREDERICK TATUM?! WHAT ARE YOU DOING HERE?
I'M HERE TO EDUCATE YOU ON THE COCOON OF PREPOSTEROUSNESS THAT'S ABOUT TO ENGULF YOU AND THE GOODY-TWO-SHOES CHILDREN OF THIS SCHOOL!
LIBRARIAN

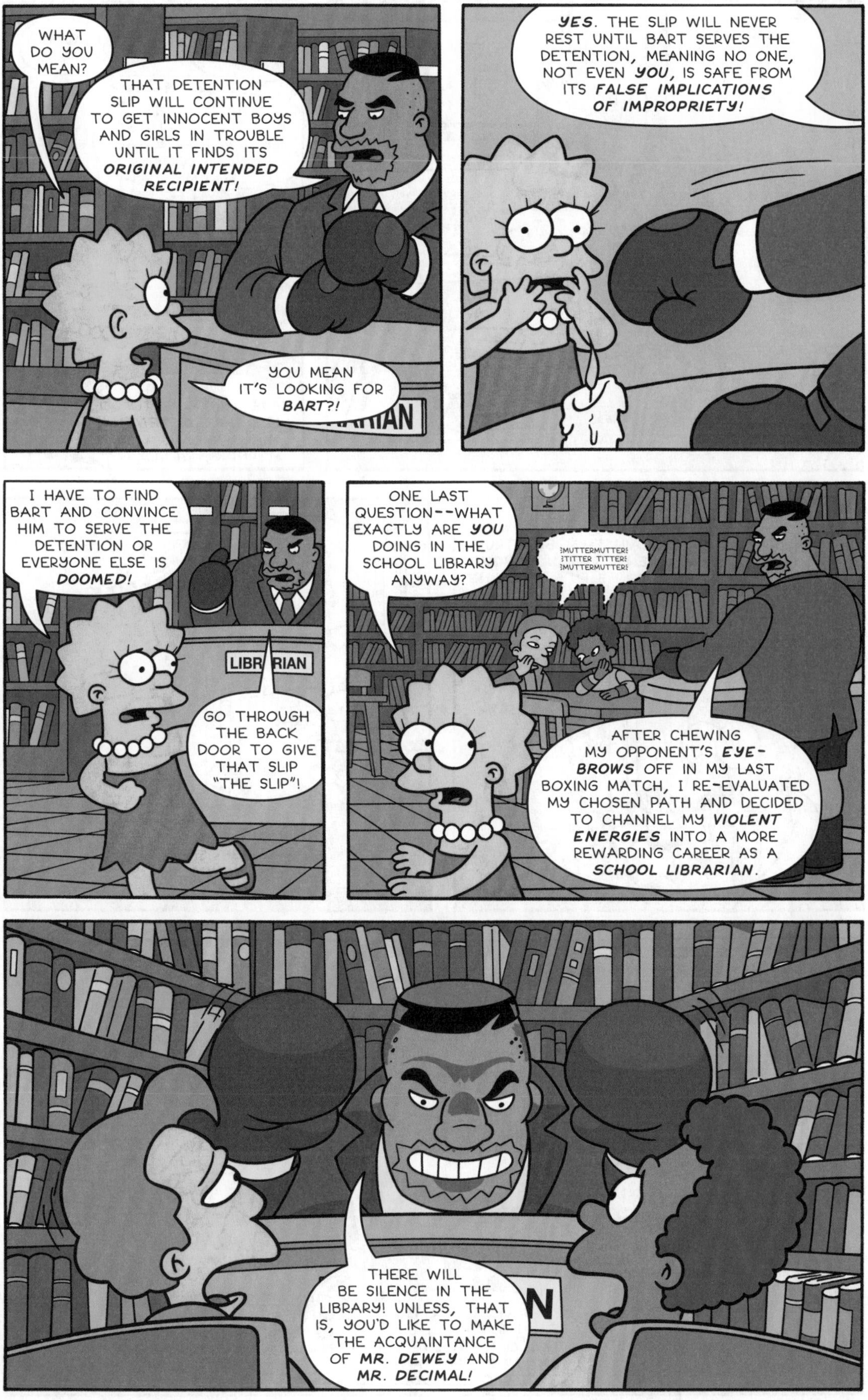
WHAT DO YOU MEAN?
THAT DETENTION SLIP WILL CONTINUE TO GET INNOCENT BOYS AND GIRLS IN TROUBLE UNTIL IT FINDS ITS ORIGINAL INTENDED RECIPIENT!
YOU MEAN IT'S LOOKING FOR BART?!
RARIAN
YES. THE SLIP WILL NEVER REST UNTIL BART SERVES THE DETENTION, MEANING NO ONE, NOT EVEN YOU, IS SAFE FROM ITS FALSE IMPLICATIONS OF IMPROPRIETY!
I HAVE TO FIND BART AND CONVINCE HIM TO SERVE THE DETENTION OR EVERYONE ELSE IS DOOMED!
LIBRARIAN
GO THROUGH THE BACK DOOR TO GIVE THAT SLIP "THE SLIP"!
ONE LAST QUESTION--WHAT EXACTLY ARE YOU DOING IN THE SCHOOL LIBRARY ANYWAY?
MUTTERMUTTER TITTER TITTER MUTTERMUTTER
AFTER CHEWING MY OPPONENT'S EYE-BROWS OFF IN MY LAST BOXING MATCH, I RE-EVALUATED MY CHOSEN PATH AND DECIDED TO CHANNEL MY VIOLENT ENERGIES INTO A MORE REWARDING CAREER AS A SCHOOL LIBRARIAN.
N
THERE WILL BE SILENCE IN THE LIBRARY! UNLESS, THAT IS, YOU'D LIKE TO MAKE THE ACQUAINTANCE OF MR. DEWEY AND MR. DECIMAL!

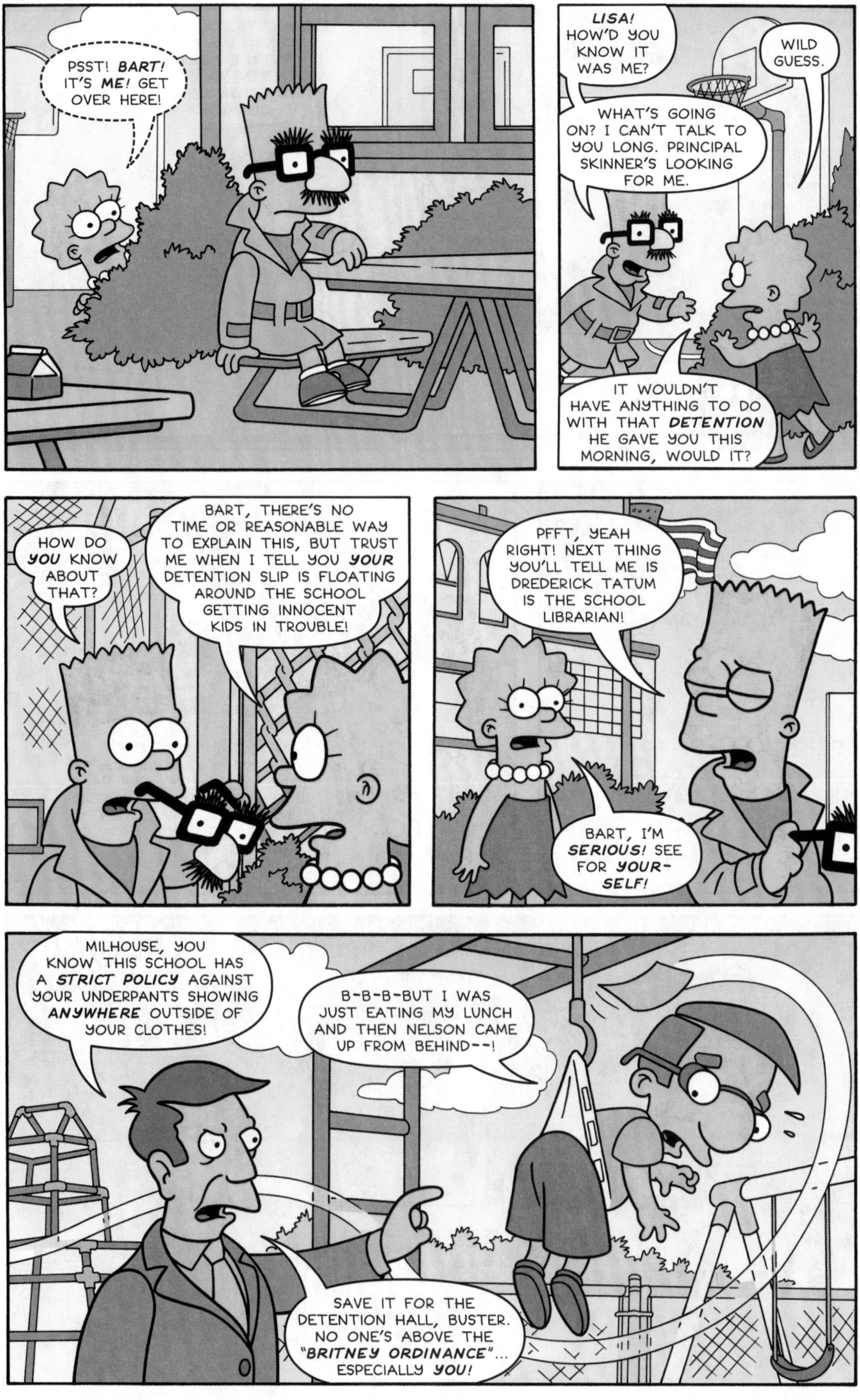
PSST! BART! IT'S ME! GET OVER HERE!
LISA! HOW'D YOU KNOW IT WAS ME?
WILD GUESS.
WHAT'S GOING ON? I CAN'T TALK TO YOU LONG. PRINCIPAL SKINNER'S LOOKING FOR ME.
IT WOULDN'T HAVE ANYTHING TO DO WITH THAT DETENTION HE GAVE YOU THIS MORNING, WOULD IT?
HOW DO YOU KNOW ABOUT THAT?
BART, THERE'S NO TIME OR REASONABLE WAY TO EXPLAIN THIS, BUT TRUST ME WHEN I TELL YOU YOUR DETENTION SLIP IS FLOATING AROUND THE SCHOOL GETTING INNOCENT KIDS IN TROUBLE!
PFFT, YEAH RIGHT! NEXT THING YOU'LL TELL ME IS DREDERICK TATUM IS THE SCHOOL LIBRARIAN!
BART, I'M SERIOUS! SEE FOR YOURSELF!
MILHOUSE, YOU KNOW THIS SCHOOL HAS A STRICT POLICY AGAINST YOUR UNDERPANTS SHOWING ANYWHERE OUTSIDE OF YOUR CLOTHES!
B-B-B-BUT I WAS JUST EATING MY LUNCH AND THEN NELSON CAME UP FROM BEHIND--!
SAVE IT FOR THE DETENTION HALL, BUSTER. NO ONE'S ABOVE THE "BRITNEY ORDINANCE"... ESPECIALLY YOU!

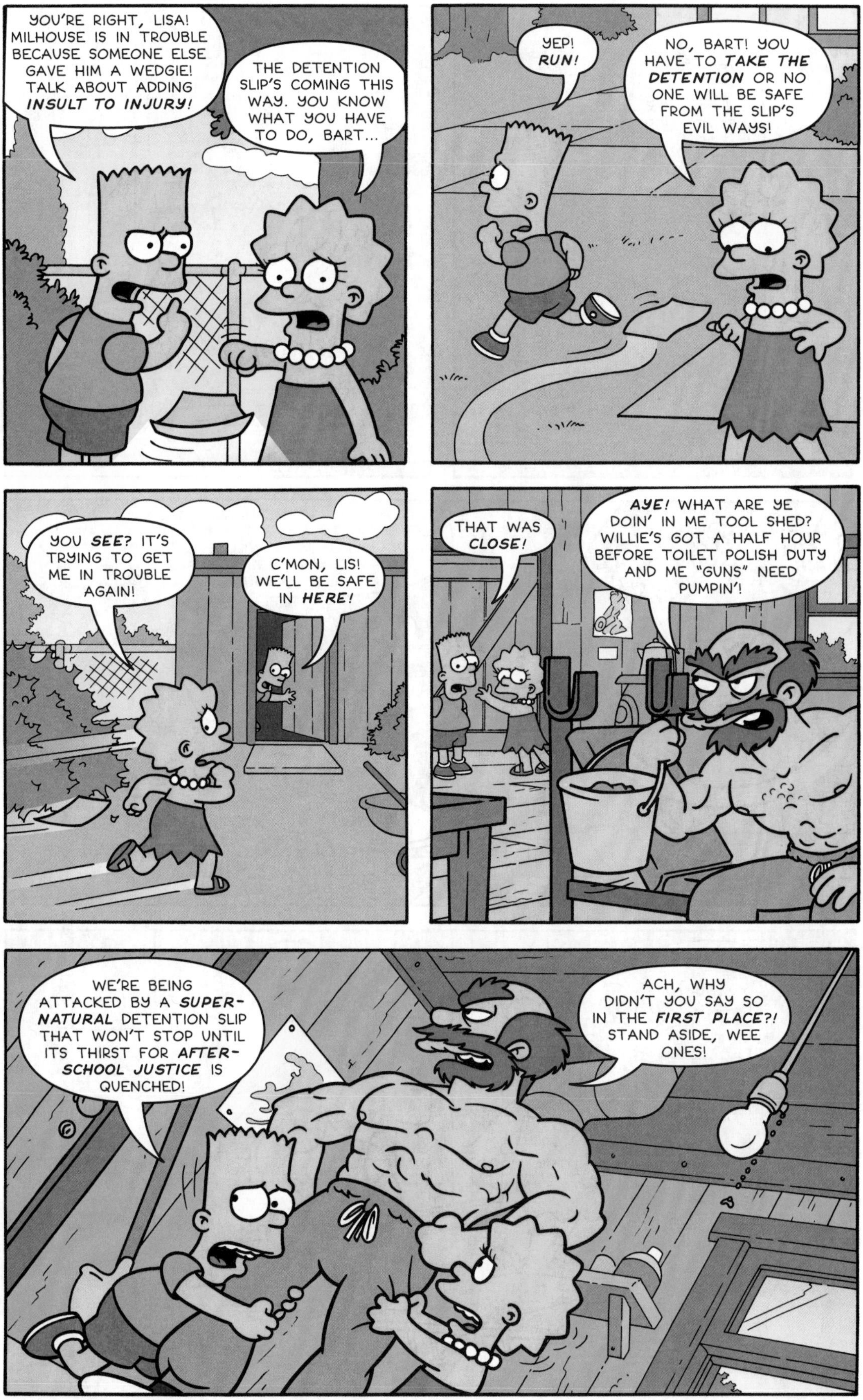
YOU'RE RIGHT, LISA! MILHOUSE IS IN TROUBLE BECAUSE SOMEONE ELSE GAVE HIM A WEDGIE! TALK ABOUT ADDING INSULT TO INJURY!
THE DETENTION SLIP'S COMING THIS WAY. YOU KNOW WHAT YOU HAVE TO DO, BART...
YEP! RUN!
NO, BART! YOU HAVE TO TAKE THE DETENTION OR NO ONE WILL BE SAFE FROM THE SLIP'S EVIL WAYS!
YOU SEE? IT'S TRYING TO GET ME IN TROUBLE AGAIN!
C'MON, LIS! WE'LL BE SAFE IN HERE!
THAT WAS CLOSE!
AYE! WHAT ARE YE DOIN' IN ME TOOL SHED? WILLIE'S GOT A HALF HOUR BEFORE TOILET POLISH DUTY AND ME "GUNS" NEED PUMPIN'!
WE'RE BEING ATTACKED BY A SUPER-NATURAL DETENTION SLIP THAT WON'T STOP UNTIL ITS THIRST FOR AFTER-SCHOOL JUSTICE IS QUENCHED!
ACH, WHY DIDN'T YOU SAY SO IN THE FIRST PLACE?! STAND ASIDE, WEE ONES!

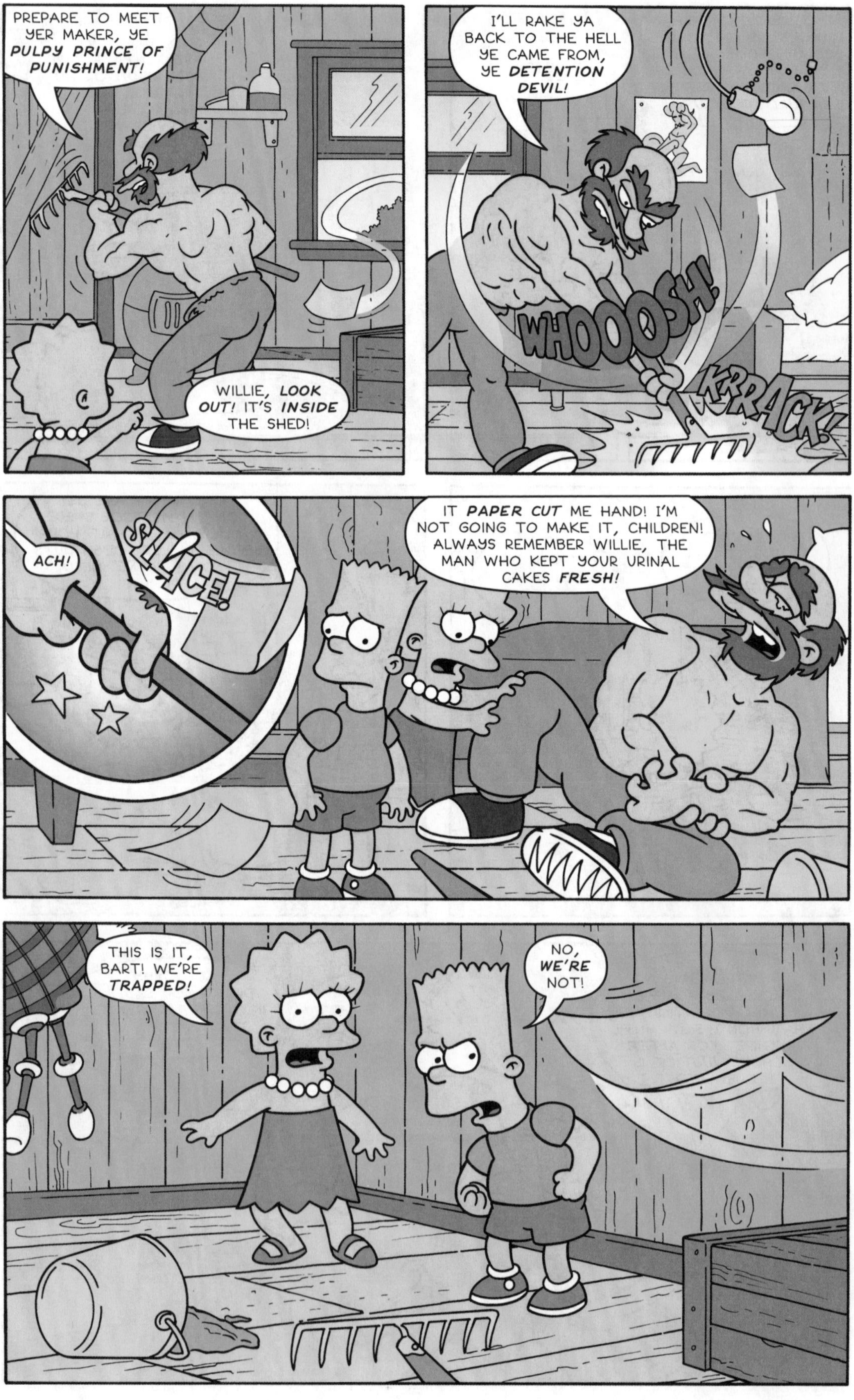
PREPARE TO MEET YER MAKER, YE PULPY PRINCE OF PUNISHMENT!
WILLIE, LOOK OUT! IT'S INSIDE THE SHED!
I'LL RAKE YA BACK TO THE HELL YE CAME FROM, YE DETENTION DEVIL!
WHOOOSH!
KRRACK!
ACH!
SLLICE!
IT PAPER CUT ME HAND! I'M NOT GOING TO MAKE IT, CHILDREN! ALWAYS REMEMBER WILLIE, THE MAN WHO KEPT YOUR URINAL CAKES FRESH!
THIS IS IT, BART! WE'RE TRAPPED!
NO, WE'RE NOT!

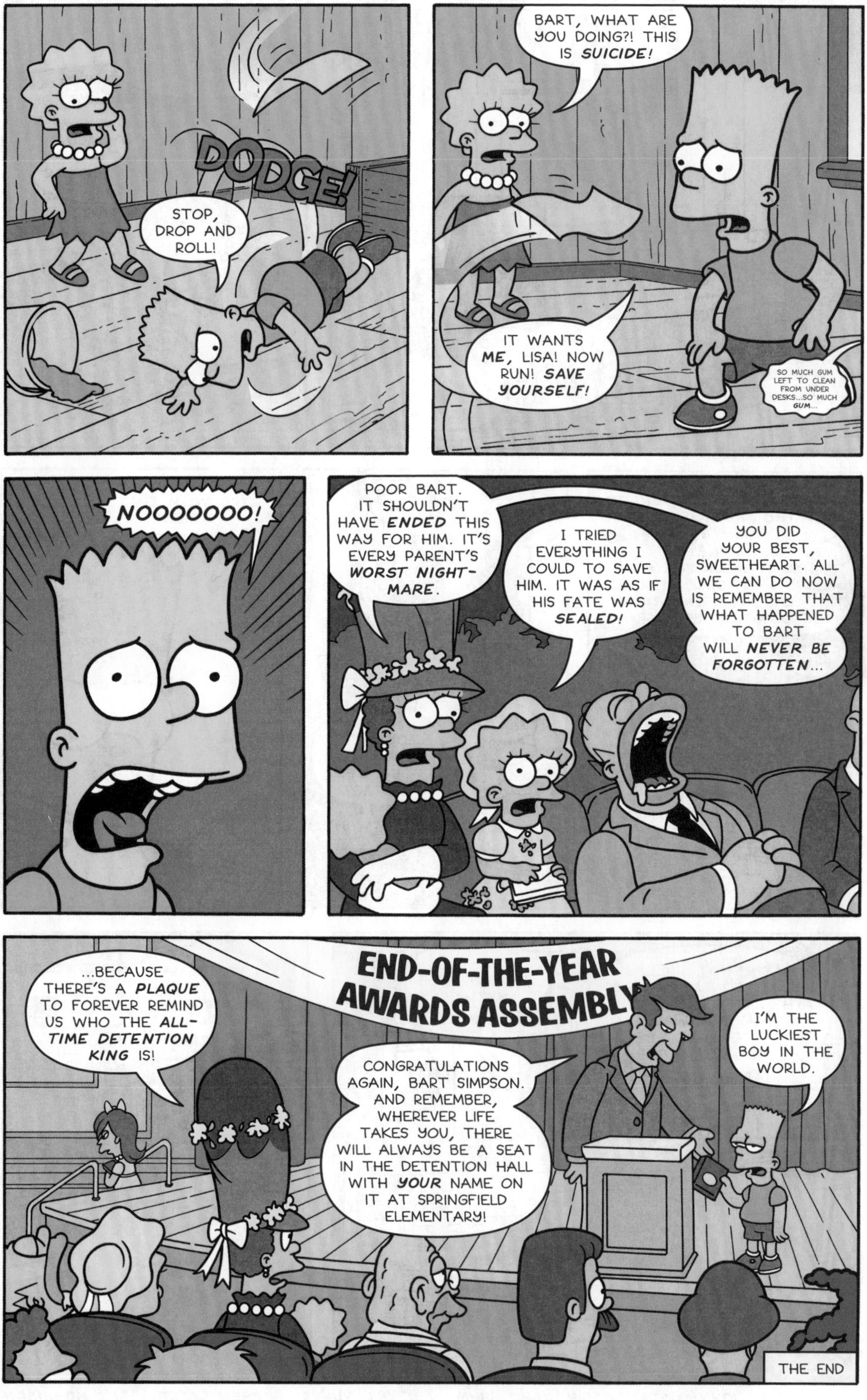
DODGE!
STOP, DROP AND ROLL!
BART, WHAT ARE YOU DOING?! THIS IS SUICIDE!
IT WANTS ME, LISA! NOW RUN! SAVE YOURSELF!
SO MUCH GUM LEFT TO CLEAN FROM UNDER DESKS...SO MUCH GUM...
NOOOOOOO!
POOR BART. IT SHOULDN'T HAVE ENDED THIS WAY FOR HIM. IT'S EVERY PARENT'S WORST NIGHT-MARE.
I TRIED EVERYTHING I COULD TO SAVE HIM. IT WAS AS IF HIS FATE WAS SEALED!
YOU DID YOUR BEST, SWEETHEART. ALL WE CAN DO NOW IS REMEMBER THAT WHAT HAPPENED TO BART WILL NEVER BE FORGOTTEN...
END-OF-THE-YEAR AWARDS ASSEMBLY
...BECAUSE THERE'S A PLAQUE TO FOREVER REMIND US WHO THE ALL-TIME DETENTION KING IS!
CONGRATULATIONS AGAIN, BART SIMPSON. AND REMEMBER, WHEREVER LIFE TAKES YOU, THERE WILL ALWAYS BE A SEAT IN THE DETENTION HALL WITH YOUR NAME ON IT AT SPRINGFIELD ELEMENTARY!
I'M THE LUCKIEST BOY IN THE WORLD.
THE END

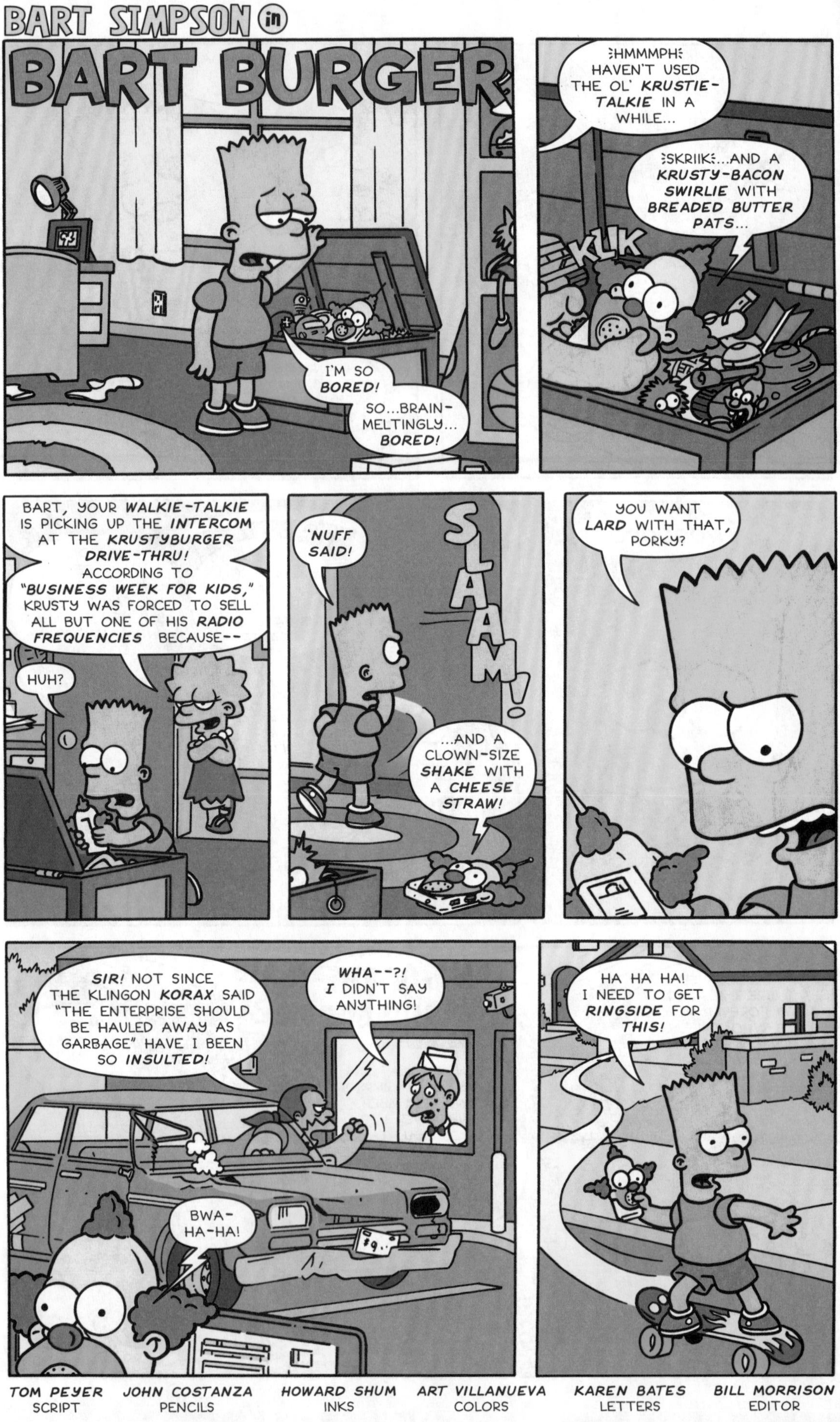
BART SIMPSON in
BART BURGER
I'M SO BORED!
SO...BRAIN-MELTINGLY... BORED!
HMMMPH HAVEN'T USED THE OL' KRUSTIE-TALKIE IN A WHILE...
KLIK
SKRIIK ...AND A KRUSTY-BACON SWIRLIE WITH BREADED BUTTER PATS...
BART, YOUR WALKIE-TALKIE IS PICKING UP THE INTERCOM AT THE KRUSTYBURGER DRIVE-THRU! ACCORDING TO "BUSINESS WEEK FOR KIDS," KRUSTY WAS FORCED TO SELL ALL BUT ONE OF HIS RADIO FREQUENCIES BECAUSE--
HUH?
'NUFF SAID!
SLAAM!
...AND A CLOWN-SIZE SHAKE WITH A CHEESE STRAW!
YOU WANT LARD WITH THAT, PORKY?
SIR! NOT SINCE THE KLINGON KORAX SAID "THE ENTERPRISE SHOULD BE HAULED AWAY AS GARBAGE" HAVE I BEEN SO INSULTED!
WHA--?! I DIDN'T SAY ANYTHING!
BWA-HA-HA!
HA HA HA! I NEED TO GET RINGSIDE FOR THIS!

TOM PEYER SCRIPT | *JOHN COSTANZA* PENCILS | *HOWARD SHUM* INKS | *ART VILLANUEVA* COLORS | *KAREN BATES* LETTERS | *BILL MORRISON* EDITOR

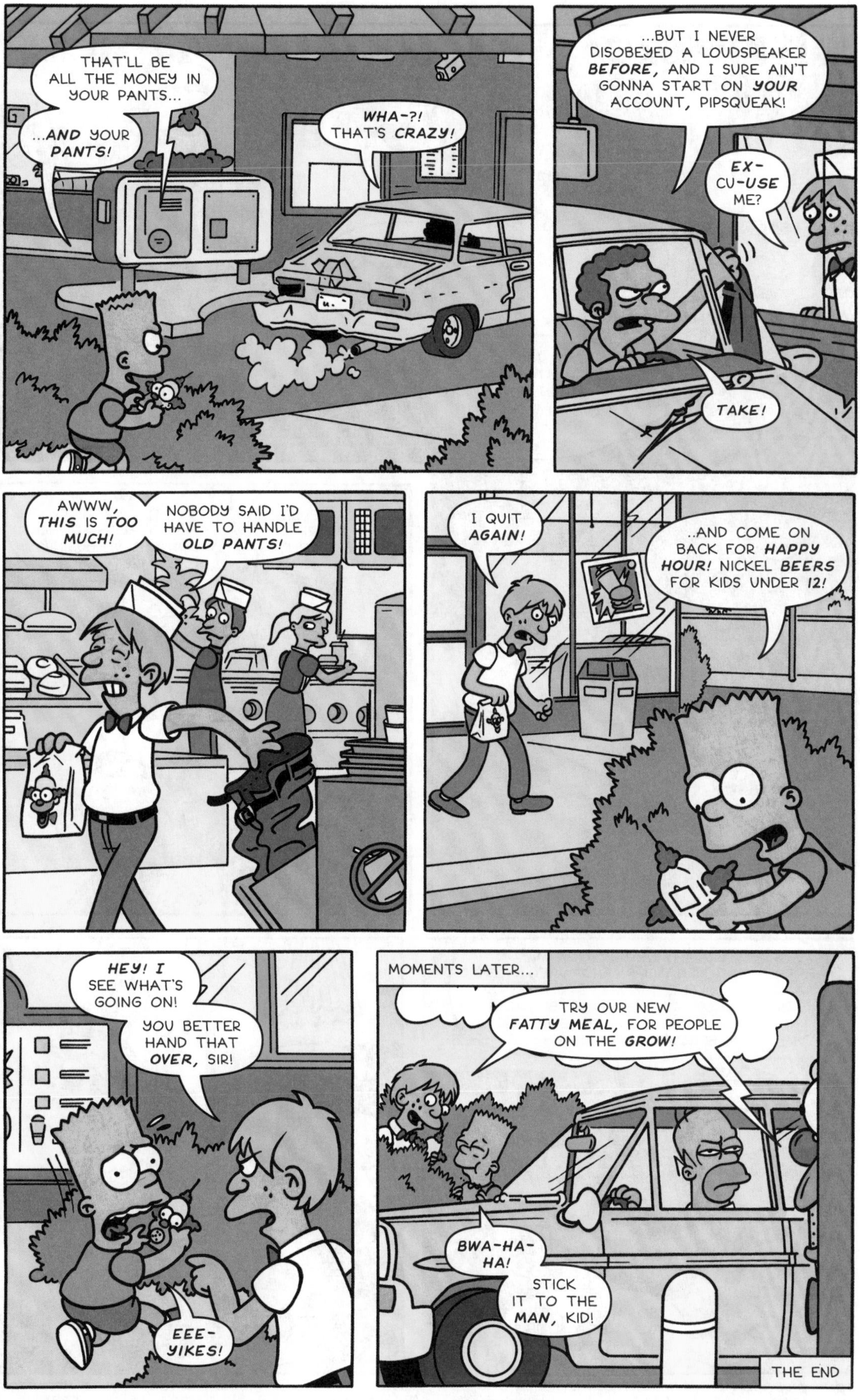
THAT'LL BE ALL THE MONEY IN YOUR PANTS...
...AND YOUR PANTS!
WHA-?! THAT'S CRAZY!
...BUT I NEVER DISOBEYED A LOUDSPEAKER BEFORE, AND I SURE AIN'T GONNA START ON YOUR ACCOUNT, PIPSQUEAK!
EX-CU-USE ME?
TAKE!
AWWW, THIS IS TOO MUCH!
NOBODY SAID I'D HAVE TO HANDLE OLD PANTS!
I QUIT AGAIN!
..AND COME ON BACK FOR HAPPY HOUR! NICKEL BEERS FOR KIDS UNDER 12!
HEY! I SEE WHAT'S GOING ON!
YOU BETTER HAND THAT OVER, SIR!
EEE-YIKES!
MOMENTS LATER...
TRY OUR NEW FATTY MEAL, FOR PEOPLE ON THE GROW!
BWA-HA-HA!
STICK IT TO THE MAN, KID!
THE END

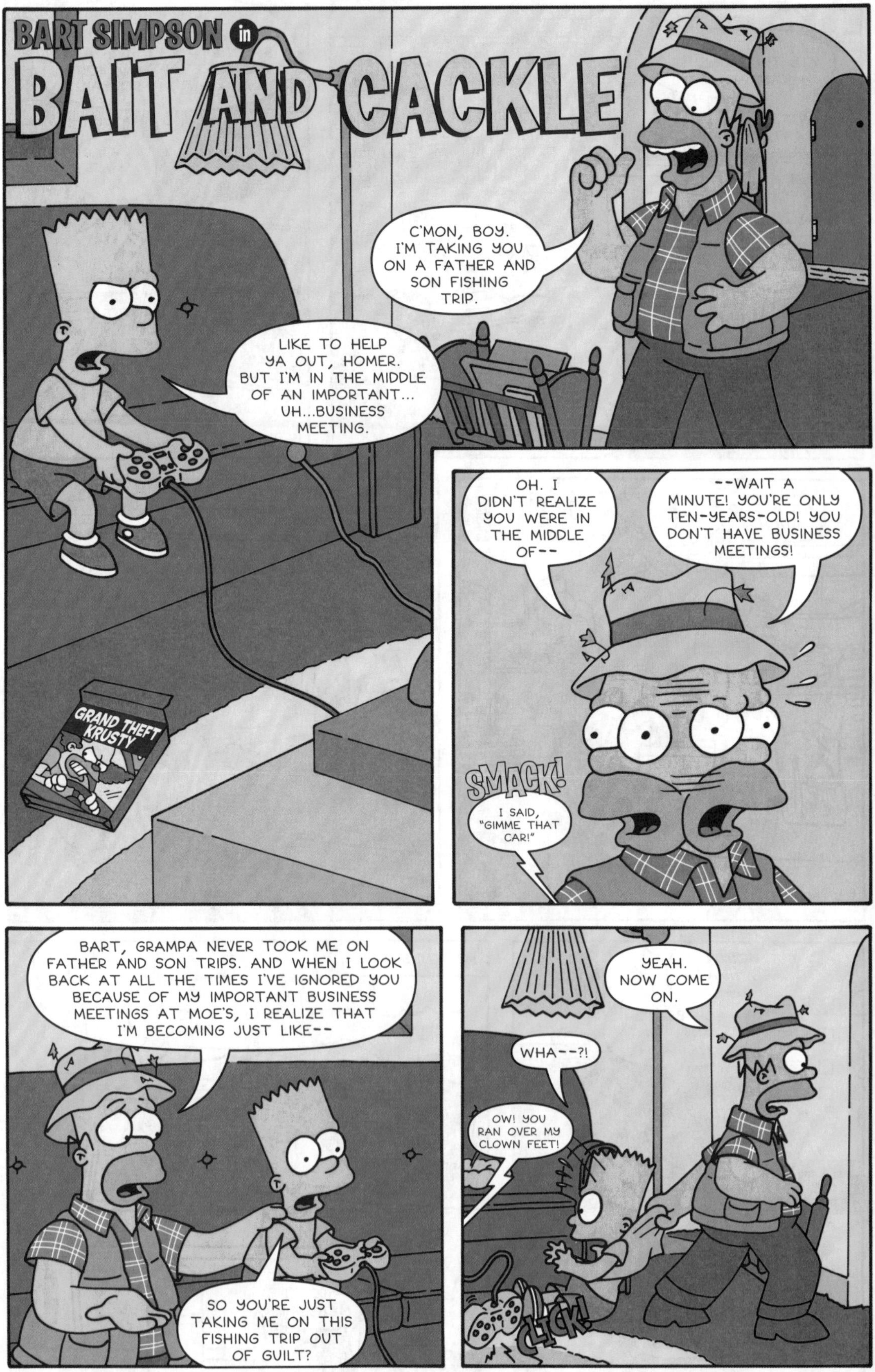
BART SIMPSON in
BAIT AND CACKLE
C'MON, BOY. I'M TAKING YOU ON A FATHER AND SON FISHING TRIP.
LIKE TO HELP YA OUT, HOMER. BUT I'M IN THE MIDDLE OF AN IMPORTANT... UH...BUSINESS MEETING.
GRAND THEFT KRUSTY
OH. I DIDN'T REALIZE YOU WERE IN THE MIDDLE OF--
--WAIT A MINUTE! YOU'RE ONLY TEN-YEARS-OLD! YOU DON'T HAVE BUSINESS MEETINGS!
SMACK!
I SAID, "GIMME THAT CAR!"
BART, GRAMPA NEVER TOOK ME ON FATHER AND SON TRIPS. AND WHEN I LOOK BACK AT ALL THE TIMES I'VE IGNORED YOU BECAUSE OF MY IMPORTANT BUSINESS MEETINGS AT MOE'S, I REALIZE THAT I'M BECOMING JUST LIKE--
SO YOU'RE JUST TAKING ME ON THIS FISHING TRIP OUT OF GUILT?
YEAH. NOW COME ON.
WHA--?!
OW! YOU RAN OVER MY CLOWN FEET!
CLICK!

TONY DIGEROLAMO STORY | *PHIL ORTIZ* PENCILS | *PATRICK OWSLEY* INKS | *NATHAN HAMILL* COLORS | *KAREN BATES* LETTERS | *BILL MORRISON* EDITOR

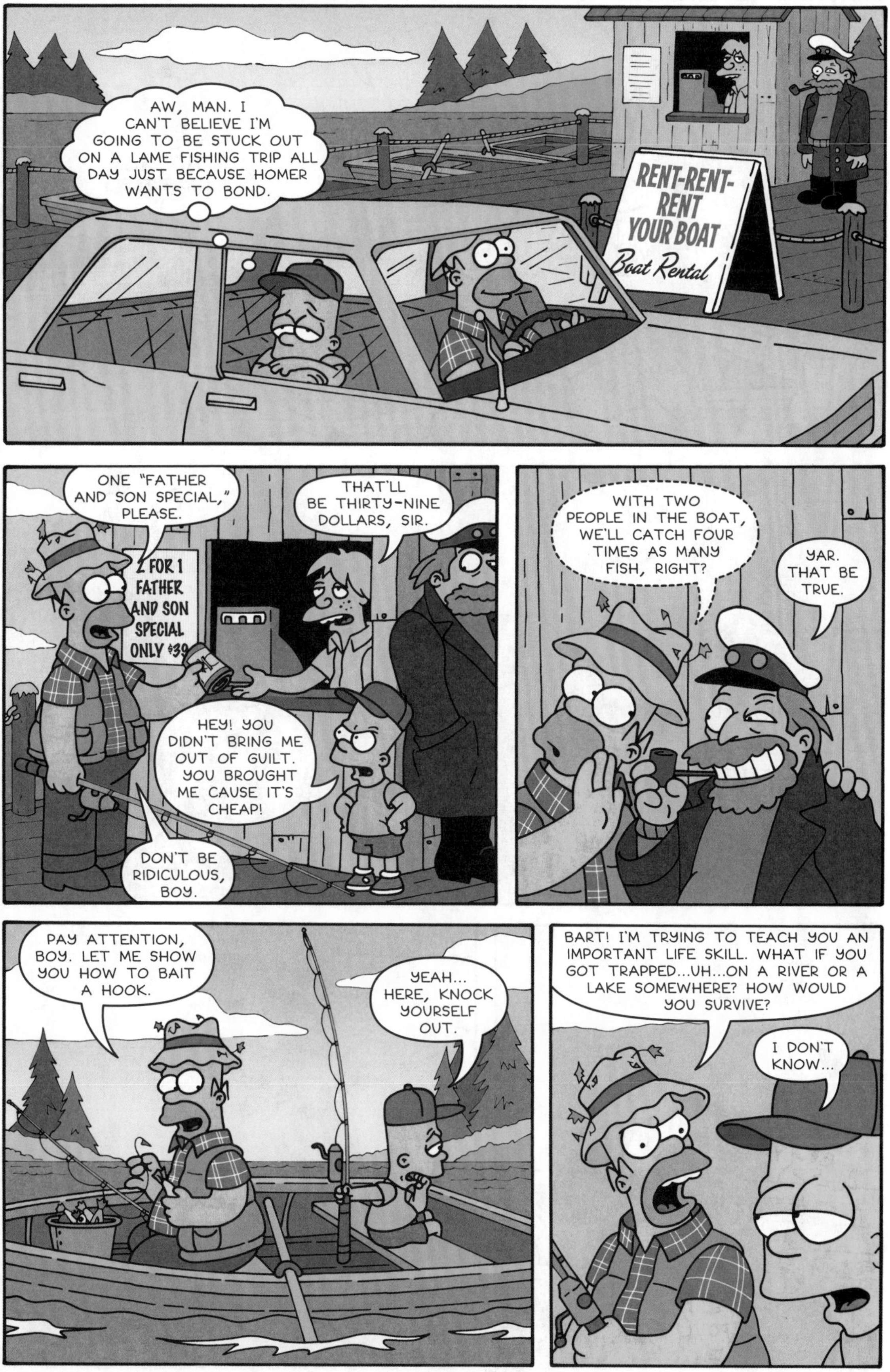
AW, MAN. I CAN'T BELIEVE I'M GOING TO BE STUCK OUT ON A LAME FISHING TRIP ALL DAY JUST BECAUSE HOMER WANTS TO BOND.
RENT-RENT-RENT YOUR BOAT
Boat Rental
ONE "FATHER AND SON SPECIAL," PLEASE.
2 FOR 1 FATHER AND SON SPECIAL ONLY $39
THAT'LL BE THIRTY-NINE DOLLARS, SIR.
HEY! YOU DIDN'T BRING ME OUT OF GUILT. YOU BROUGHT ME CAUSE IT'S CHEAP!
DON'T BE RIDICULOUS, BOY.
WITH TWO PEOPLE IN THE BOAT, WE'LL CATCH FOUR TIMES AS MANY FISH, RIGHT?
YAR. THAT BE TRUE.
PAY ATTENTION, BOY. LET ME SHOW YOU HOW TO BAIT A HOOK.
YEAH... HERE, KNOCK YOURSELF OUT.
BART! I'M TRYING TO TEACH YOU AN IMPORTANT LIFE SKILL. WHAT IF YOU GOT TRAPPED...UH...ON A RIVER OR A LAKE SOMEWHERE? HOW WOULD YOU SURVIVE?
I DON'T KNOW...

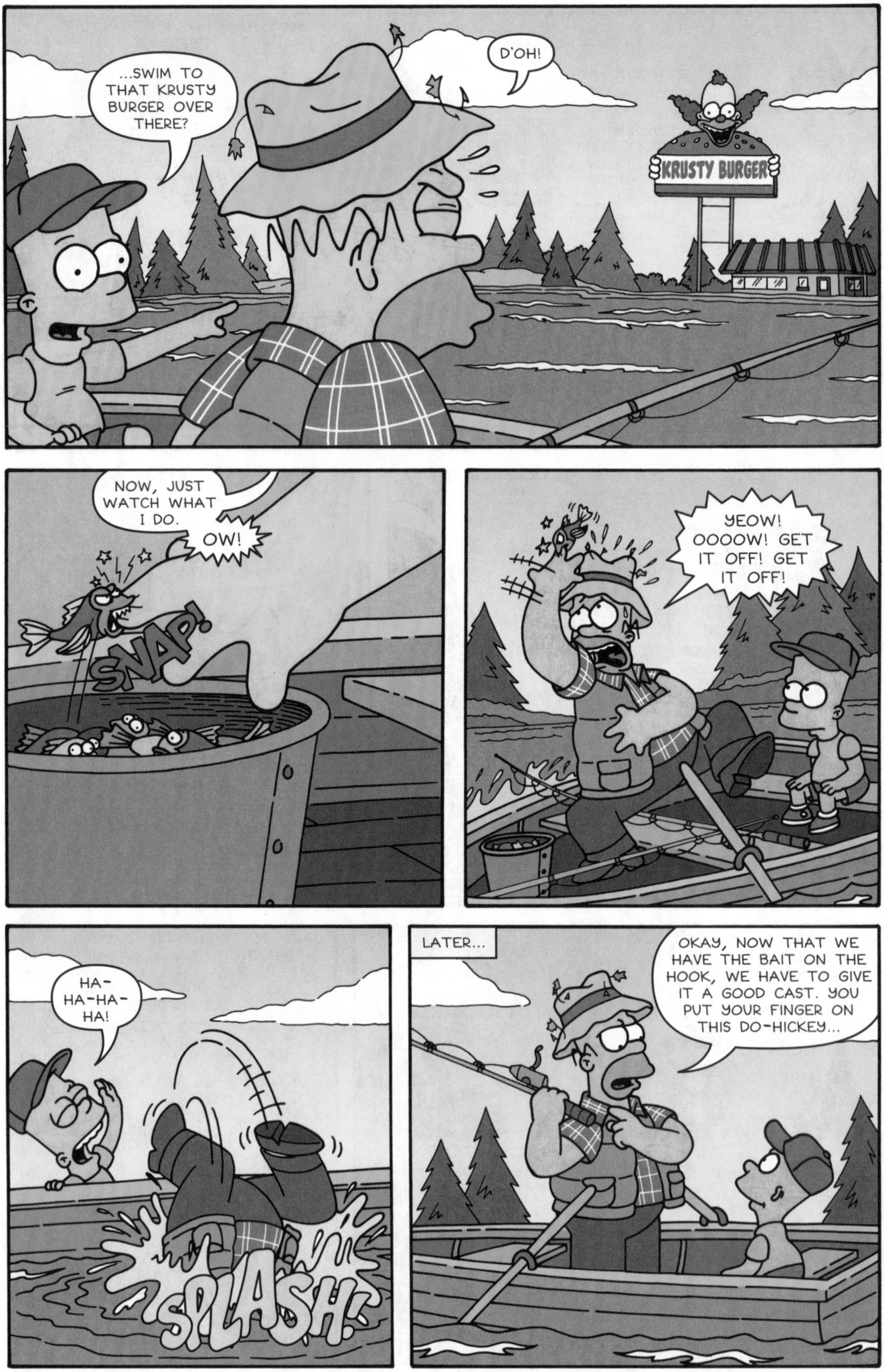
...SWIM TO THAT KRUSTY BURGER OVER THERE?
D'OH!
KRUSTY BURGER
NOW, JUST WATCH WHAT I DO.
OW!
SNAP!
YEOW! OOOOW! GET IT OFF! GET IT OFF!
HA-HA-HA-HA!
SPLASH!
LATER...
OKAY, NOW THAT WE HAVE THE BAIT ON THE HOOK, WE HAVE TO GIVE IT A GOOD CAST. YOU PUT YOUR FINGER ON THIS DO-HICKEY...

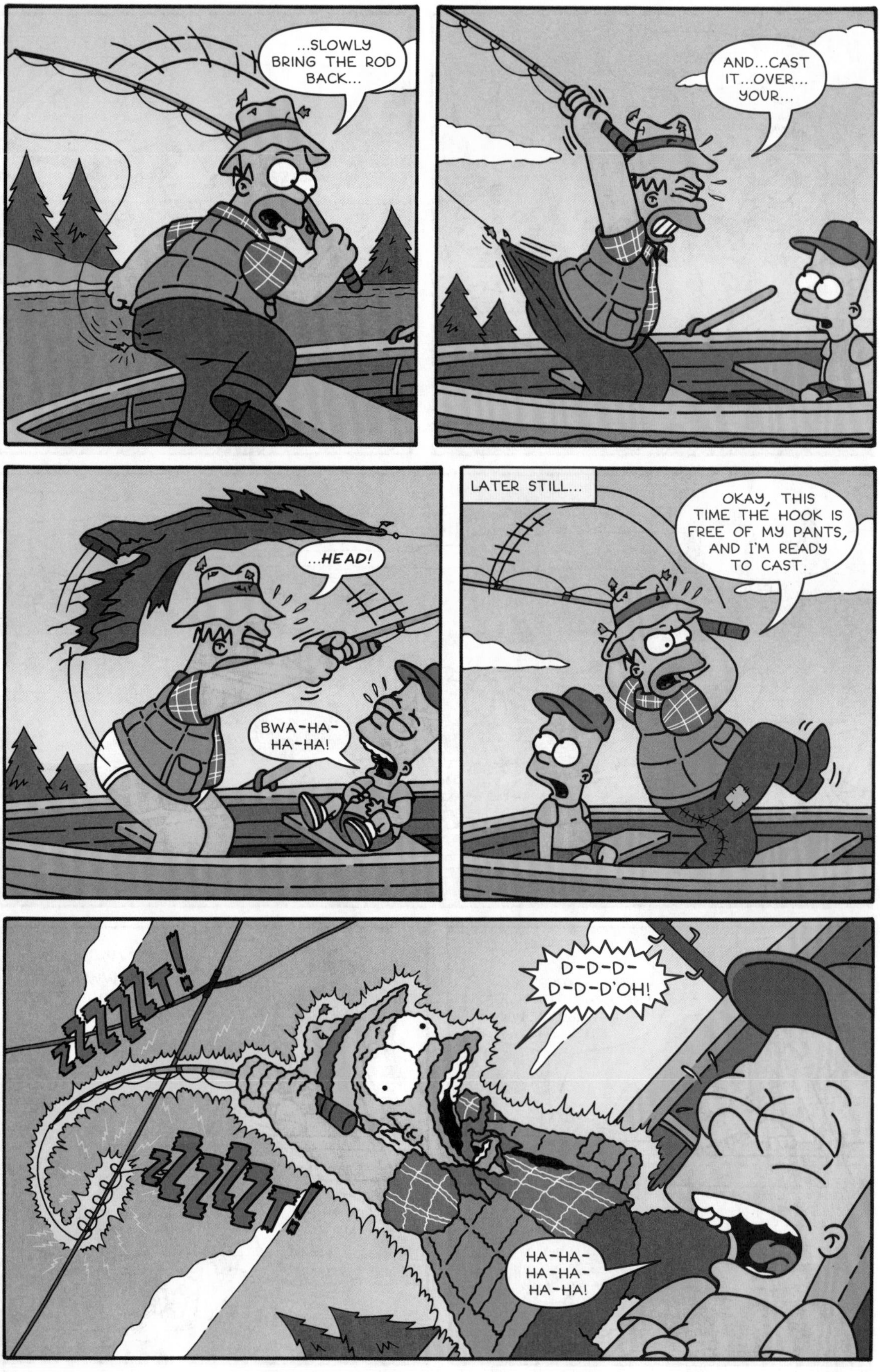
...SLOWLY BRING THE ROD BACK...
AND...CAST IT...OVER... YOUR...
...HEAD!
BWA-HA-HA-HA!
LATER STILL...
OKAY, THIS TIME THE HOOK IS FREE OF MY PANTS, AND I'M READY TO CAST.
ZZZZZZT!
D-D-D-D-D-D'OH!
ZZZZZZT!
HA-HA-HA-HA-HA-HA!

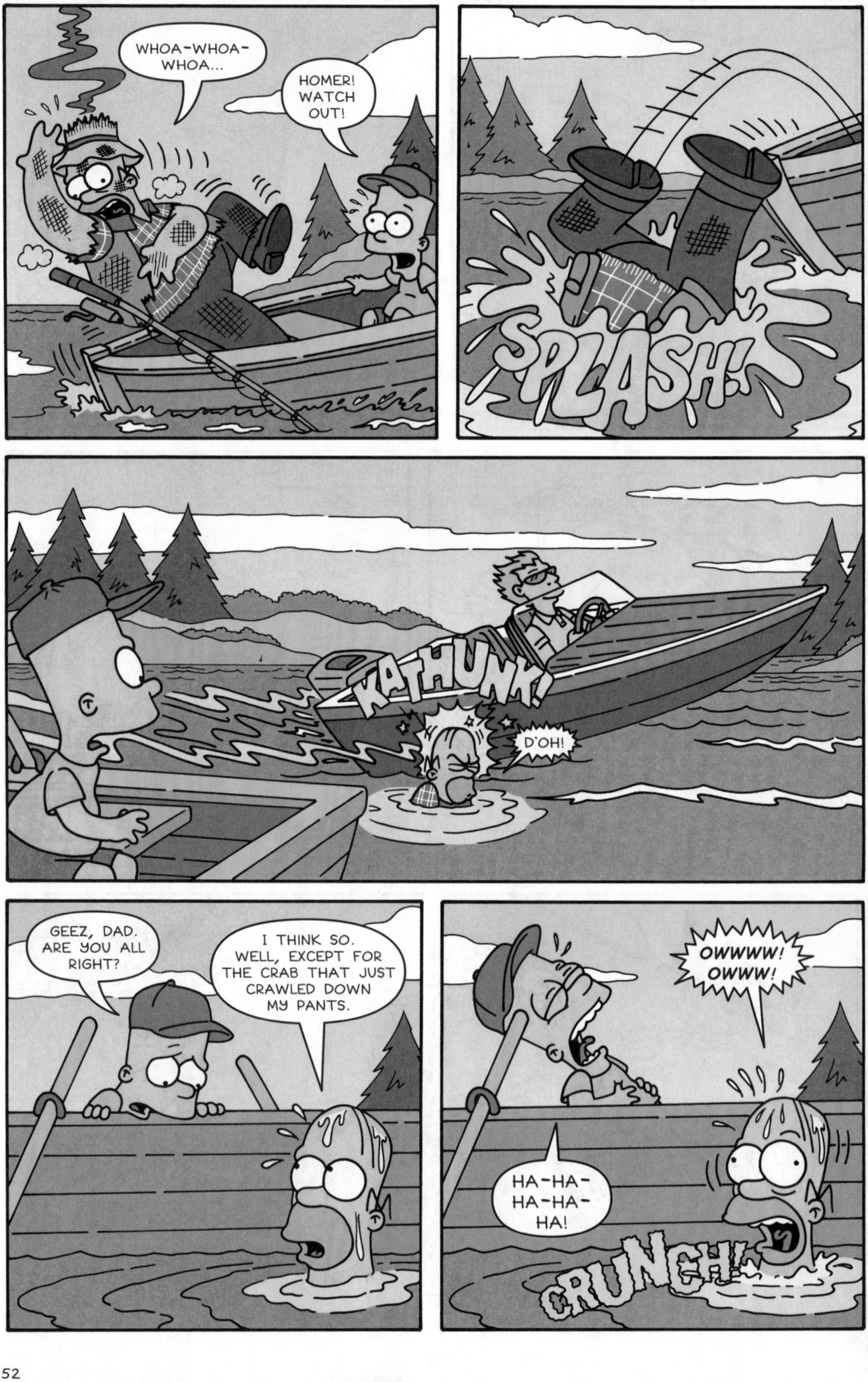
WHOA-WHOA-WHOA...
HOMER! WATCH OUT!
SPLASH!
KATHUNK!
D'OH!
GEEZ, DAD. ARE YOU ALL RIGHT?
I THINK SO. WELL, EXCEPT FOR THE CRAB THAT JUST CRAWLED DOWN MY PANTS.
OWWWW! OWWW!
HA-HA-HA-HA-HA!
CRUNCH!

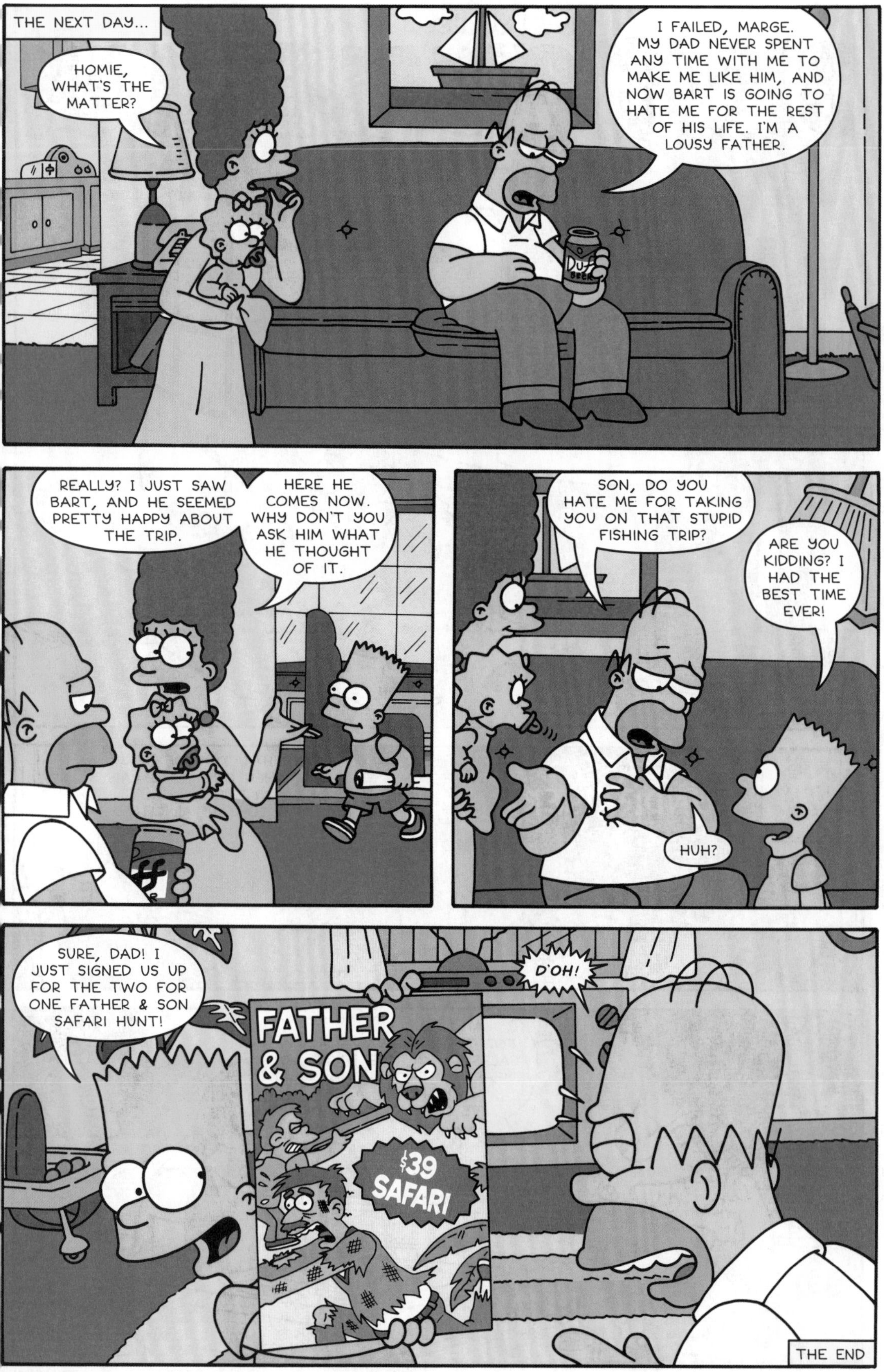
THE NEXT DAY...
HOMIE, WHAT'S THE MATTER?
I FAILED, MARGE. MY DAD NEVER SPENT ANY TIME WITH ME TO MAKE ME LIKE HIM, AND NOW BART IS GOING TO HATE ME FOR THE REST OF HIS LIFE. I'M A LOUSY FATHER.
REALLY? I JUST SAW BART, AND HE SEEMED PRETTY HAPPY ABOUT THE TRIP.
HERE HE COMES NOW. WHY DON'T YOU ASK HIM WHAT HE THOUGHT OF IT.
SON, DO YOU HATE ME FOR TAKING YOU ON THAT STUPID FISHING TRIP?
ARE YOU KIDDING? I HAD THE BEST TIME EVER!
HUH?
SURE, DAD! I JUST SIGNED US UP FOR THE TWO FOR ONE FATHER & SON SAFARI HUNT!
FATHER & SON
$39 SAFARI
D'OH!
THE END

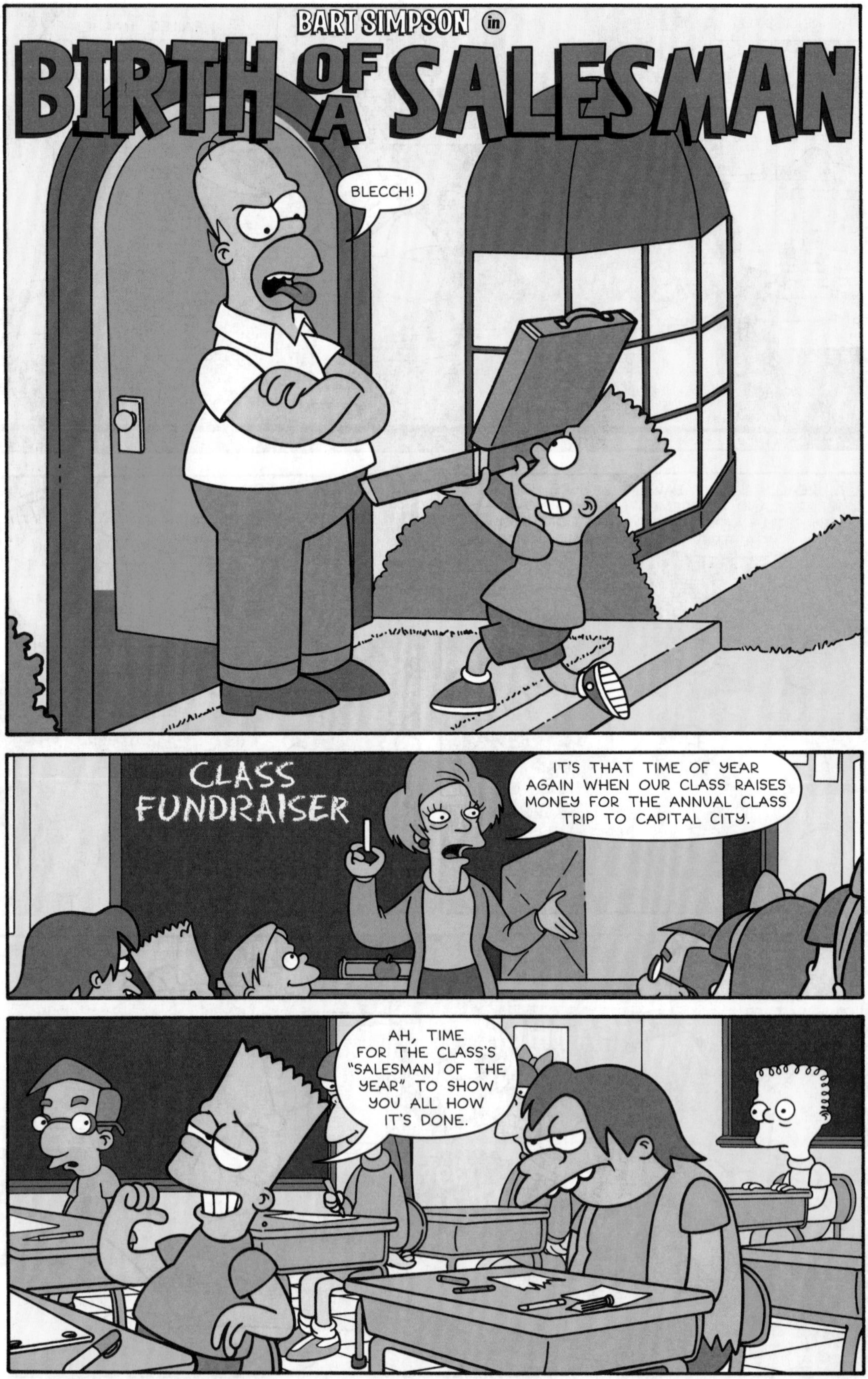
BART SIMPSON in
BIRTH OF A SALESMAN
BLECCH!
CLASS FUNDRAISER
IT'S THAT TIME OF YEAR AGAIN WHEN OUR CLASS RAISES MONEY FOR THE ANNUAL CLASS TRIP TO CAPITAL CITY.
AH, TIME FOR THE CLASS'S "SALESMAN OF THE YEAR" TO SHOW YOU ALL HOW IT'S DONE.

JAMES W. BATES SCRIPT **JOHN DELANEY** PENCILS **PHYLLIS NOVIN** INKS **ART VILLANUEVA** COLORS **KAREN BATES** LETTERS **BILL MORRISON** EDITOR

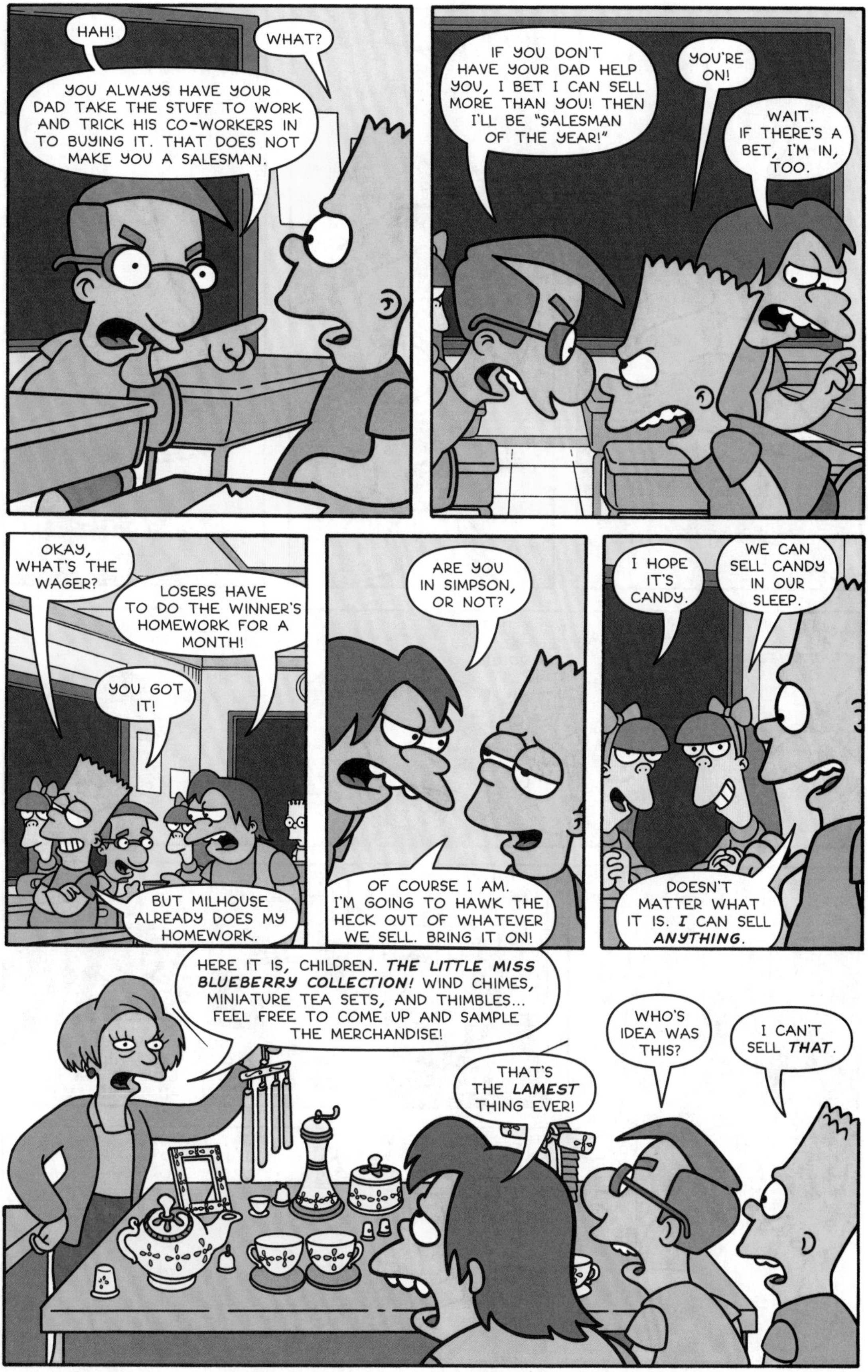
HAH!
WHAT?
YOU ALWAYS HAVE YOUR DAD TAKE THE STUFF TO WORK AND TRICK HIS CO-WORKERS IN TO BUYING IT. THAT DOES NOT MAKE YOU A SALESMAN.
IF YOU DON'T HAVE YOUR DAD HELP YOU, I BET I CAN SELL MORE THAN YOU! THEN I'LL BE "SALESMAN OF THE YEAR!"
YOU'RE ON!
WAIT. IF THERE'S A BET, I'M IN, TOO.
OKAY, WHAT'S THE WAGER?
LOSERS HAVE TO DO THE WINNER'S HOMEWORK FOR A MONTH!
YOU GOT IT!
BUT MILHOUSE ALREADY DOES MY HOMEWORK.
ARE YOU IN SIMPSON, OR NOT?
OF COURSE I AM. I'M GOING TO HAWK THE HECK OUT OF WHATEVER WE SELL. BRING IT ON!
I HOPE IT'S CANDY.
WE CAN SELL CANDY IN OUR SLEEP.
DOESN'T MATTER WHAT IT IS. *I* CAN SELL ***ANYTHING***.
HERE IT IS, CHILDREN. ***THE LITTLE MISS BLUEBERRY COLLECTION!*** WIND CHIMES, MINIATURE TEA SETS, AND THIMBLES... FEEL FREE TO COME UP AND SAMPLE THE MERCHANDISE!
THAT'S THE ***LAMEST*** THING EVER!
WHO'S IDEA WAS THIS?
I CAN'T SELL ***THAT***.

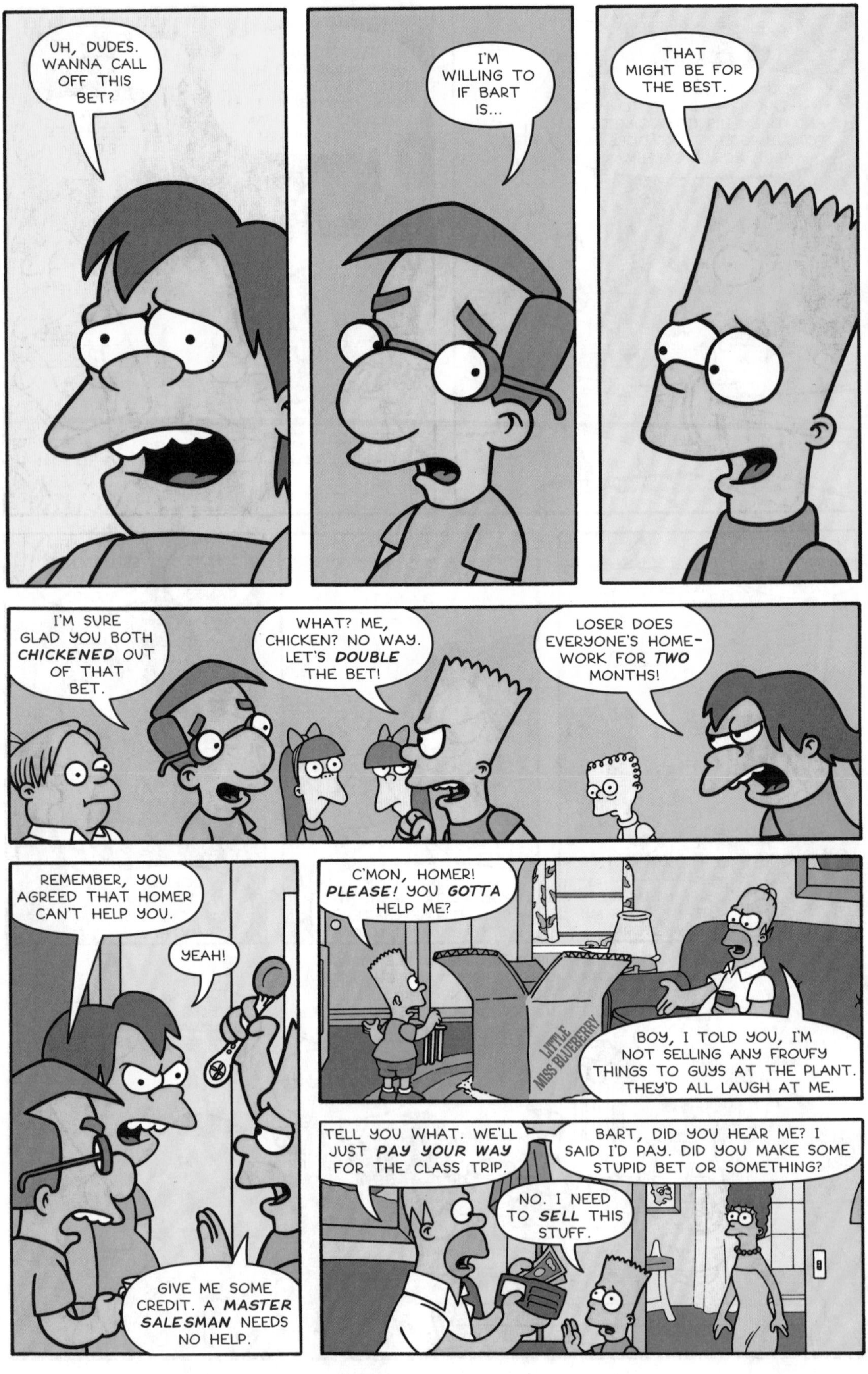
UH, DUDES. WANNA CALL OFF THIS BET?
I'M WILLING TO IF BART IS...
THAT MIGHT BE FOR THE BEST.
I'M SURE GLAD YOU BOTH **CHICKENED** OUT OF THAT BET.
WHAT? ME, CHICKEN? NO WAY. LET'S **DOUBLE** THE BET!
LOSER DOES EVERYONE'S HOME-WORK FOR **TWO** MONTHS!
REMEMBER, YOU AGREED THAT HOMER CAN'T HELP YOU.
YEAH!
GIVE ME SOME CREDIT. A **MASTER SALESMAN** NEEDS NO HELP.
C'MON, HOMER! **PLEASE!** YOU **GOTTA** HELP ME?
LITTLE MISS BLUEBERRY
BOY, I TOLD YOU, I'M NOT SELLING ANY FROUFY THINGS TO GUYS AT THE PLANT. THEY'D ALL LAUGH AT ME.
TELL YOU WHAT. WE'LL JUST **PAY YOUR WAY** FOR THE CLASS TRIP.
BART, DID YOU HEAR ME? I SAID I'D PAY. DID YOU MAKE SOME STUPID BET OR SOMETHING?
NO. I NEED TO **SELL** THIS STUFF.

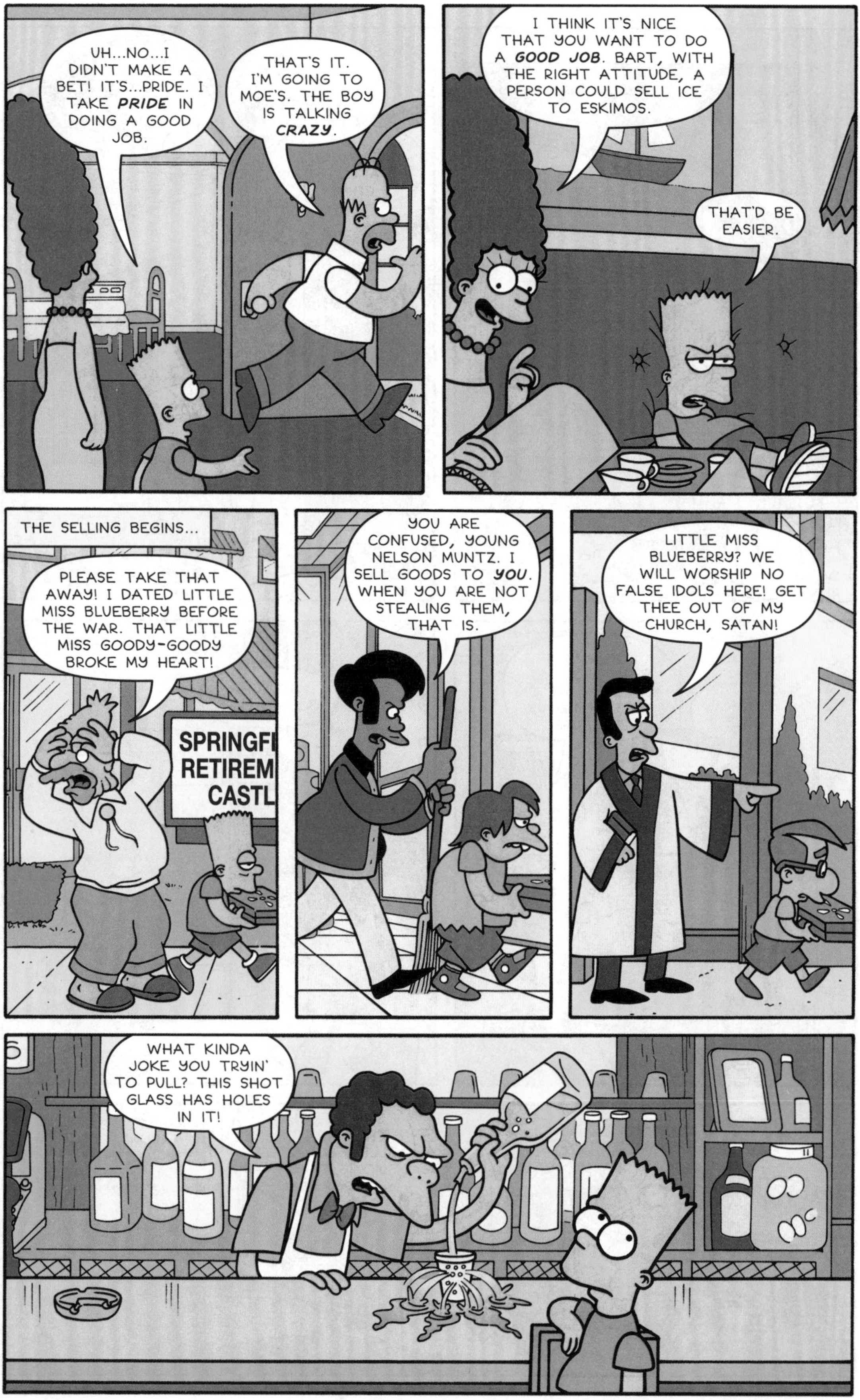
UH...NO...I DIDN'T MAKE A BET! IT'S...PRIDE. I TAKE **PRIDE** IN DOING A GOOD JOB.
THAT'S IT. I'M GOING TO MOE'S. THE BOY IS TALKING **CRAZY**.
I THINK IT'S NICE THAT YOU WANT TO DO A **GOOD JOB**. BART, WITH THE RIGHT ATTITUDE, A PERSON COULD SELL ICE TO ESKIMOS.
THAT'D BE EASIER.
THE SELLING BEGINS...
PLEASE TAKE THAT AWAY! I DATED LITTLE MISS BLUEBERRY BEFORE THE WAR. THAT LITTLE MISS GOODY-GOODY BROKE MY HEART!
SPRINGFI
RETIREM
CASTL
YOU ARE CONFUSED, YOUNG NELSON MUNTZ. I SELL GOODS TO **YOU**. WHEN YOU ARE NOT STEALING THEM, THAT IS.
LITTLE MISS BLUEBERRY? WE WILL WORSHIP NO FALSE IDOLS HERE! GET THEE OUT OF MY CHURCH, SATAN!
WHAT KINDA JOKE YOU TRYIN' TO PULL? THIS SHOT GLASS HAS HOLES IN IT!

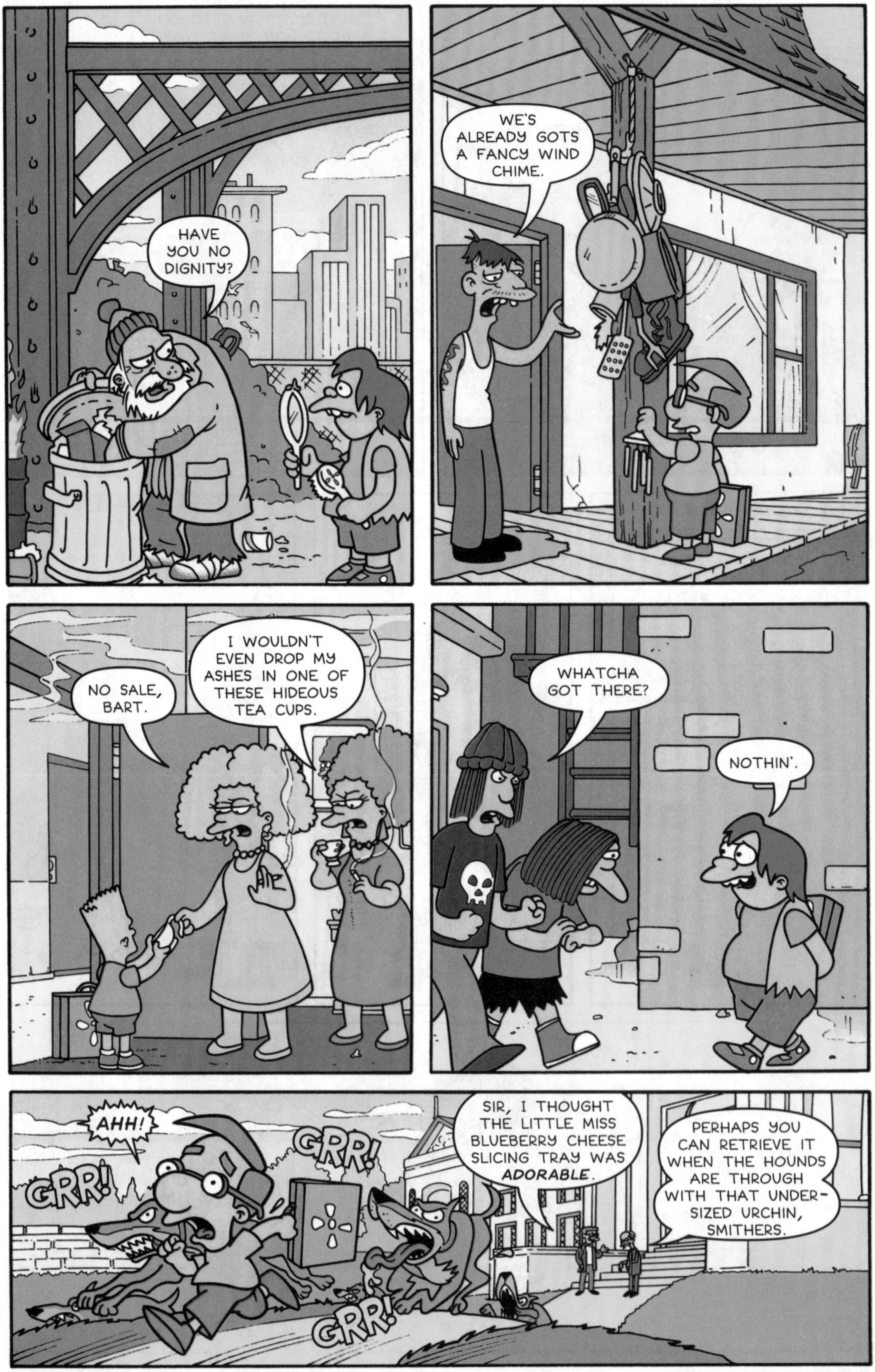
HAVE YOU NO DIGNITY?
WE'S ALREADY GOTS A FANCY WIND CHIME.
NO SALE, BART.
I WOULDN'T EVEN DROP MY ASHES IN ONE OF THESE HIDEOUS TEA CUPS.
WHATCHA GOT THERE?
NOTHIN'.
AHH!
GRR!
GRR!
GRR!
SIR, I THOUGHT THE LITTLE MISS BLUEBERRY CHEESE SLICING TRAY WAS ADORABLE.
PERHAPS YOU CAN RETRIEVE IT WHEN THE HOUNDS ARE THROUGH WITH THAT UNDER-SIZED URCHIN, SMITHERS.

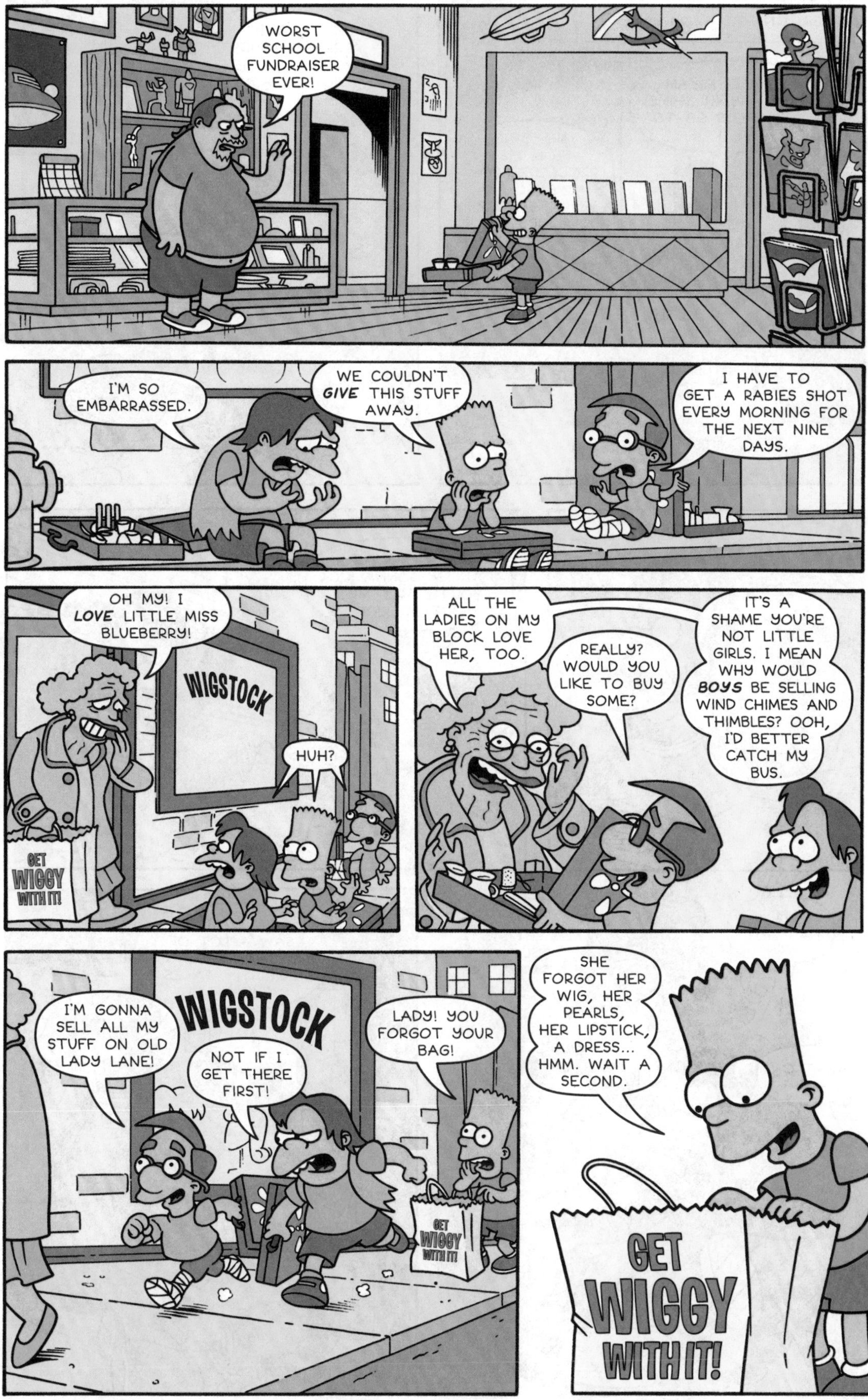
WORST SCHOOL FUNDRAISER EVER!
I'M SO EMBARRASSED.
WE COULDN'T GIVE THIS STUFF AWAY.
I HAVE TO GET A RABIES SHOT EVERY MORNING FOR THE NEXT NINE DAYS.
OH MY! I LOVE LITTLE MISS BLUEBERRY!
WIGSTOCK
HUH?
GET WIGGY WITH IT!
ALL THE LADIES ON MY BLOCK LOVE HER, TOO.
REALLY? WOULD YOU LIKE TO BUY SOME?
IT'S A SHAME YOU'RE NOT LITTLE GIRLS. I MEAN WHY WOULD BOYS BE SELLING WIND CHIMES AND THIMBLES? OOH, I'D BETTER CATCH MY BUS.
WIGSTOCK
I'M GONNA SELL ALL MY STUFF ON OLD LADY LANE!
NOT IF I GET THERE FIRST!
LADY! YOU FORGOT YOUR BAG!
GET WIGGY WITH IT!
SHE FORGOT HER WIG, HER PEARLS, HER LIPSTICK, A DRESS... HMM. WAIT A SECOND.
GET WIGGY WITH IT!

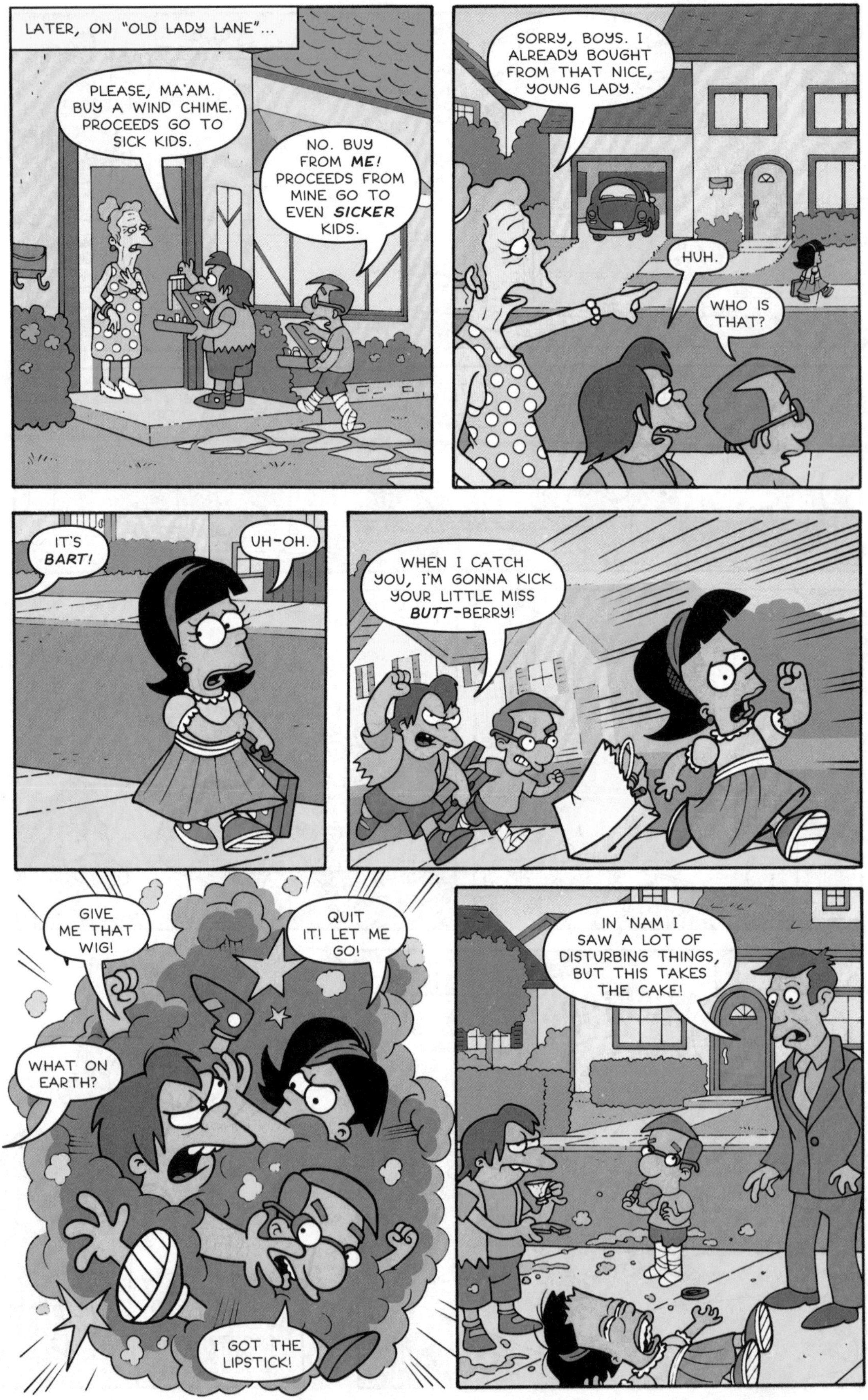
LATER, ON "OLD LADY LANE"...
PLEASE, MA'AM. BUY A WIND CHIME. PROCEEDS GO TO SICK KIDS.
NO. BUY FROM ME! PROCEEDS FROM MINE GO TO EVEN SICKER KIDS.
SORRY, BOYS. I ALREADY BOUGHT FROM THAT NICE, YOUNG LADY.
HUH.
WHO IS THAT?
IT'S BART!
UH-OH.
WHEN I CATCH YOU, I'M GONNA KICK YOUR LITTLE MISS BUTT-BERRY!
GIVE ME THAT WIG!
QUIT IT! LET ME GO!
WHAT ON EARTH?
I GOT THE LIPSTICK!
IN 'NAM I SAW A LOT OF DISTURBING THINGS, BUT THIS TAKES THE CAKE!

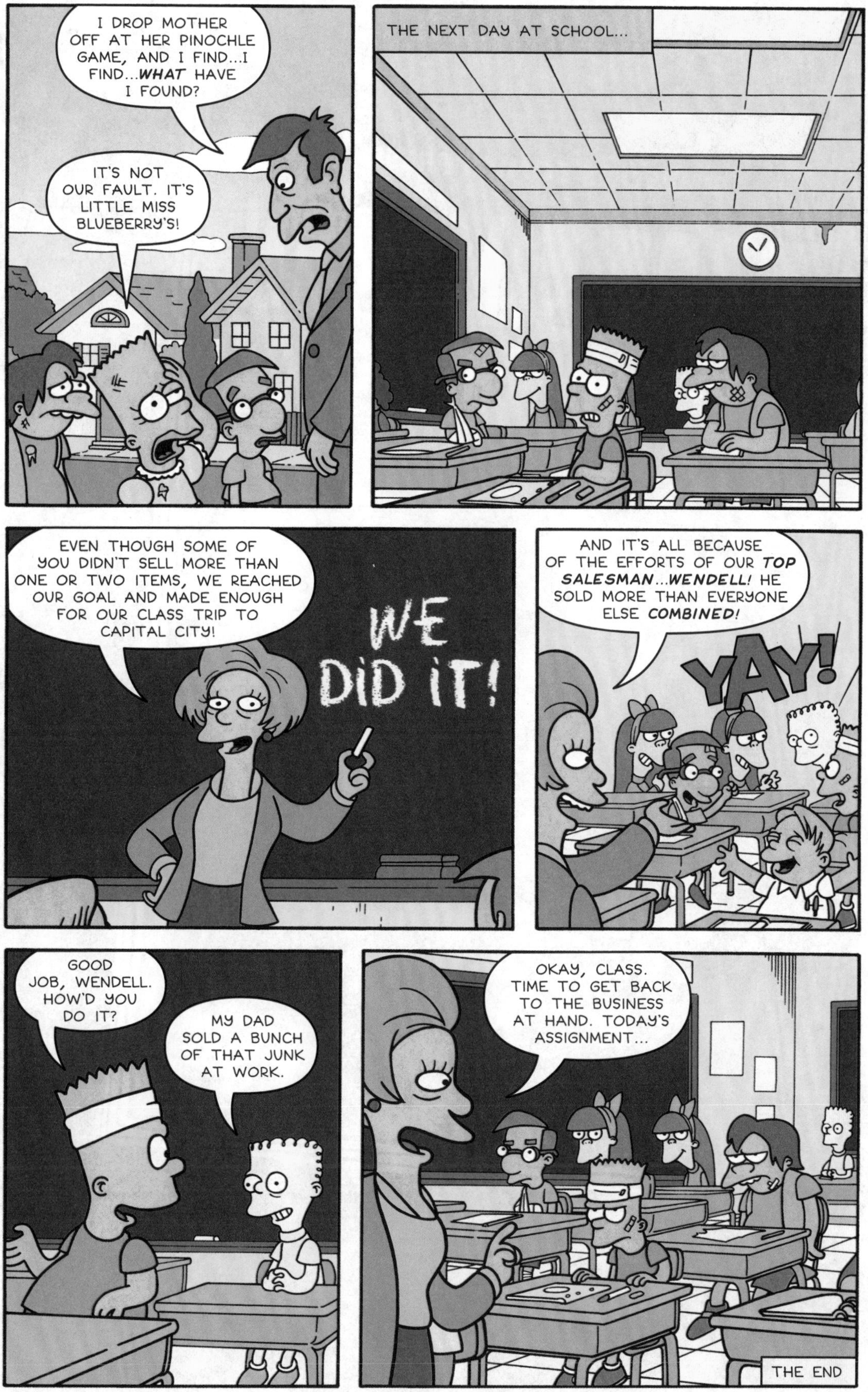
I DROP MOTHER OFF AT HER PINOCHLE GAME, AND I FIND...I FIND...WHAT HAVE I FOUND?
IT'S NOT OUR FAULT. IT'S LITTLE MISS BLUEBERRY'S!
THE NEXT DAY AT SCHOOL...
EVEN THOUGH SOME OF YOU DIDN'T SELL MORE THAN ONE OR TWO ITEMS, WE REACHED OUR GOAL AND MADE ENOUGH FOR OUR CLASS TRIP TO CAPITAL CITY!
WE DiD iT!
AND IT'S ALL BECAUSE OF THE EFFORTS OF OUR TOP SALESMAN...WENDELL! HE SOLD MORE THAN EVERYONE ELSE COMBINED!
YAY!
GOOD JOB, WENDELL. HOW'D YOU DO IT?
MY DAD SOLD A BUNCH OF THAT JUNK AT WORK.
OKAY, CLASS. TIME TO GET BACK TO THE BUSINESS AT HAND. TODAY'S ASSIGNMENT...
THE END

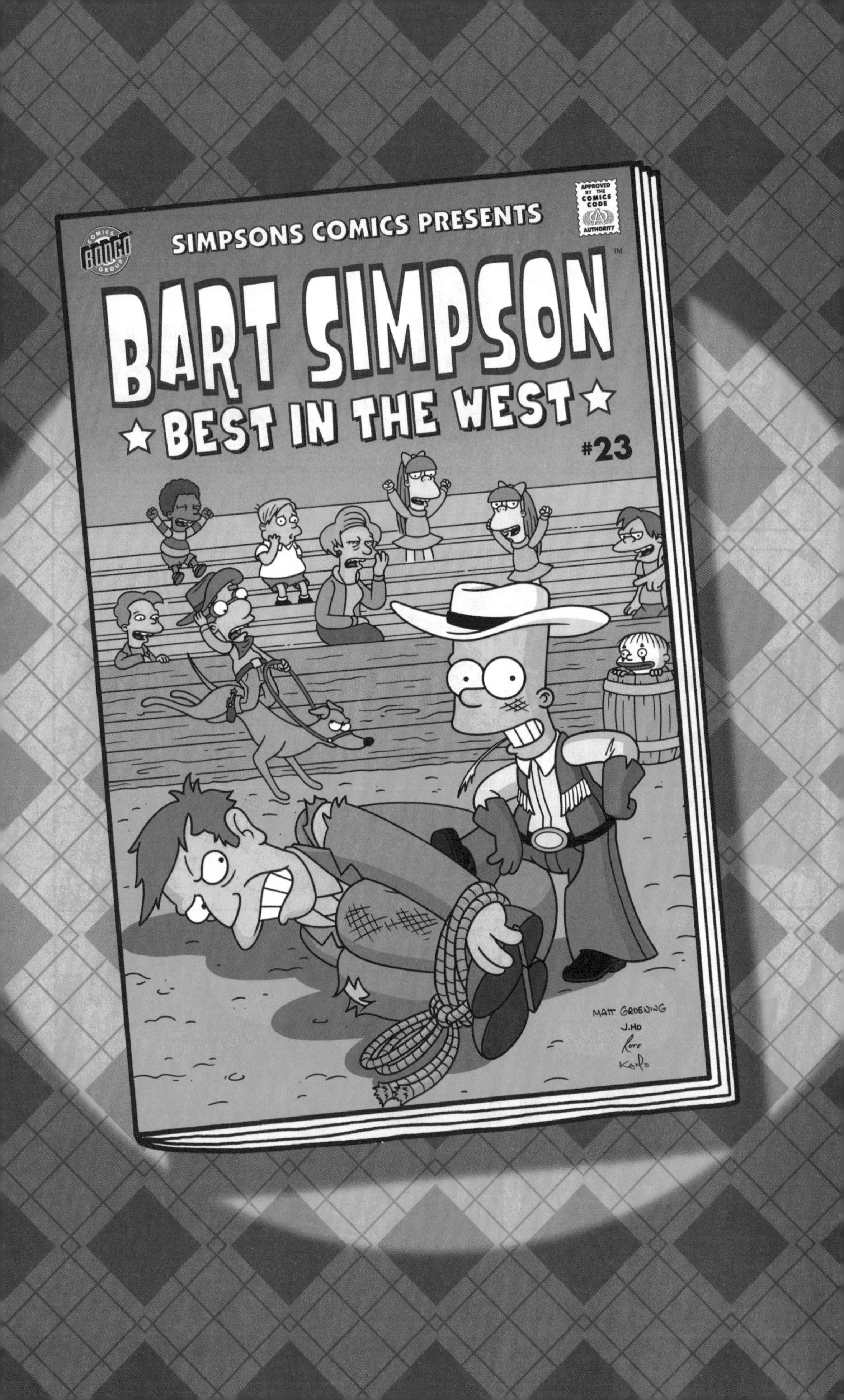
SIMPSONS COMICS PRESENTS
APPROVED BY THE COMICS CODE AUTHORITY
BART SIMPSON
BEST IN THE WEST
#23
MATT GROENING
J.HO

BART SIMPSON
in
BART VS. THE ONE-MAN SCHOOL

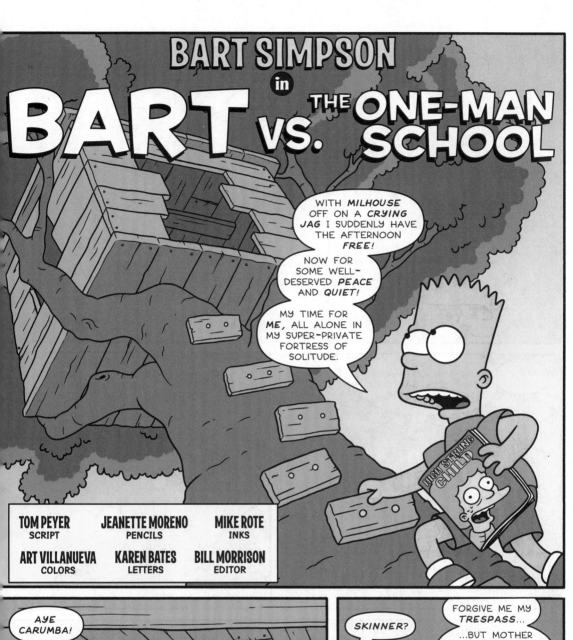

WITH *MILHOUSE* OFF ON A *CRYING JAG* I SUDDENLY HAVE THE AFTERNOON *FREE!*

NOW FOR SOME WELL-DESERVED *PEACE* AND *QUIET!*

MY TIME FOR *ME*, ALL ALONE IN MY SUPER-PRIVATE FORTRESS OF SOLITUDE.

HIGH-STRUNG CHILD

TOM PEYER SCRIPT	**JEANETTE MORENO** PENCILS	**MIKE ROTE** INKS
ART VILLANUEVA COLORS	**KAREN BATES** LETTERS	**BILL MORRISON** EDITOR

AYE CARUMBA!

HELLO, BART.

SKINNER?

FORGIVE ME MY *TRESPASS*...

...BUT MOTHER *INSISTED* YOU WOULDN'T WANT TO BE SEEN IN *PUBLIC* WITH YOUR *PRINCIPAL!*

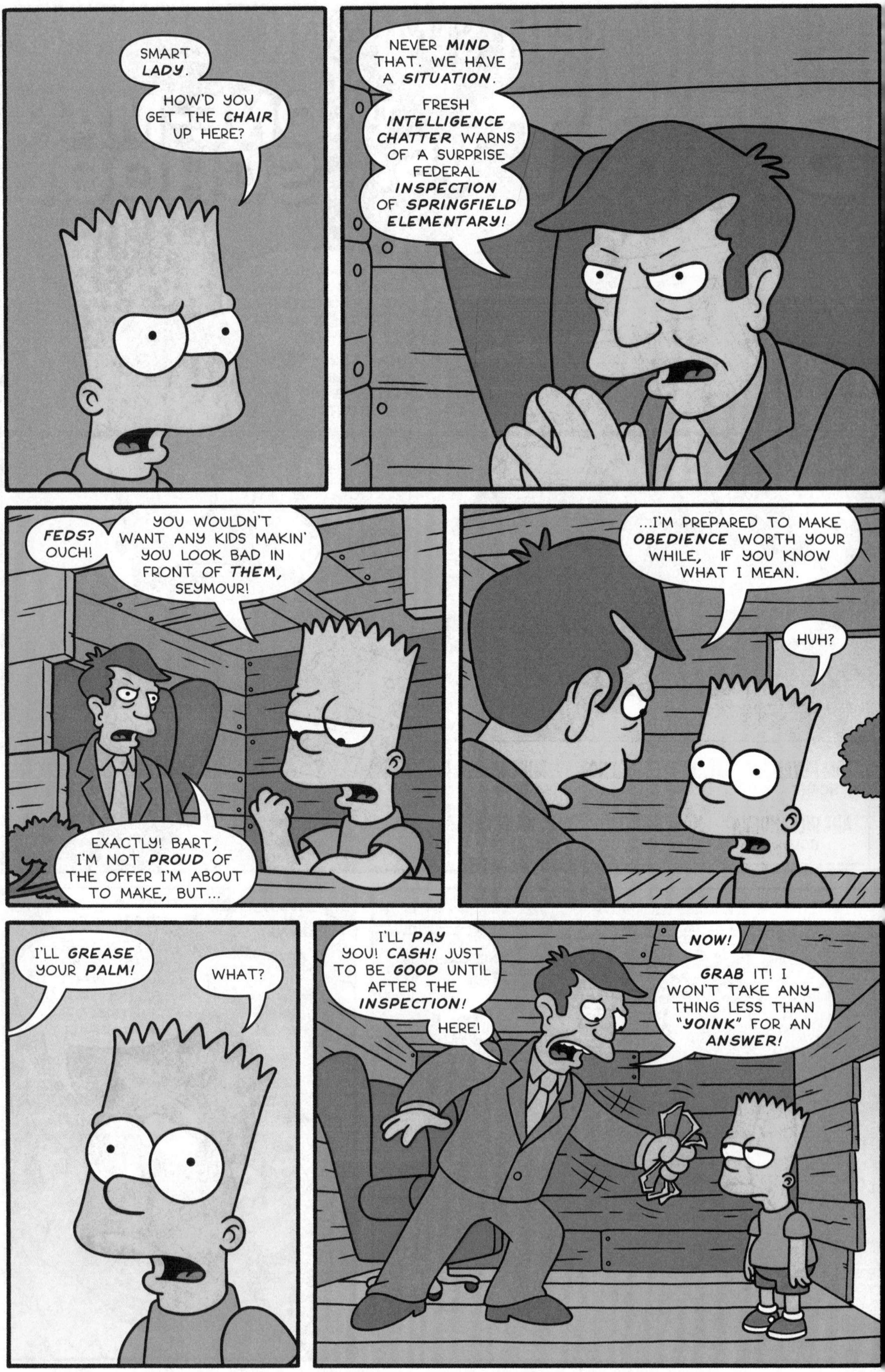
SMART LADY.
HOW'D YOU GET THE CHAIR UP HERE?
NEVER MIND THAT. WE HAVE A SITUATION.
FRESH INTELLIGENCE CHATTER WARNS OF A SURPRISE FEDERAL INSPECTION OF SPRINGFIELD ELEMENTARY!
FEDS? OUCH!
YOU WOULDN'T WANT ANY KIDS MAKIN' YOU LOOK BAD IN FRONT OF THEM, SEYMOUR!
EXACTLY! BART, I'M NOT PROUD OF THE OFFER I'M ABOUT TO MAKE, BUT...
...I'M PREPARED TO MAKE OBEDIENCE WORTH YOUR WHILE, IF YOU KNOW WHAT I MEAN.
HUH?
I'LL GREASE YOUR PALM!
WHAT?
I'LL PAY YOU! CASH! JUST TO BE GOOD UNTIL AFTER THE INSPECTION!
HERE!
NOW!
GRAB IT! I WON'T TAKE ANYTHING LESS THAN "YOINK" FOR AN ANSWER!

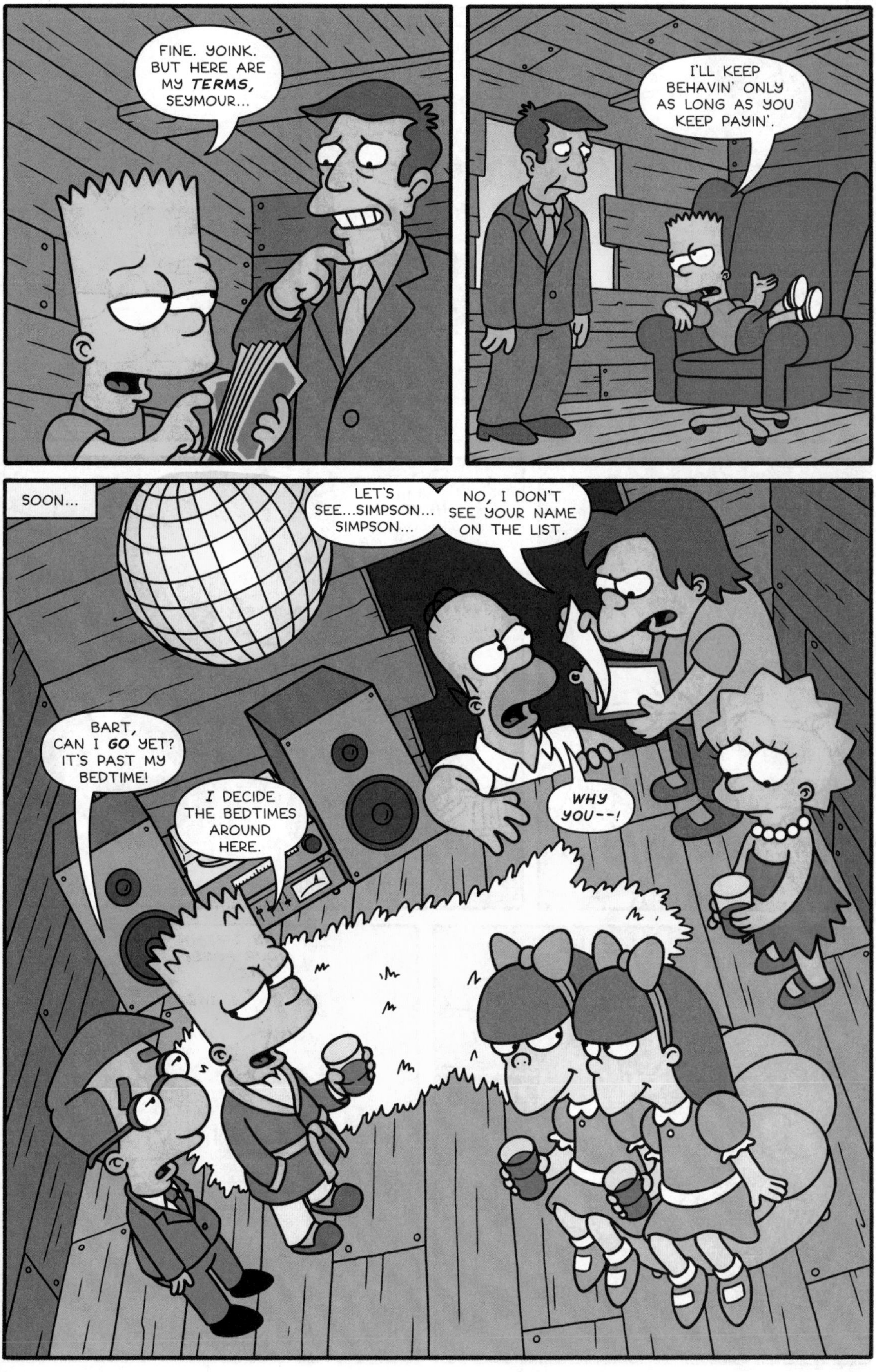
FINE. YOINK. BUT HERE ARE MY ***TERMS,*** SEYMOUR...
I'LL KEEP BEHAVIN' ONLY AS LONG AS YOU KEEP PAYIN'.
SOON...
LET'S SEE...SIMPSON... SIMPSON...
NO, I DON'T SEE YOUR NAME ON THE LIST.
BART, CAN I ***GO*** YET? IT'S PAST MY BEDTIME!
I DECIDE THE BEDTIMES AROUND HERE.
WHY YOU--!

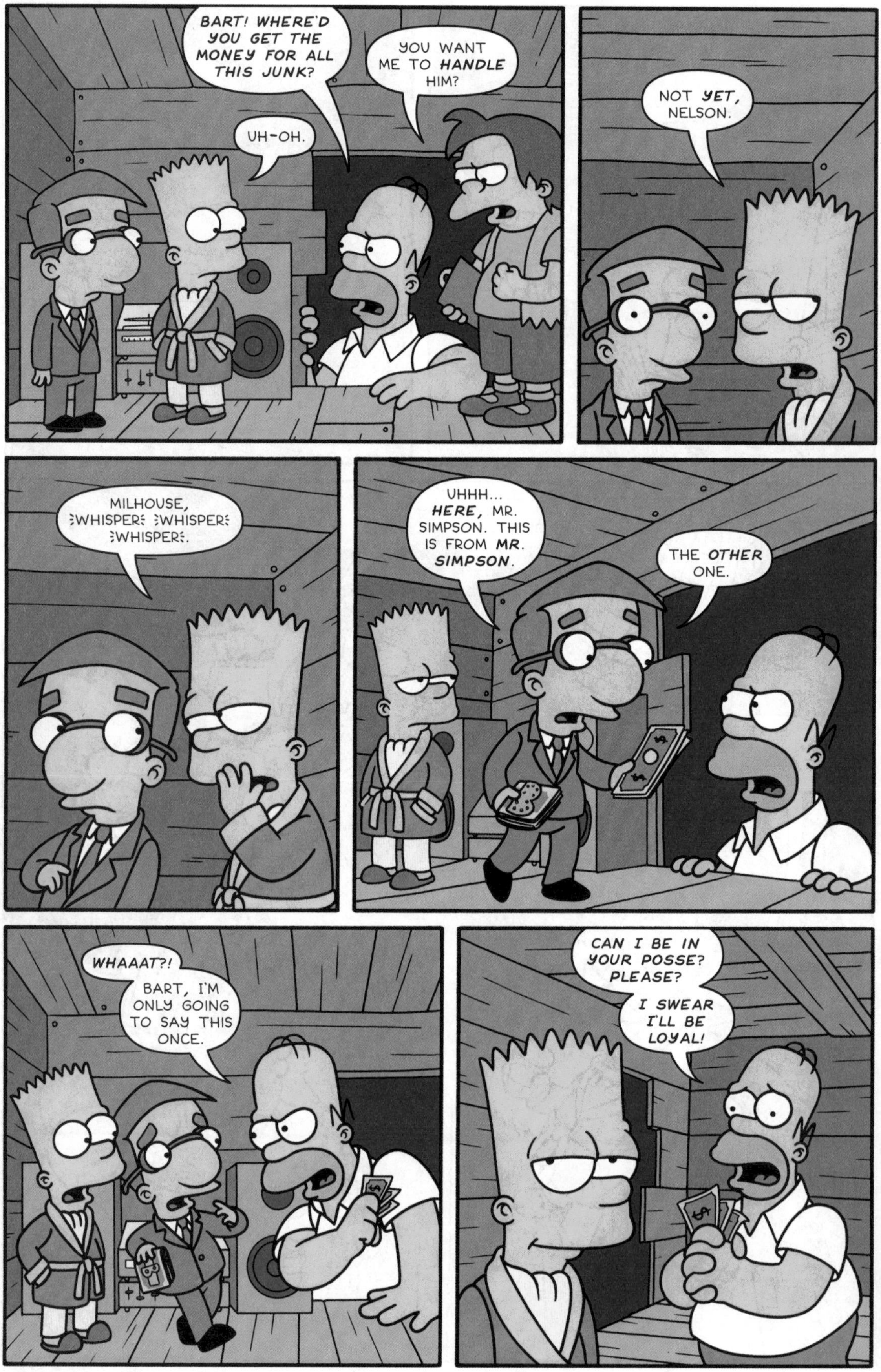
BART! WHERE'D YOU GET THE MONEY FOR ALL THIS JUNK?
UH-OH.
YOU WANT ME TO HANDLE HIM?
NOT YET, NELSON.
MILHOUSE, WHISPER WHISPER WHISPER.
UHHH... HERE, MR. SIMPSON. THIS IS FROM MR. SIMPSON.
THE OTHER ONE.
WHAAAT?!
BART, I'M ONLY GOING TO SAY THIS ONCE.
CAN I BE IN YOUR POSSE? PLEASE?
I SWEAR I'LL BE LOYAL!

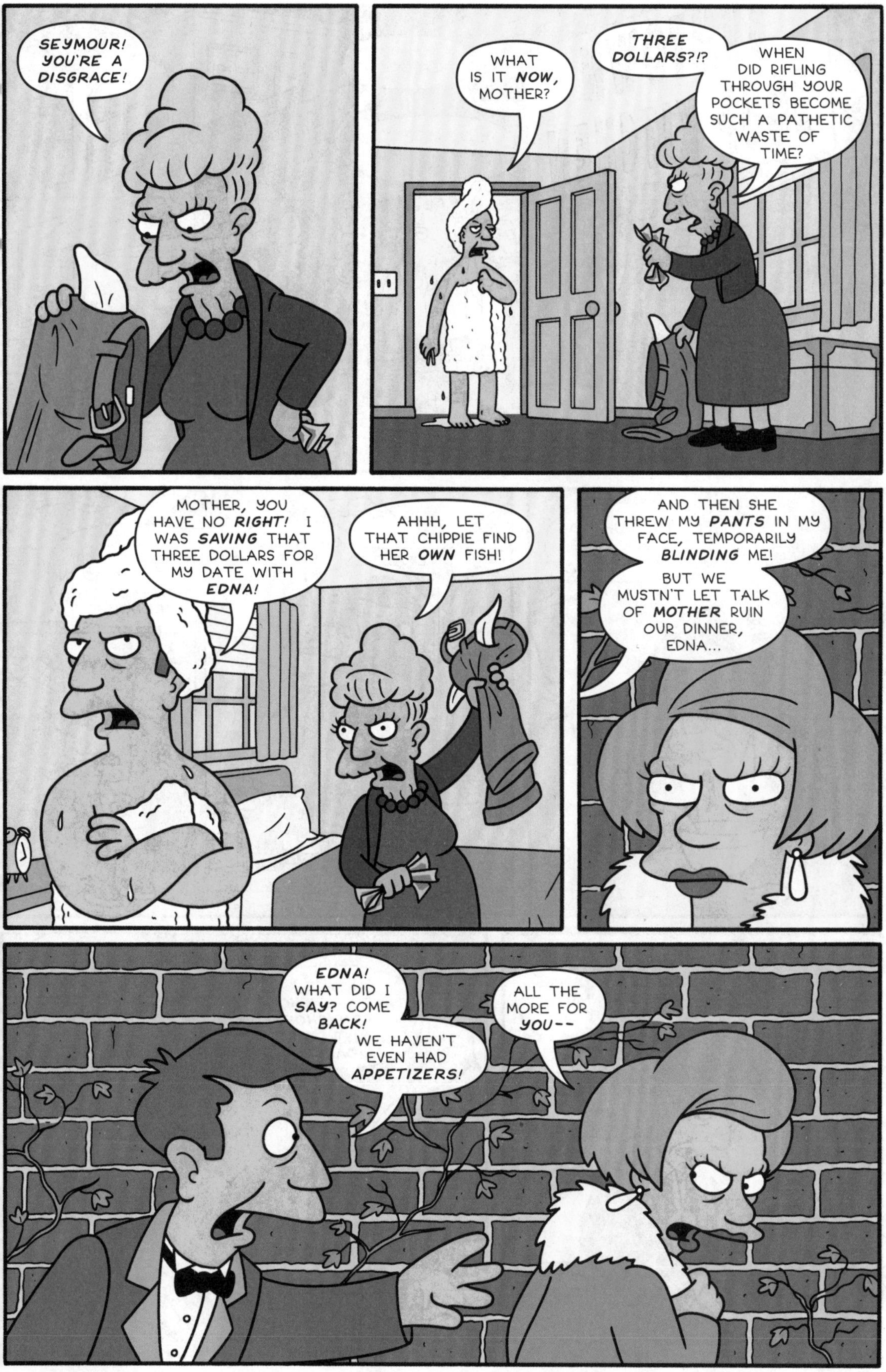
SEYMOUR! YOU'RE A DISGRACE!
WHAT IS IT NOW, MOTHER?
THREE DOLLARS?!?
WHEN DID RIFLING THROUGH YOUR POCKETS BECOME SUCH A PATHETIC WASTE OF TIME?
MOTHER, YOU HAVE NO RIGHT! I WAS SAVING THAT THREE DOLLARS FOR MY DATE WITH EDNA!
AHHH, LET THAT CHIPPIE FIND HER OWN FISH!
AND THEN SHE THREW MY PANTS IN MY FACE, TEMPORARILY BLINDING ME!
BUT WE MUSTN'T LET TALK OF MOTHER RUIN OUR DINNER, EDNA...
EDNA! WHAT DID I SAY? COME BACK!
WE HAVEN'T EVEN HAD APPETIZERS!
ALL THE MORE FOR YOU--

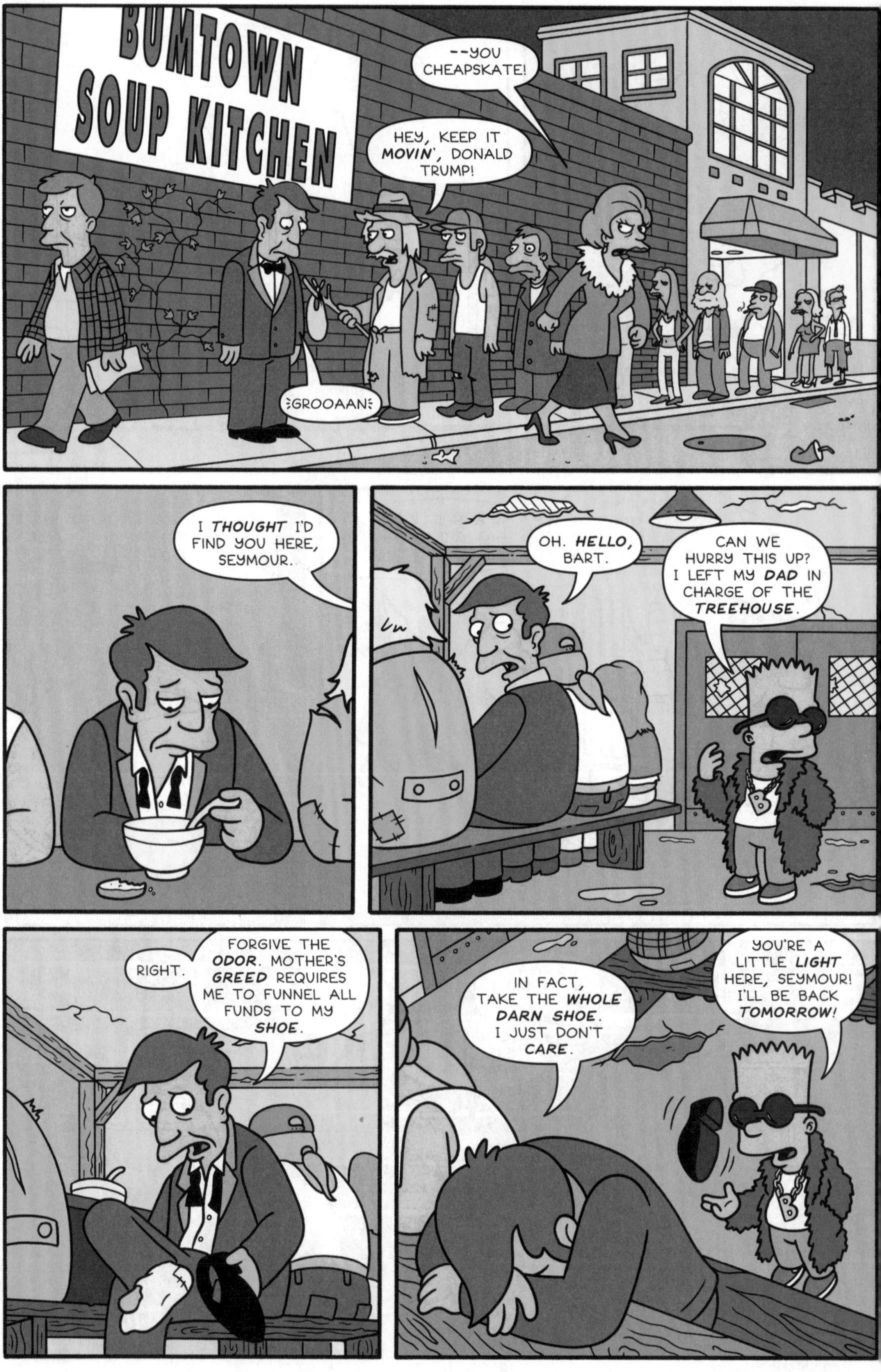
BUMTOWN SOUP KITCHEN
--YOU CHEAPSKATE!
HEY, KEEP IT MOVIN', DONALD TRUMP!
GROOAAN
I THOUGHT I'D FIND YOU HERE, SEYMOUR.
OH. HELLO, BART.
CAN WE HURRY THIS UP? I LEFT MY DAD IN CHARGE OF THE TREEHOUSE.
RIGHT.
FORGIVE THE ODOR. MOTHER'S GREED REQUIRES ME TO FUNNEL ALL FUNDS TO MY SHOE.
IN FACT, TAKE THE WHOLE DARN SHOE. I JUST DON'T CARE.
YOU'RE A LITTLE LIGHT HERE, SEYMOUR! I'LL BE BACK TOMORROW!

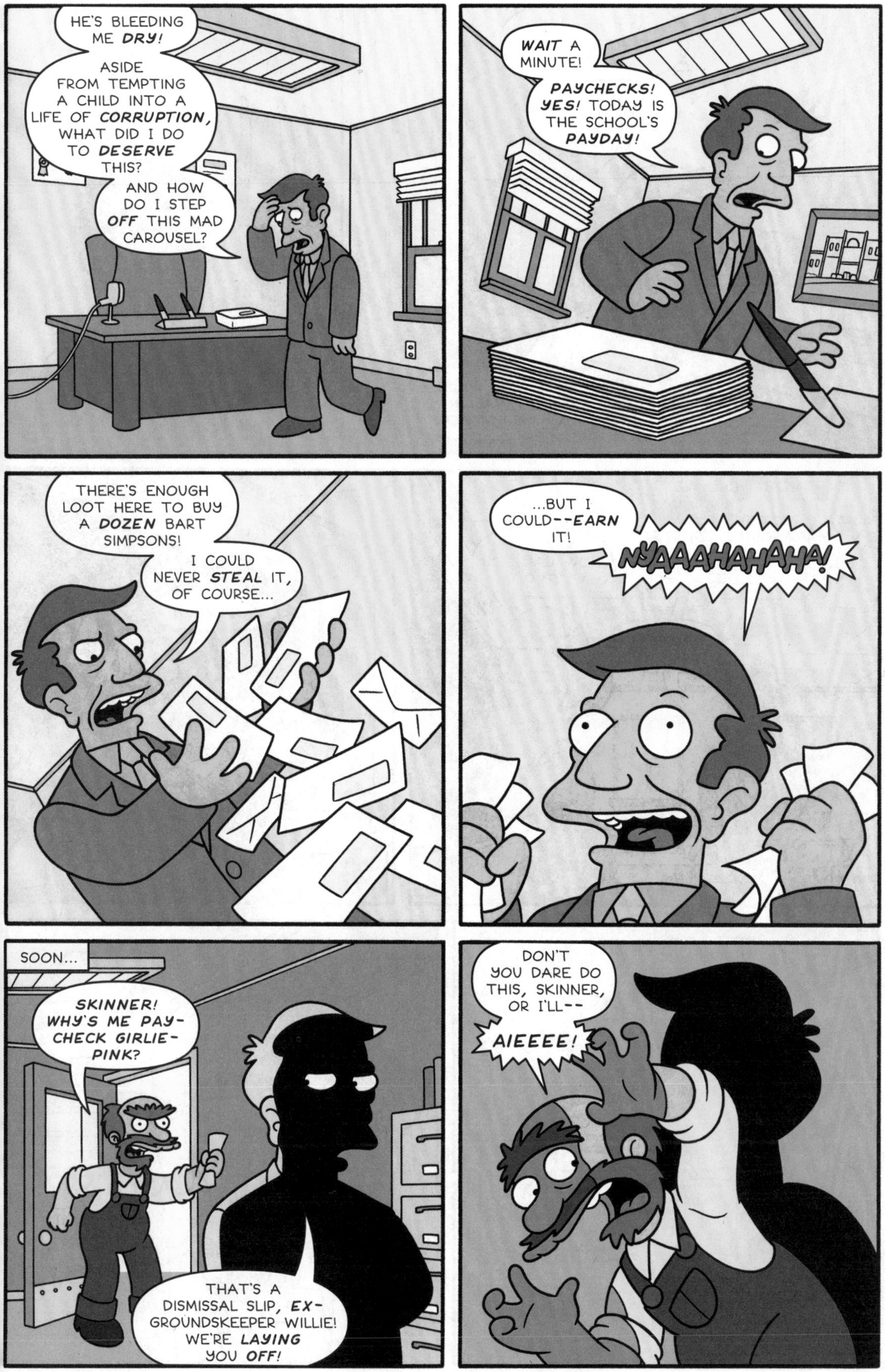
HE'S BLEEDING ME DRY!
ASIDE FROM TEMPTING A CHILD INTO A LIFE OF CORRUPTION, WHAT DID I DO TO DESERVE THIS?
AND HOW DO I STEP OFF THIS MAD CAROUSEL?
WAIT A MINUTE!
PAYCHECKS! YES! TODAY IS THE SCHOOL'S PAYDAY!
THERE'S ENOUGH LOOT HERE TO BUY A DOZEN BART SIMPSONS!
I COULD NEVER STEAL IT, OF COURSE...
...BUT I COULD--EARN IT!
NYAAAHAHAHA!
SOON...
SKINNER! WHY'S ME PAY-CHECK GIRLIE-PINK?
THAT'S A DISMISSAL SLIP, EX-GROUNDSKEEPER WILLIE! WE'RE LAYING YOU OFF!
DON'T YOU DARE DO THIS, SKINNER, OR I'LL--
AIEEEE!

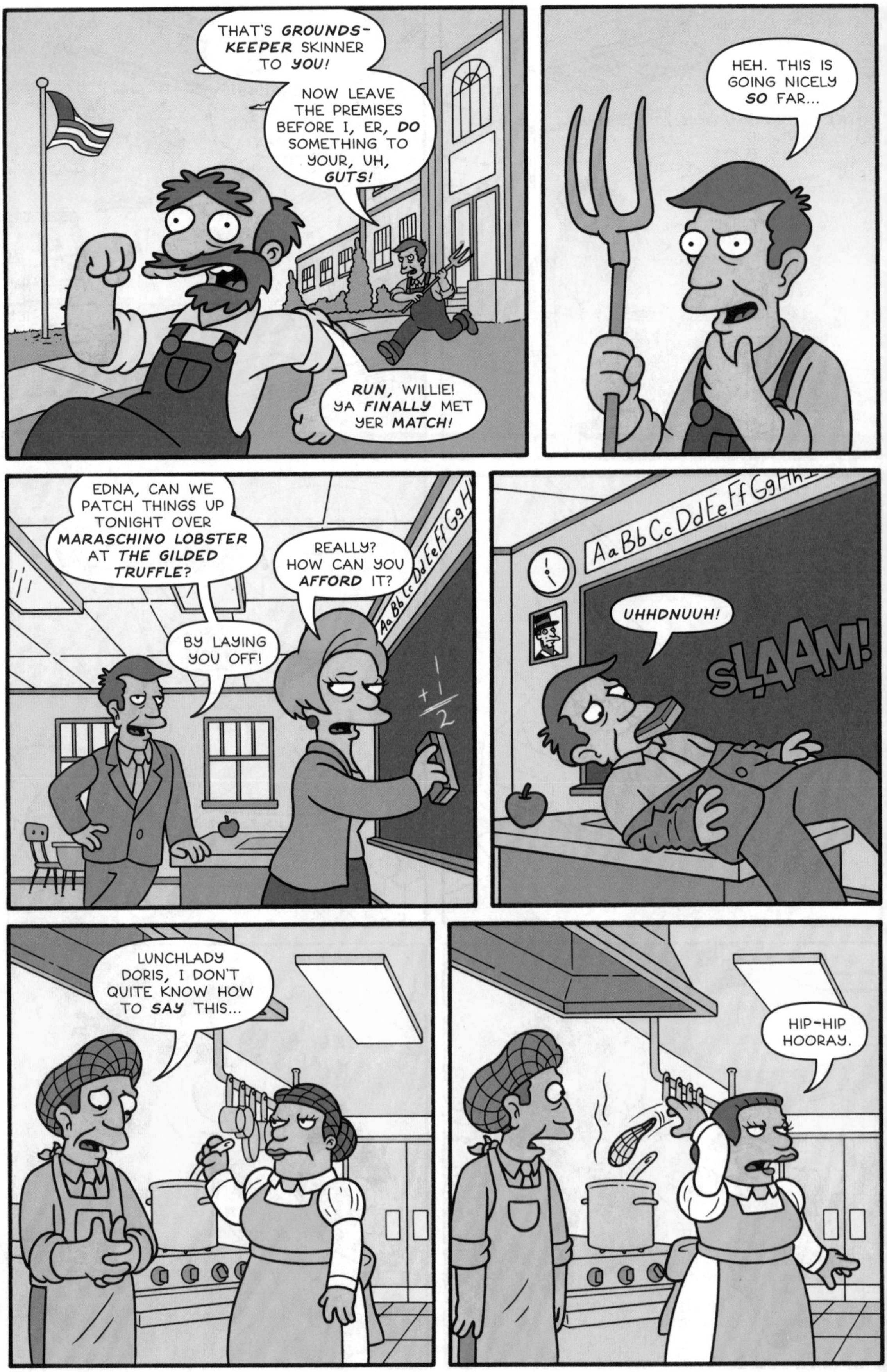
THAT'S GROUNDS-KEEPER SKINNER TO YOU!
NOW LEAVE THE PREMISES BEFORE I, ER, DO SOMETHING TO YOUR, UH, GUTS!
RUN, WILLIE! YA FINALLY MET YER MATCH!
HEH. THIS IS GOING NICELY SO FAR...
EDNA, CAN WE PATCH THINGS UP TONIGHT OVER MARASCHINO LOBSTER AT THE GILDED TRUFFLE?
REALLY? HOW CAN YOU AFFORD IT?
BY LAYING YOU OFF!
Aa Bb Cc Dd Ee Ff Gg Hh
UHHDNUUH!
SLAAM!
LUNCHLADY DORIS, I DON'T QUITE KNOW HOW TO SAY THIS...
HIP-HIP HOORAY.

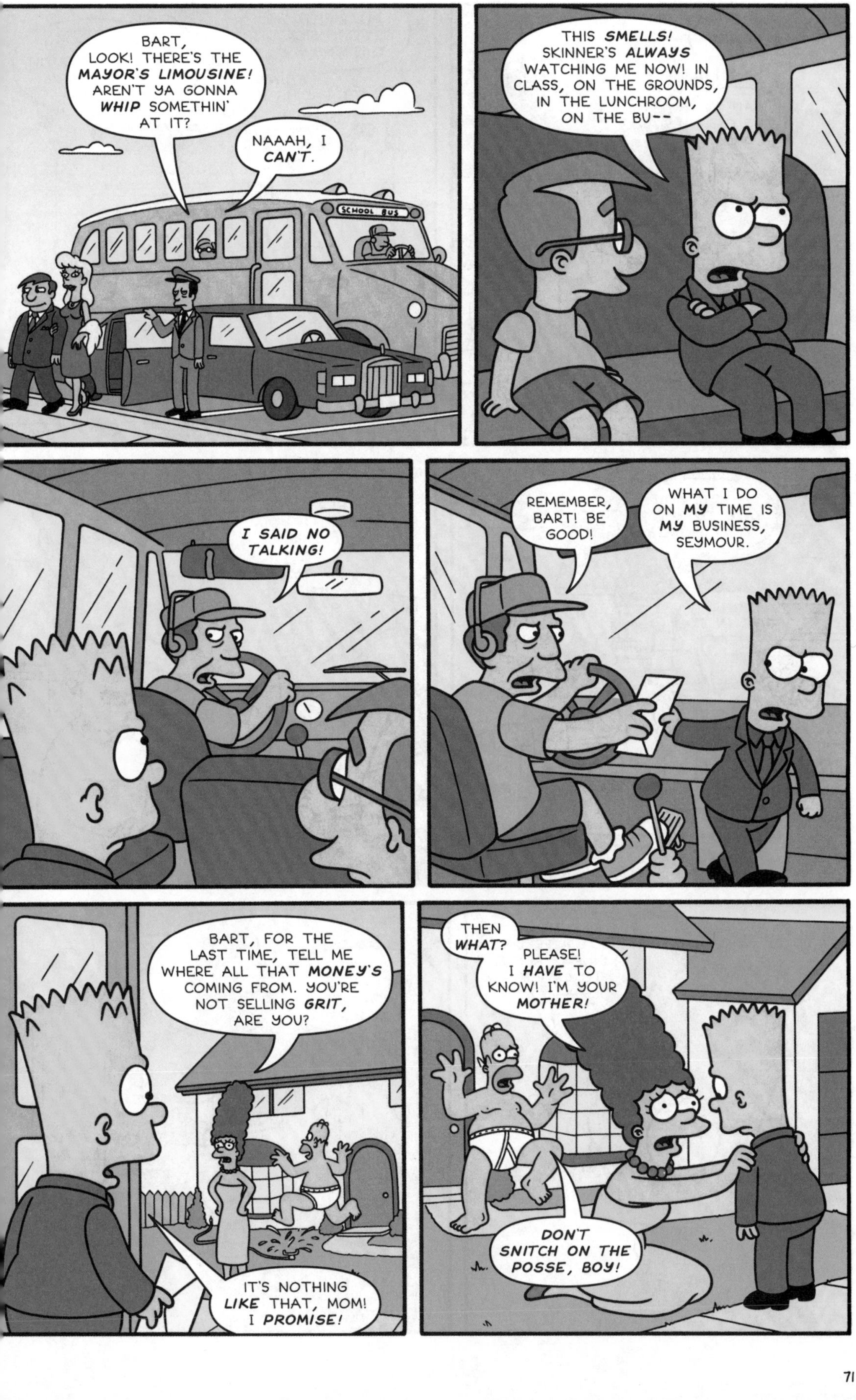
BART, LOOK! THERE'S THE **MAYOR'S LIMOUSINE!** AREN'T YA GONNA **WHIP** SOMETHIN' AT IT?
NAAAH, I **CAN'T**.
SCHOOL BUS
THIS **SMELLS!** SKINNER'S **ALWAYS** WATCHING ME NOW! IN CLASS, ON THE GROUNDS, IN THE LUNCHROOM, ON THE BU--
I SAID NO TALKING!
REMEMBER, BART! BE GOOD!
WHAT I DO ON **MY** TIME IS **MY** BUSINESS, SEYMOUR.
BART, FOR THE LAST TIME, TELL ME WHERE ALL THAT **MONEY'S** COMING FROM. YOU'RE NOT SELLING **GRIT**, ARE YOU?
IT'S NOTHING **LIKE** THAT, MOM! I **PROMISE!**
THEN **WHAT?**
PLEASE! I **HAVE** TO KNOW! I'M YOUR **MOTHER!**
DON'T SNITCH ON THE POSSE, BOY!

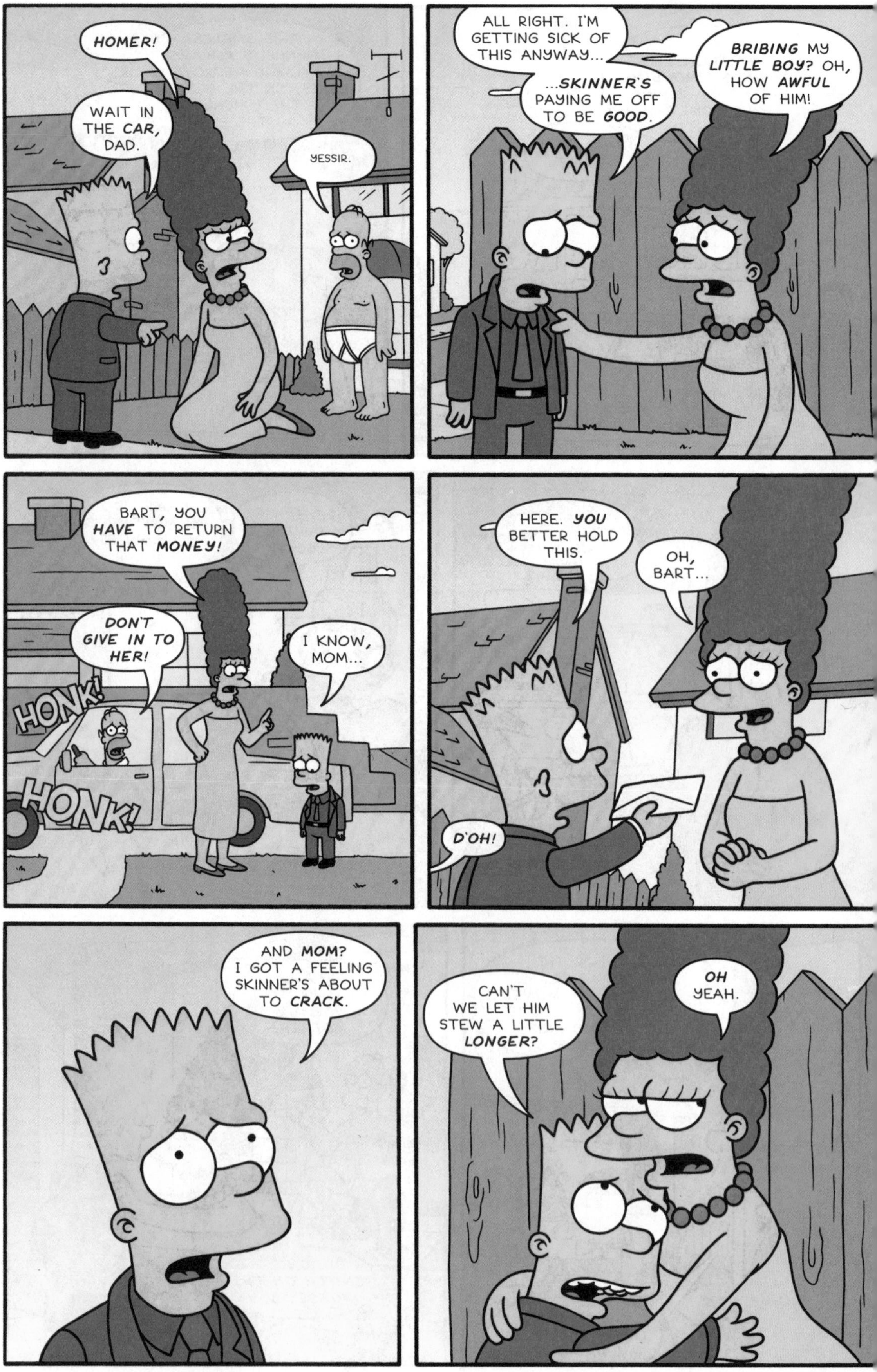
HOMER!
WAIT IN THE CAR, DAD.
YESSIR.
ALL RIGHT. I'M GETTING SICK OF THIS ANYWAY...
...SKINNER'S PAYING ME OFF TO BE GOOD.
BRIBING MY LITTLE BOY? OH, HOW AWFUL OF HIM!
BART, YOU HAVE TO RETURN THAT MONEY!
DON'T GIVE IN TO HER!
HONK!
HONK!
I KNOW, MOM...
HERE. YOU BETTER HOLD THIS.
OH, BART...
D'OH!
AND MOM? I GOT A FEELING SKINNER'S ABOUT TO CRACK.
CAN'T WE LET HIM STEW A LITTLE LONGER?
OH YEAH.

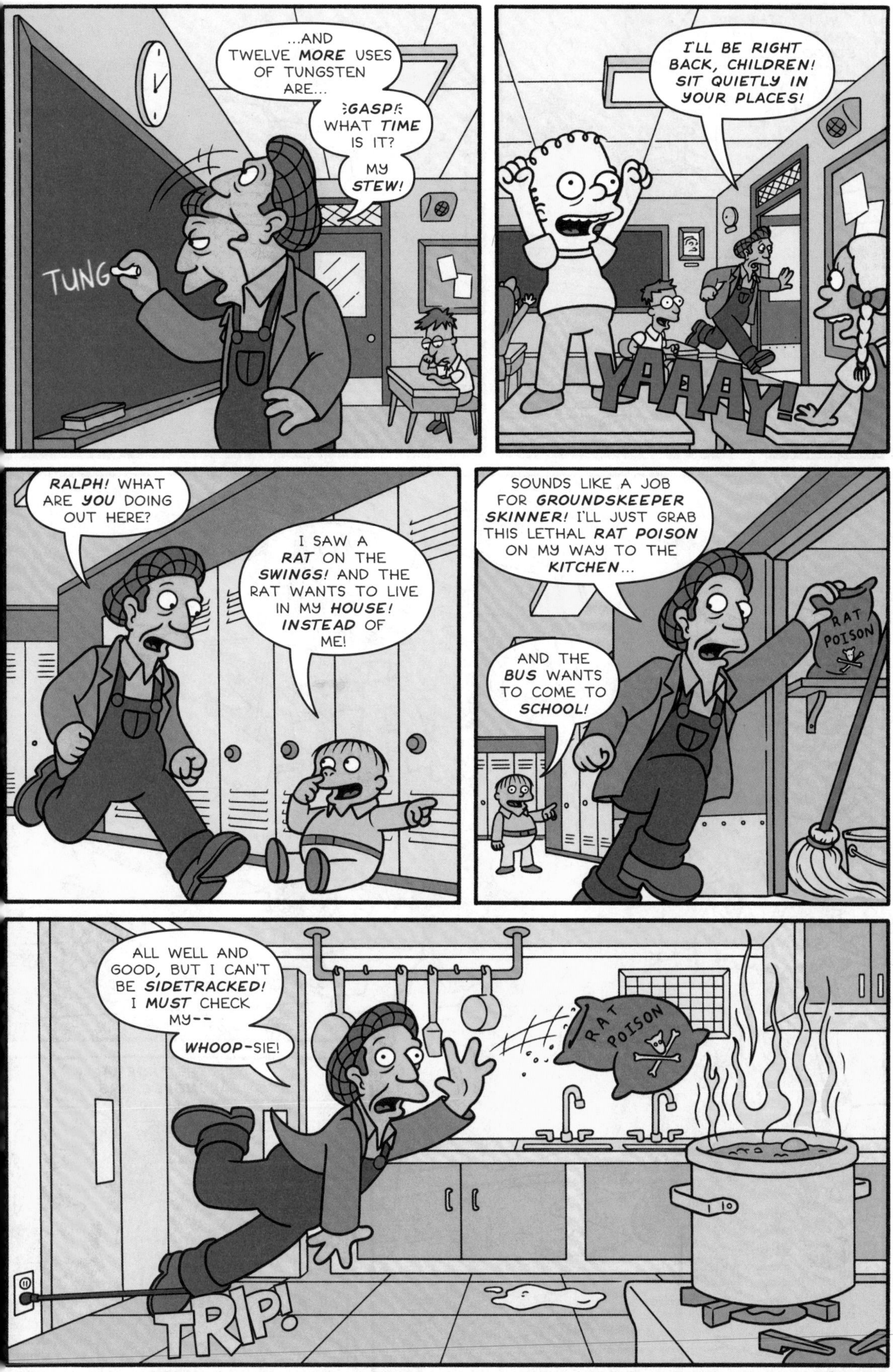
...AND TWELVE MORE USES OF TUNGSTEN ARE...
TUNG
GASP! WHAT TIME IS IT?
MY STEW!
I'LL BE RIGHT BACK, CHILDREN! SIT QUIETLY IN YOUR PLACES!
YAAAY!
RALPH! WHAT ARE YOU DOING OUT HERE?
I SAW A RAT ON THE SWINGS! AND THE RAT WANTS TO LIVE IN MY HOUSE! INSTEAD OF ME!
SOUNDS LIKE A JOB FOR GROUNDSKEEPER SKINNER! I'LL JUST GRAB THIS LETHAL RAT POISON ON MY WAY TO THE KITCHEN...
RAT POISON
AND THE BUS WANTS TO COME TO SCHOOL!
ALL WELL AND GOOD, BUT I CAN'T BE SIDETRACKED! I MUST CHECK MY--
WHOOP-SIE!
RAT POISON
TRIP!

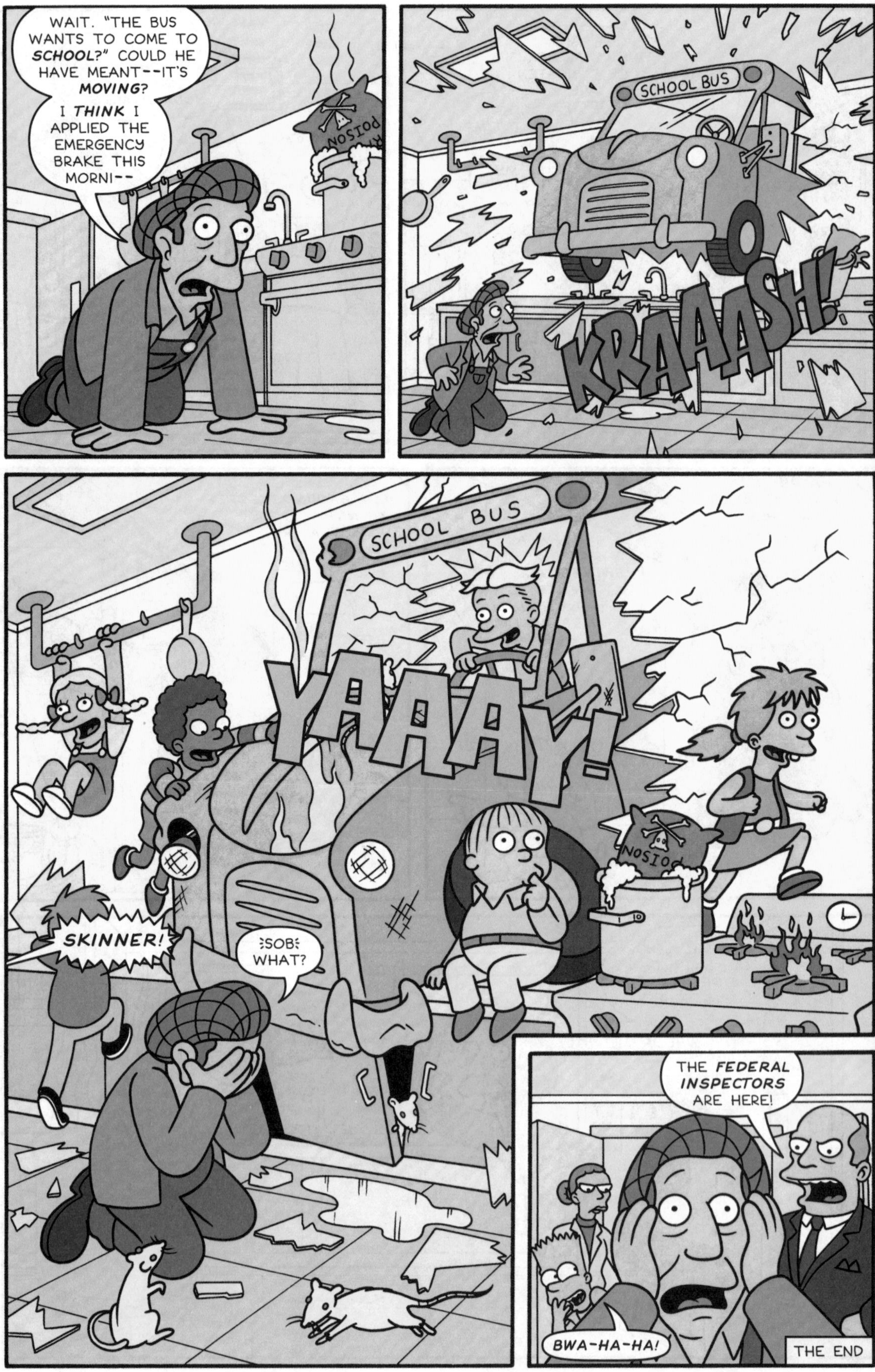
WAIT. "THE BUS WANTS TO COME TO SCHOOL?" COULD HE HAVE MEANT--IT'S MOVING?
I THINK I APPLIED THE EMERGENCY BRAKE THIS MORNI--
POISON
SCHOOL BUS
KRAAASH!
SCHOOL BUS
YAAAY!
POISON
SKINNER!
SOB WHAT?
THE FEDERAL INSPECTORS ARE HERE!
BWA-HA-HA!
THE END

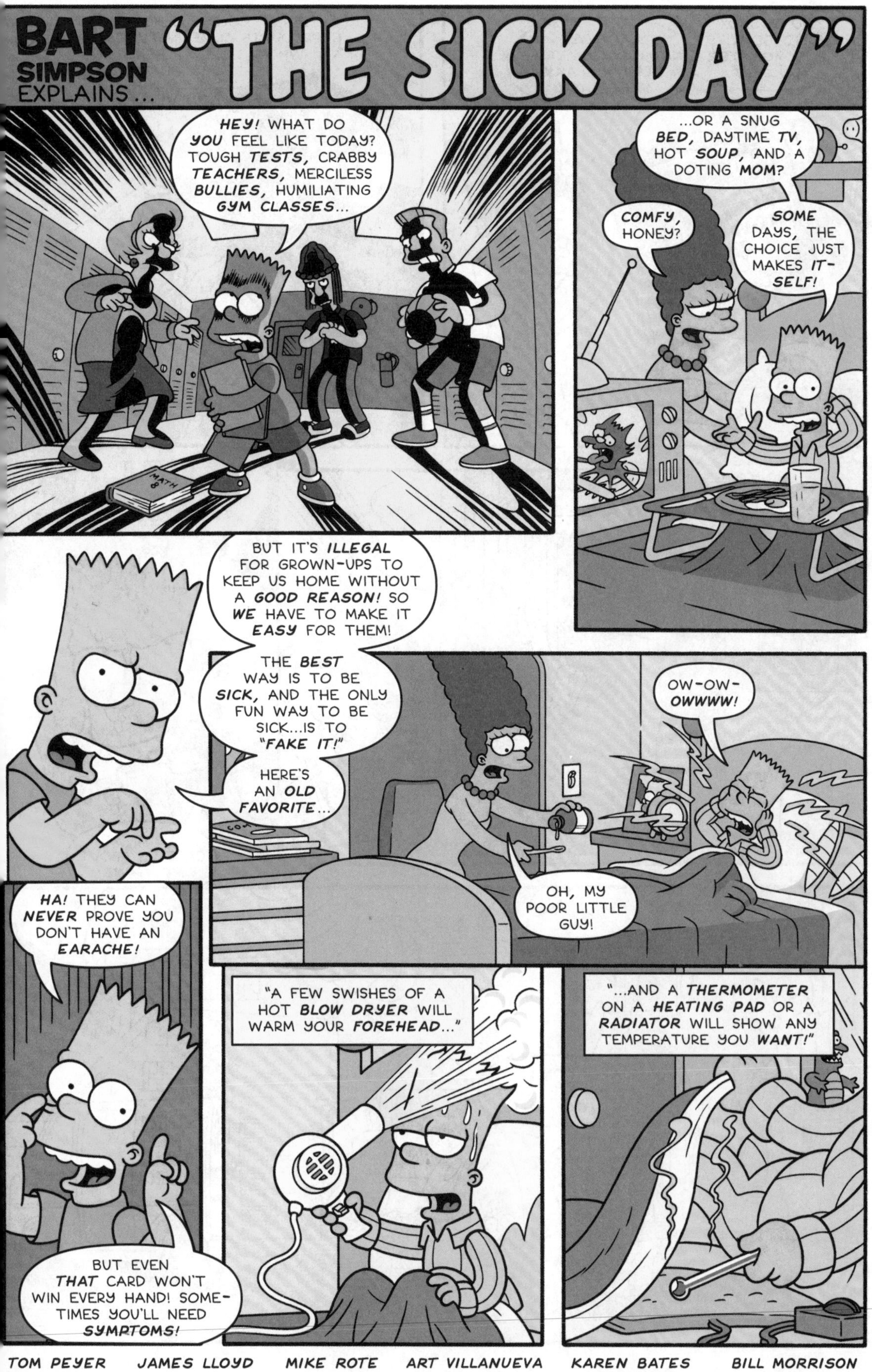
BART SIMPSON EXPLAINS...
"THE SICK DAY"
HEY! WHAT DO YOU FEEL LIKE TODAY? TOUGH TESTS, CRABBY TEACHERS, MERCILESS BULLIES, HUMILIATING GYM CLASSES...
MATH 8
...OR A SNUG BED, DAYTIME TV, HOT SOUP, AND A DOTING MOM?
COMFY, HONEY?
SOME DAYS, THE CHOICE JUST MAKES IT-SELF!
BUT IT'S ILLEGAL FOR GROWN-UPS TO KEEP US HOME WITHOUT A GOOD REASON! SO WE HAVE TO MAKE IT EASY FOR THEM!
THE BEST WAY IS TO BE SICK, AND THE ONLY FUN WAY TO BE SICK...IS TO "FAKE IT!"
HERE'S AN OLD FAVORITE...
OW-OW-OWWWW!
OH, MY POOR LITTLE GUY!
HA! THEY CAN NEVER PROVE YOU DON'T HAVE AN EARACHE!
BUT EVEN THAT CARD WON'T WIN EVERY HAND! SOME-TIMES YOU'LL NEED SYMPTOMS!
"A FEW SWISHES OF A HOT BLOW DRYER WILL WARM YOUR FOREHEAD..."
"...AND A THERMOMETER ON A HEATING PAD OR A RADIATOR WILL SHOW ANY TEMPERATURE YOU WANT!"

TOM PEYER SCRIPT · JAMES LLOYD PENCILS · MIKE ROTE INKS · ART VILLANUEVA COLORS · KAREN BATES LETTERS · BILL MORRISON EDITOR

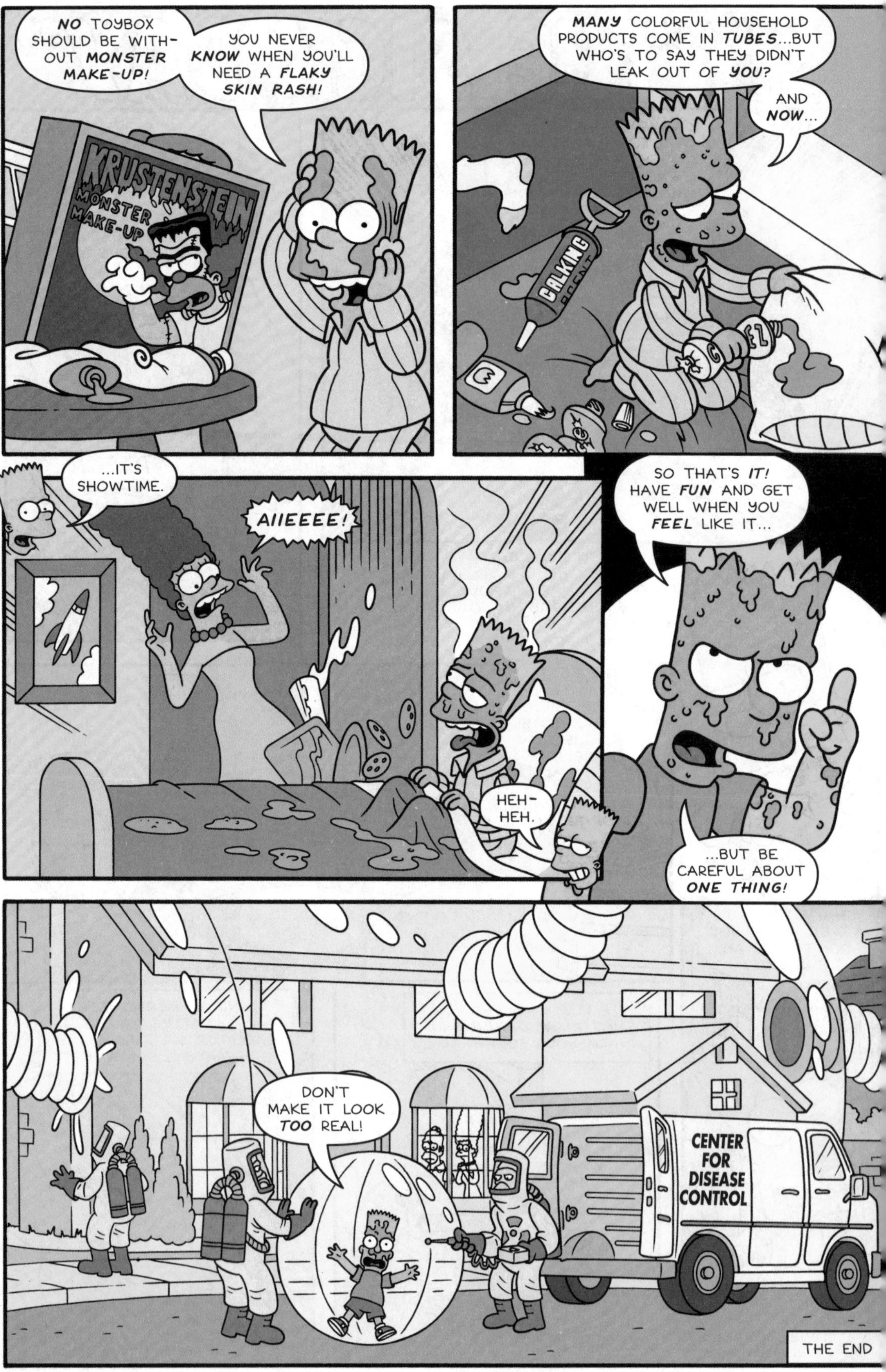
NO TOYBOX SHOULD BE WITH-OUT MONSTER MAKE-UP!
YOU NEVER KNOW WHEN YOU'LL NEED A FLAKY SKIN RASH!
KRUSTENSTEIN MONSTER MAKE-UP
MANY COLORFUL HOUSEHOLD PRODUCTS COME IN TUBES...BUT WHO'S TO SAY THEY DIDN'T LEAK OUT OF YOU?
AND NOW...
CALKING
...IT'S SHOWTIME.
AIIEEEE!
HEH-HEH.
SO THAT'S IT! HAVE FUN AND GET WELL WHEN YOU FEEL LIKE IT...
...BUT BE CAREFUL ABOUT ONE THING!
DON'T MAKE IT LOOK TOO REAL!
CENTER FOR DISEASE CONTROL
THE END

The Simpsons in SPECIAL DELIVERY

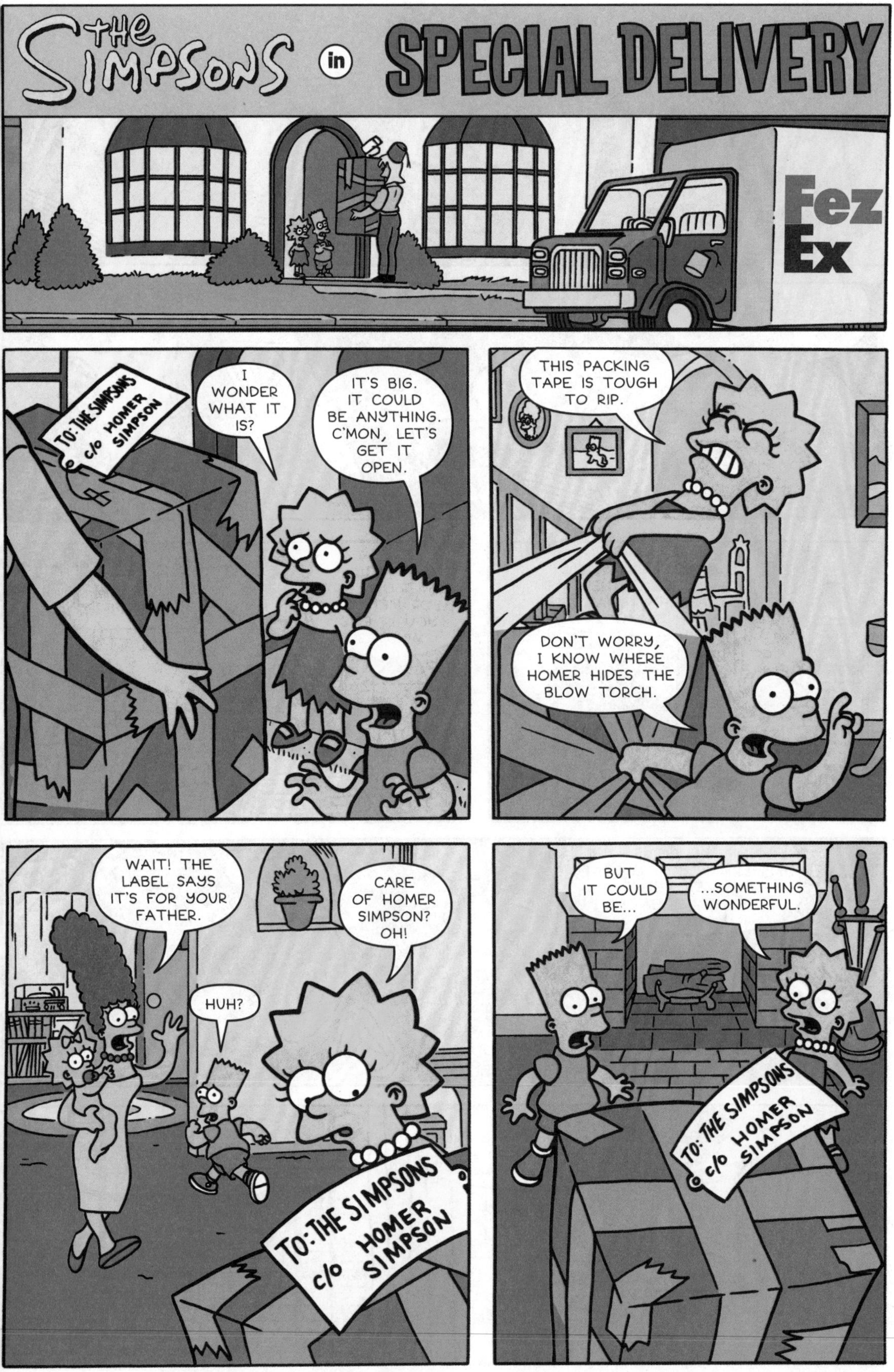
Fez Ex
TO: THE SIMPSONS c/o HOMER SIMPSON
I WONDER WHAT IT IS?
IT'S BIG. IT COULD BE ANYTHING. C'MON, LET'S GET IT OPEN.
THIS PACKING TAPE IS TOUGH TO RIP.
DON'T WORRY, I KNOW WHERE HOMER HIDES THE BLOW TORCH.
WAIT! THE LABEL SAYS IT'S FOR YOUR FATHER.
HUH?
CARE OF HOMER SIMPSON? OH!
TO: THE SIMPSONS c/o HOMER SIMPSON
BUT IT COULD BE...
...SOMETHING WONDERFUL.
TO: THE SIMPSONS c/o HOMER SIMPSON

JAMES BATES SCRIPT *JOHN DELANEY* PENCILS *HOWARD SHUM* INKS *ART VILLANUEVA* COLORS *KAREN BATES* LETTERS *BILL MORRISON* EDITOR

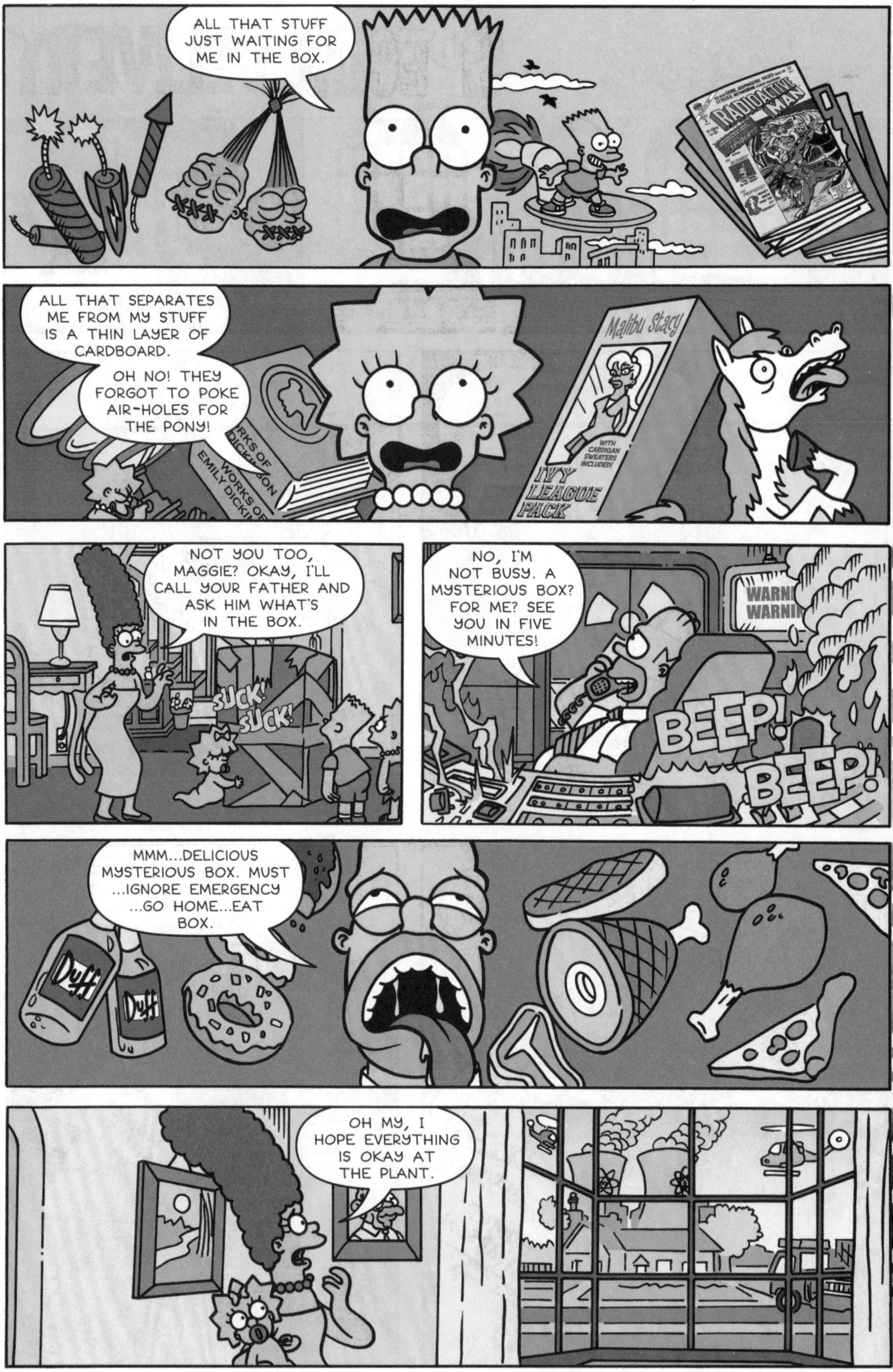
ALL THAT STUFF JUST WAITING FOR ME IN THE BOX.
RADIOACTIVE MAN
ALL THAT SEPARATES ME FROM MY STUFF IS A THIN LAYER OF CARDBOARD.
OH NO! THEY FORGOT TO POKE AIR-HOLES FOR THE PONY!
Malibu Stacy
WITH CARDIGAN SWEATERS INCLUDED!
IVY LEAGUE PACK
NOT YOU TOO, MAGGIE? OKAY, I'LL CALL YOUR FATHER AND ASK HIM WHAT'S IN THE BOX.
SUCK! SUCK!
NO, I'M NOT BUSY. A MYSTERIOUS BOX? FOR ME? SEE YOU IN FIVE MINUTES!
BEEP! BEEP!
MMM...DELICIOUS MYSTERIOUS BOX. MUST ...IGNORE EMERGENCY ...GO HOME...EAT BOX.
Duff
Duff
OH MY, I HOPE EVERYTHING IS OKAY AT THE PLANT.

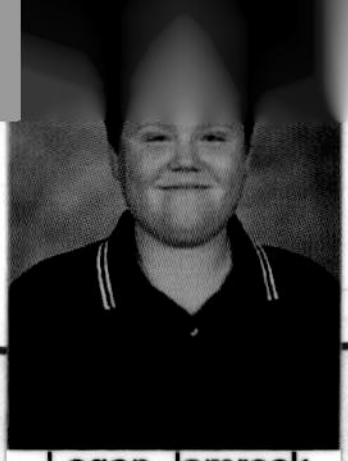
Logan Jamrock

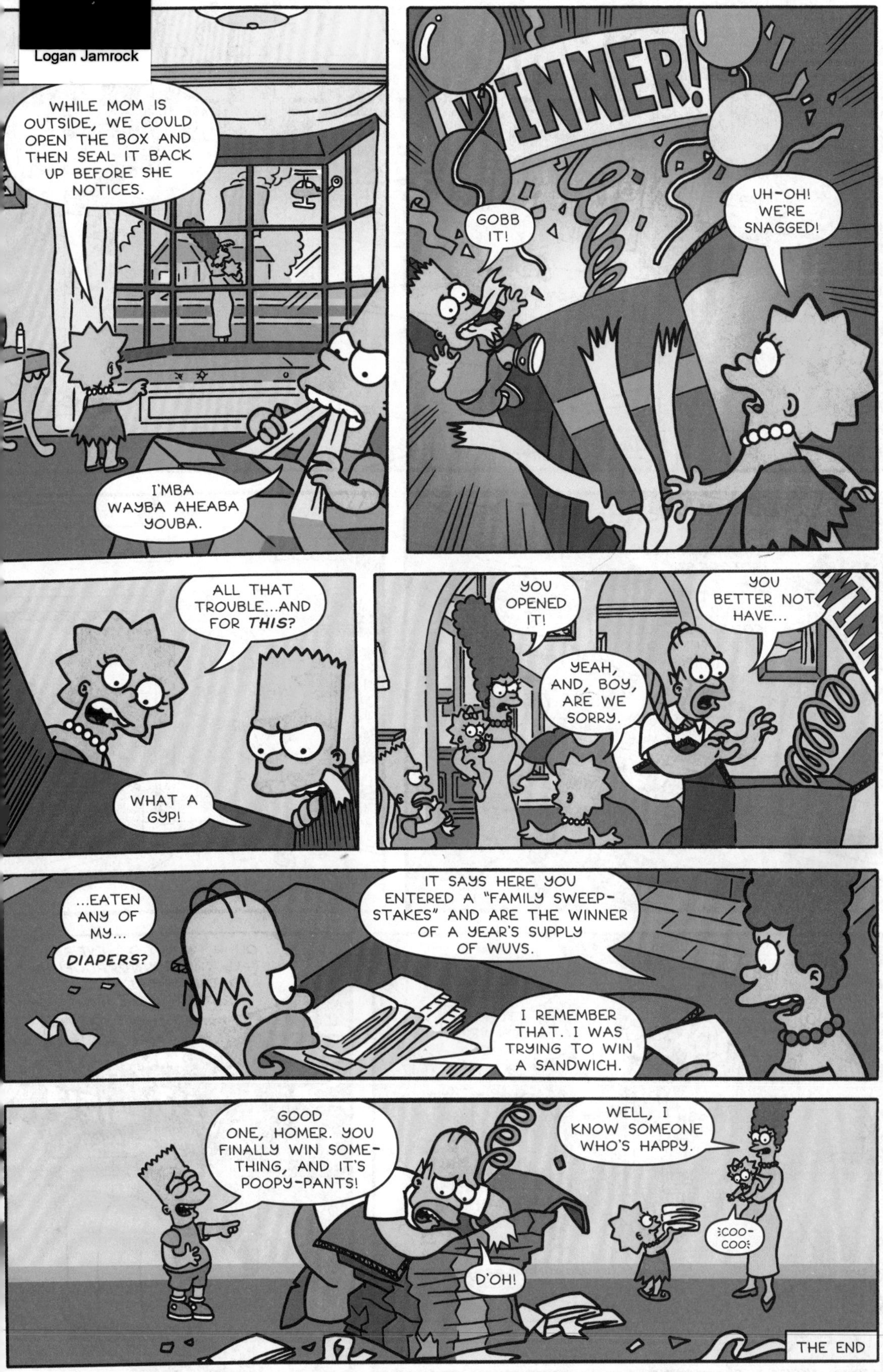

WHILE MOM IS OUTSIDE, WE COULD OPEN THE BOX AND THEN SEAL IT BACK UP BEFORE SHE NOTICES.
I'MBA WAYBA AHEABA YOUBA.
GOBB IT!
UH-OH! WE'RE SNAGGED!
ALL THAT TROUBLE...AND FOR *THIS?*
WHAT A GYP!
YOU OPENED IT!
YOU BETTER NOT HAVE...
YEAH, AND, BOY, ARE WE SORRY.
...EATEN ANY OF MY... ***DIAPERS?***
IT SAYS HERE YOU ENTERED A "FAMILY SWEEP-STAKES" AND ARE THE WINNER OF A YEAR'S SUPPLY OF WUVS.
I REMEMBER THAT. I WAS TRYING TO WIN A SANDWICH.
GOOD ONE, HOMER. YOU FINALLY WIN SOME-THING, AND IT'S POOPY-PANTS!
WELL, I KNOW SOMEONE WHO'S HAPPY.
D'OH!
COO-COO!
THE END

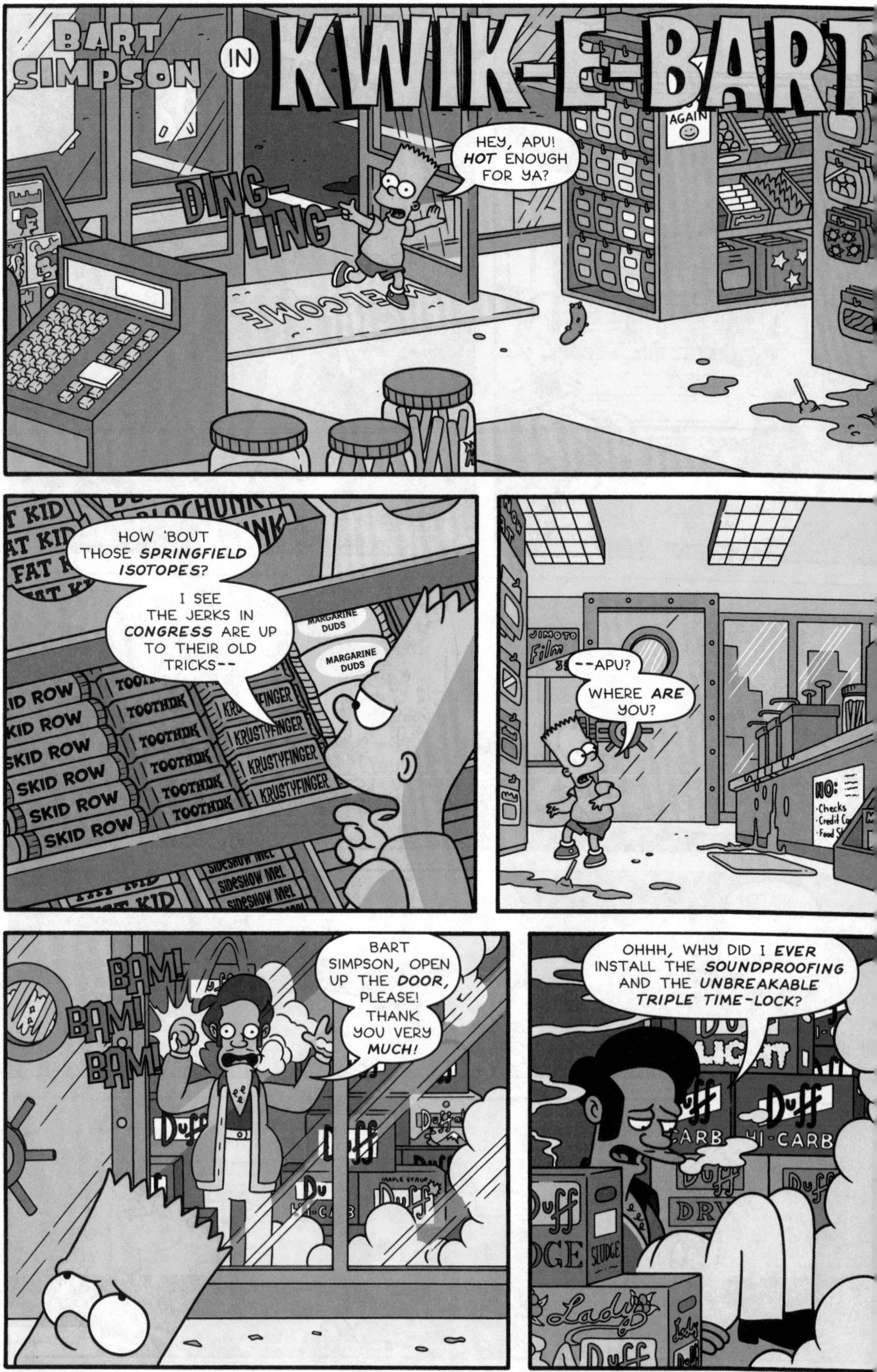
BART SIMPSON IN KWIK-E-BART
AGAIN
HEY, APU! HOT ENOUGH FOR YA?
DING-LING
WELCOME
FAT KID
HOW 'BOUT THOSE SPRINGFIELD ISOTOPES?
I SEE THE JERKS IN CONGRESS ARE UP TO THEIR OLD TRICKS--
MARGARINE DUDS
SKID ROW
TOOTHDK
KRUSTYFINGER
SIDESHOW MEL
JIMOTO Film
--APU?
WHERE ARE YOU?
NO: Checks Credit Ca Food St
BAM! BAM! BAM!
BART SIMPSON, OPEN UP THE DOOR, PLEASE! THANK YOU VERY MUCH!
Duff
MAPLE SYRUP Duff
OHHH, WHY DID I EVER INSTALL THE SOUNDPROOFING AND THE UNBREAKABLE TRIPLE TIME-LOCK?
Duff LIGHT
Duff HI-CARB
SLUDGE
Lady Duff

TOM PEYER SCRIPT JAMES LLOYD PENCILS MIKE ROTE INKS NATHAN HAMILL COLORS KAREN BATES LETTERS BILL MORRISON EDITOR

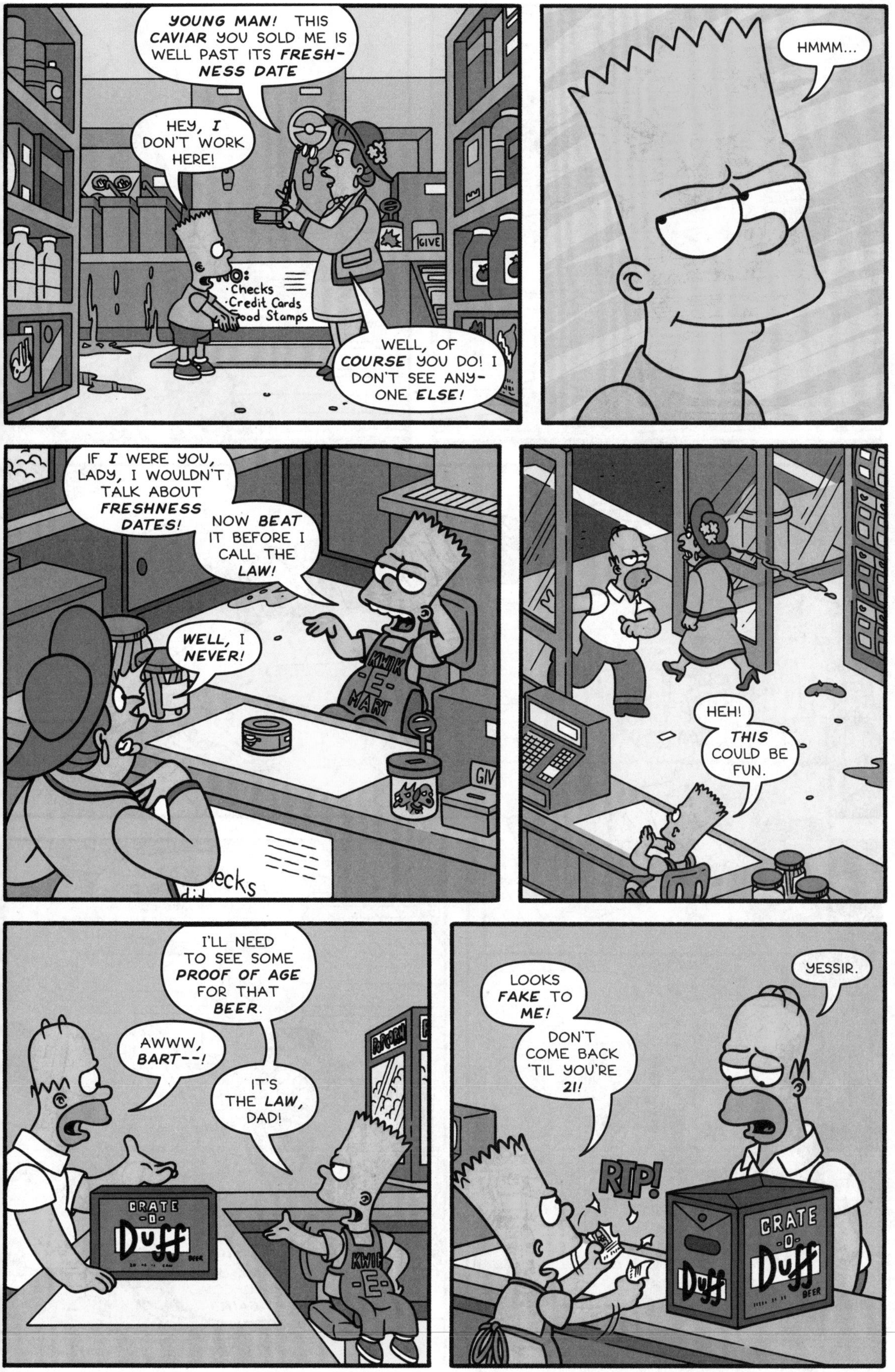
YOUNG MAN! THIS CAVIAR YOU SOLD ME IS WELL PAST ITS FRESHNESS DATE
HEY, I DON'T WORK HERE!
·Checks
·Credit Cards
GIVE
WELL, OF COURSE YOU DO! I DON'T SEE ANYONE ELSE!
HMMM...
IF I WERE YOU, LADY, I WOULDN'T TALK ABOUT FRESHNESS DATES!
NOW BEAT IT BEFORE I CALL THE LAW!
WELL, I NEVER!
KWIK-E-MART
HEH! THIS COULD BE FUN.
I'LL NEED TO SEE SOME PROOF OF AGE FOR THAT BEER.
AWWW, BART--!
IT'S THE LAW, DAD!
CRATE-O-DUFF
LOOKS FAKE TO ME!
DON'T COME BACK 'TIL YOU'RE 21!
YESSIR.
RIP!
CRATE-O-DUFF BEER

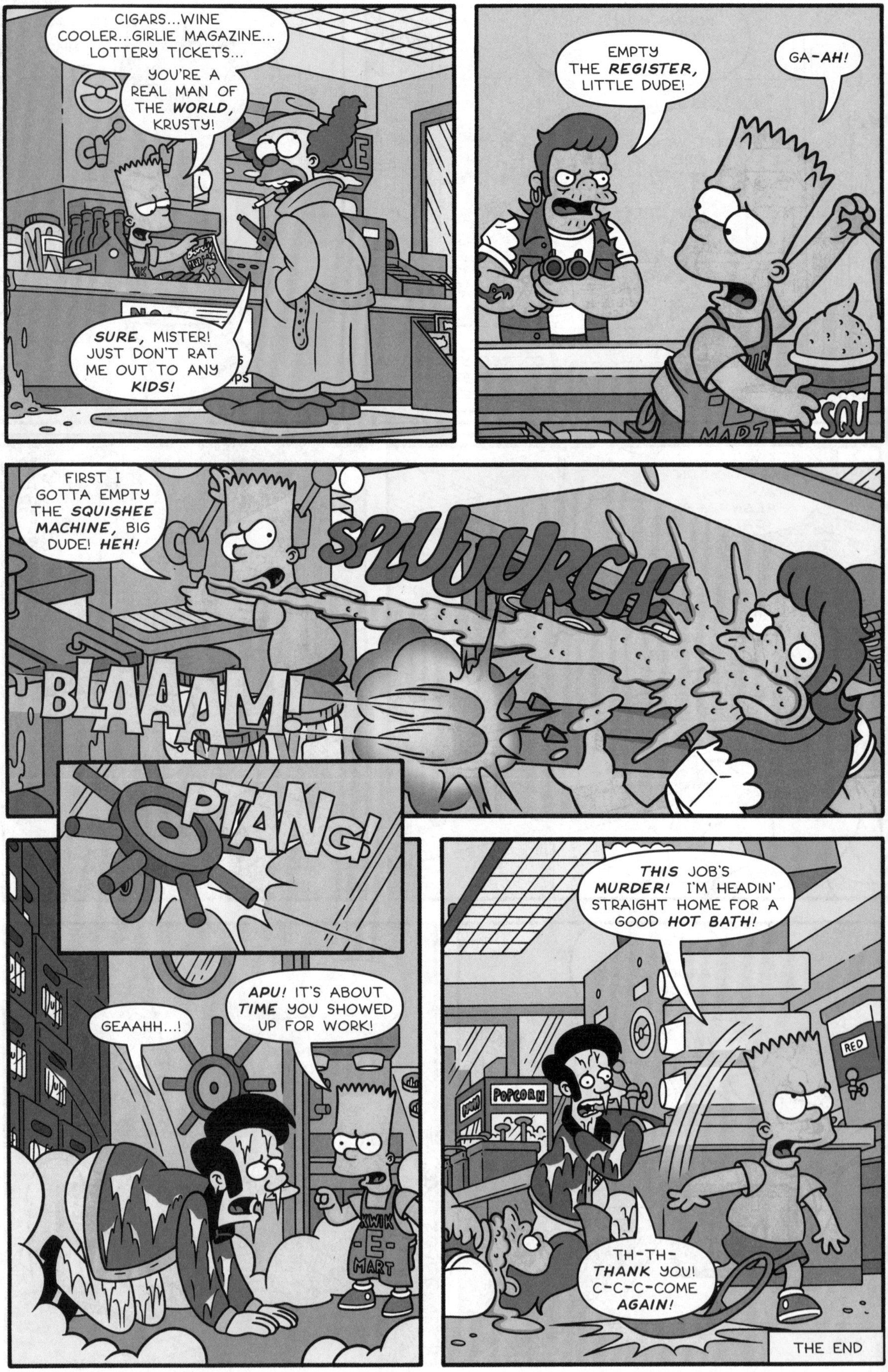
CIGARS...WINE COOLER...GIRLIE MAGAZINE... LOTTERY TICKETS...
YOU'RE A REAL MAN OF THE WORLD, KRUSTY!
SURE, MISTER! JUST DON'T RAT ME OUT TO ANY KIDS!
EMPTY THE REGISTER, LITTLE DUDE!
GA-AH!
FIRST I GOTTA EMPTY THE SQUISHEE MACHINE, BIG DUDE! HEH!
SPLUUURCH!
BLAAAM!
PTANG!
GEAAHH...!
APU! IT'S ABOUT TIME YOU SHOWED UP FOR WORK!
THIS JOB'S MURDER! I'M HEADIN' STRAIGHT HOME FOR A GOOD HOT BATH!
TH-TH-THANK YOU! C-C-C-COME AGAIN!
THE END

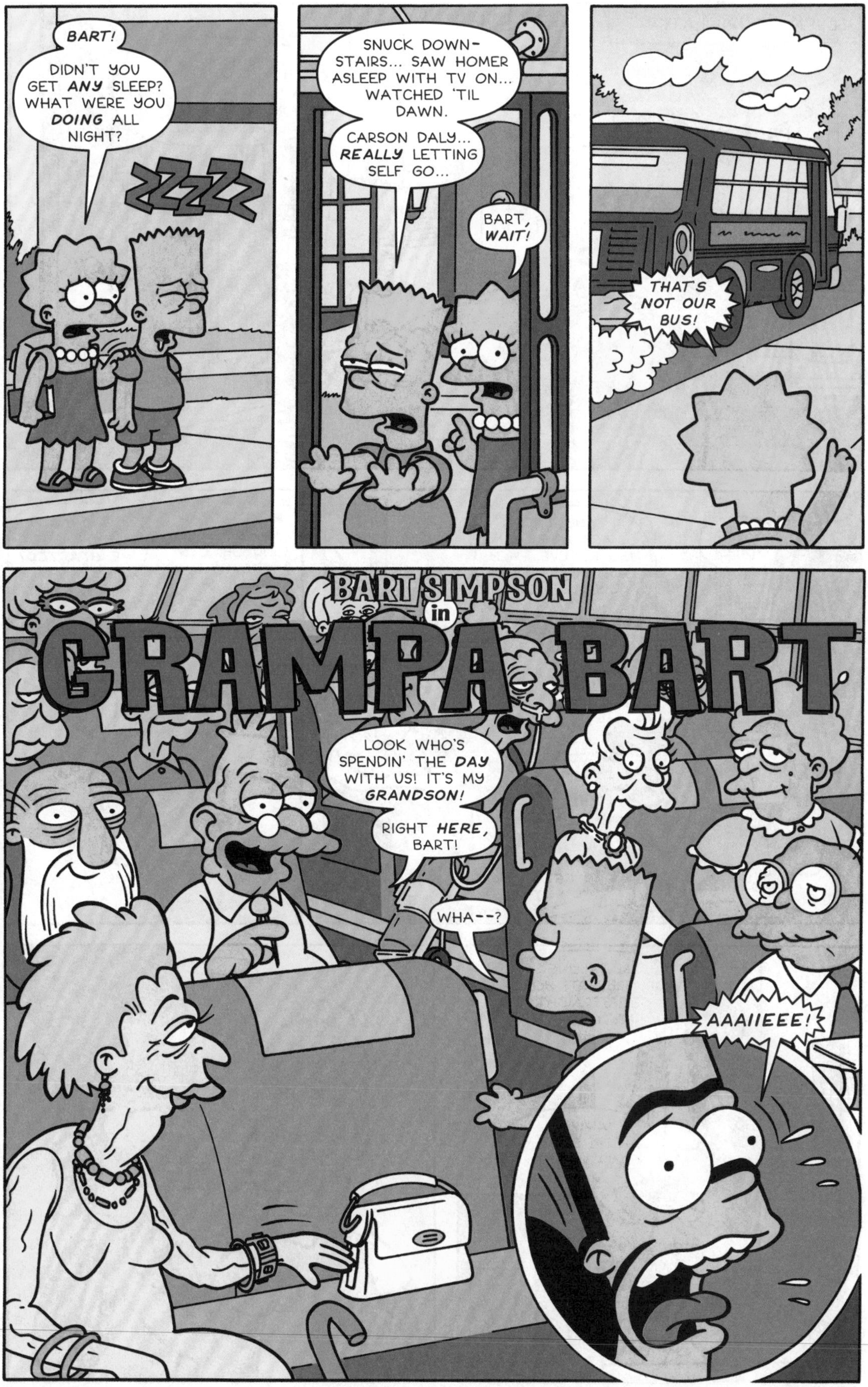
BART!
DIDN'T YOU GET ANY SLEEP? WHAT WERE YOU DOING ALL NIGHT?
ZZZZZ
SNUCK DOWNSTAIRS... SAW HOMER ASLEEP WITH TV ON... WATCHED 'TIL DAWN.
CARSON DALY... REALLY LETTING SELF GO...
BART, WAIT!
THAT'S NOT OUR BUS!
BART SIMPSON in
GRAMPA BART
LOOK WHO'S SPENDIN' THE DAY WITH US! IT'S MY GRANDSON!
RIGHT HERE, BART!
WHA--?
AAAIIEEE!

TOM PEYER SCRIPT · **JOHN COSTANZA** PENCILS · **HOWARD SHUM** INKS · **ART VILLANUEVA** COLORS · **KAREN BATES** LETTERS · **BILL MORRISON** EDITOR

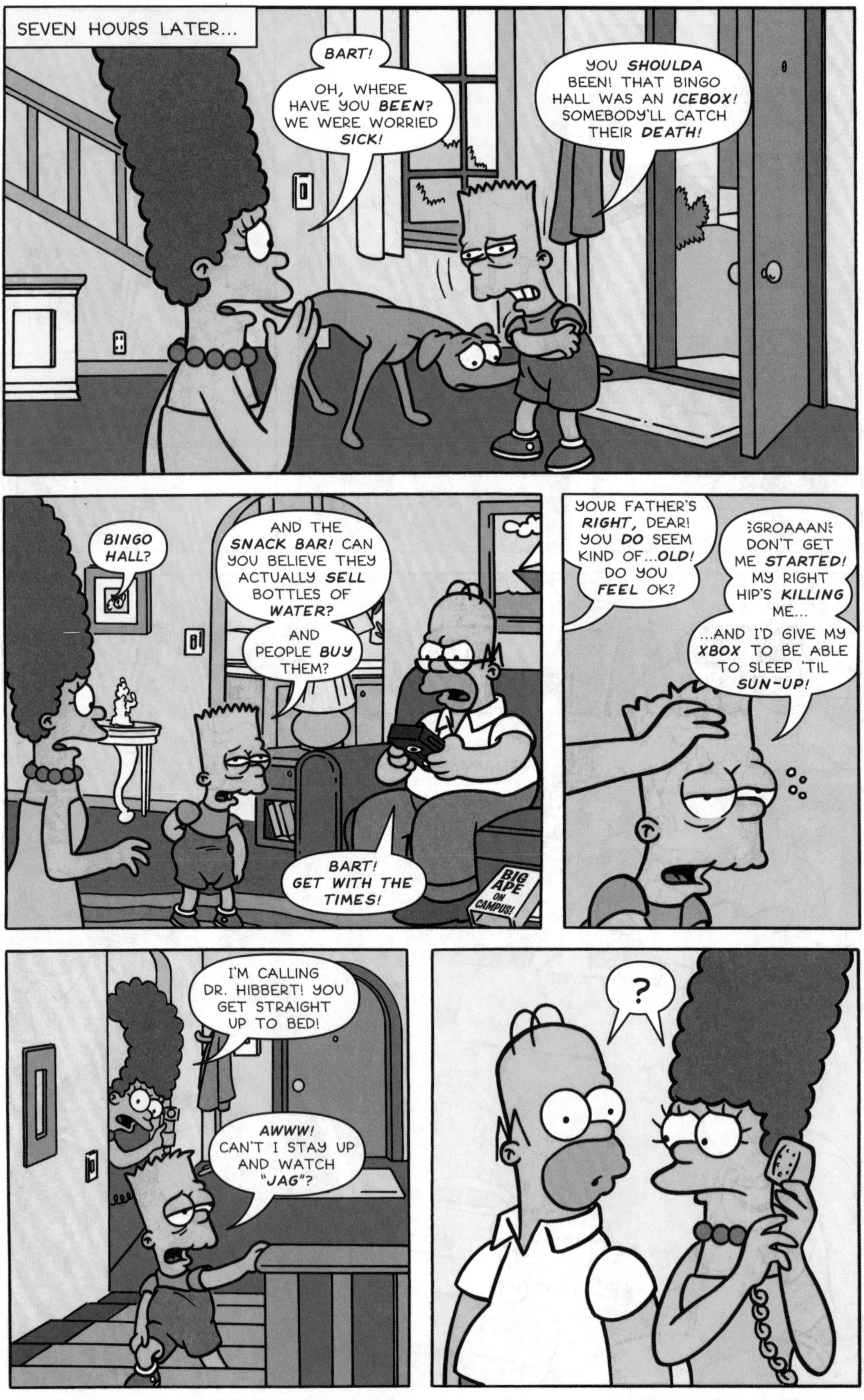
SEVEN HOURS LATER...
BART!
OH, WHERE HAVE YOU BEEN? WE WERE WORRIED SICK!
YOU SHOULDA BEEN! THAT BINGO HALL WAS AN ICEBOX! SOMEBODY'LL CATCH THEIR DEATH!
BINGO HALL?
AND THE SNACK BAR! CAN YOU BELIEVE THEY ACTUALLY SELL BOTTLES OF WATER?
AND PEOPLE BUY THEM?
BART! GET WITH THE TIMES!
BIG APE ON CAMPUS!
YOUR FATHER'S RIGHT, DEAR! YOU DO SEEM KIND OF...OLD! DO YOU FEEL OK?
GROAAAN
DON'T GET ME STARTED! MY RIGHT HIP'S KILLING ME...
...AND I'D GIVE MY XBOX TO BE ABLE TO SLEEP 'TIL SUN-UP!
I'M CALLING DR. HIBBERT! YOU GET STRAIGHT UP TO BED!
AWWW! CAN'T I STAY UP AND WATCH "JAG"?
?

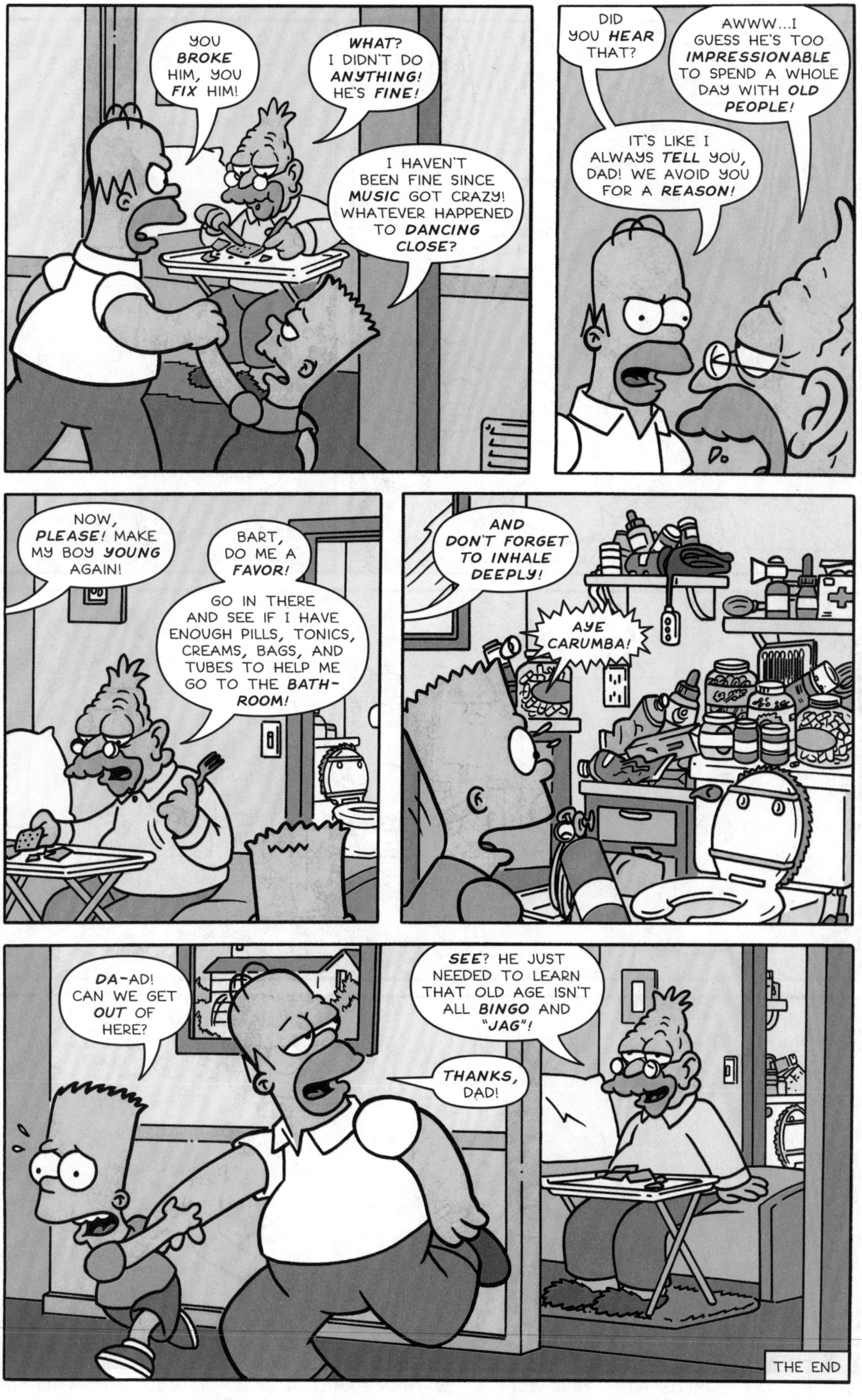
YOU BROKE HIM, YOU FIX HIM!
WHAT? I DIDN'T DO ANYTHING! HE'S FINE!
I HAVEN'T BEEN FINE SINCE MUSIC GOT CRAZY! WHATEVER HAPPENED TO DANCING CLOSE?
DID YOU HEAR THAT?
AWWW...I GUESS HE'S TOO IMPRESSIONABLE TO SPEND A WHOLE DAY WITH OLD PEOPLE!
IT'S LIKE I ALWAYS TELL YOU, DAD! WE AVOID YOU FOR A REASON!
NOW, PLEASE! MAKE MY BOY YOUNG AGAIN!
BART, DO ME A FAVOR!
GO IN THERE AND SEE IF I HAVE ENOUGH PILLS, TONICS, CREAMS, BAGS, AND TUBES TO HELP ME GO TO THE BATH-ROOM!
AND DON'T FORGET TO INHALE DEEPLY!
AYE CARUMBA!
DA-AD! CAN WE GET OUT OF HERE?
SEE? HE JUST NEEDED TO LEARN THAT OLD AGE ISN'T ALL BINGO AND "JAG"!
THANKS, DAD!
THE END

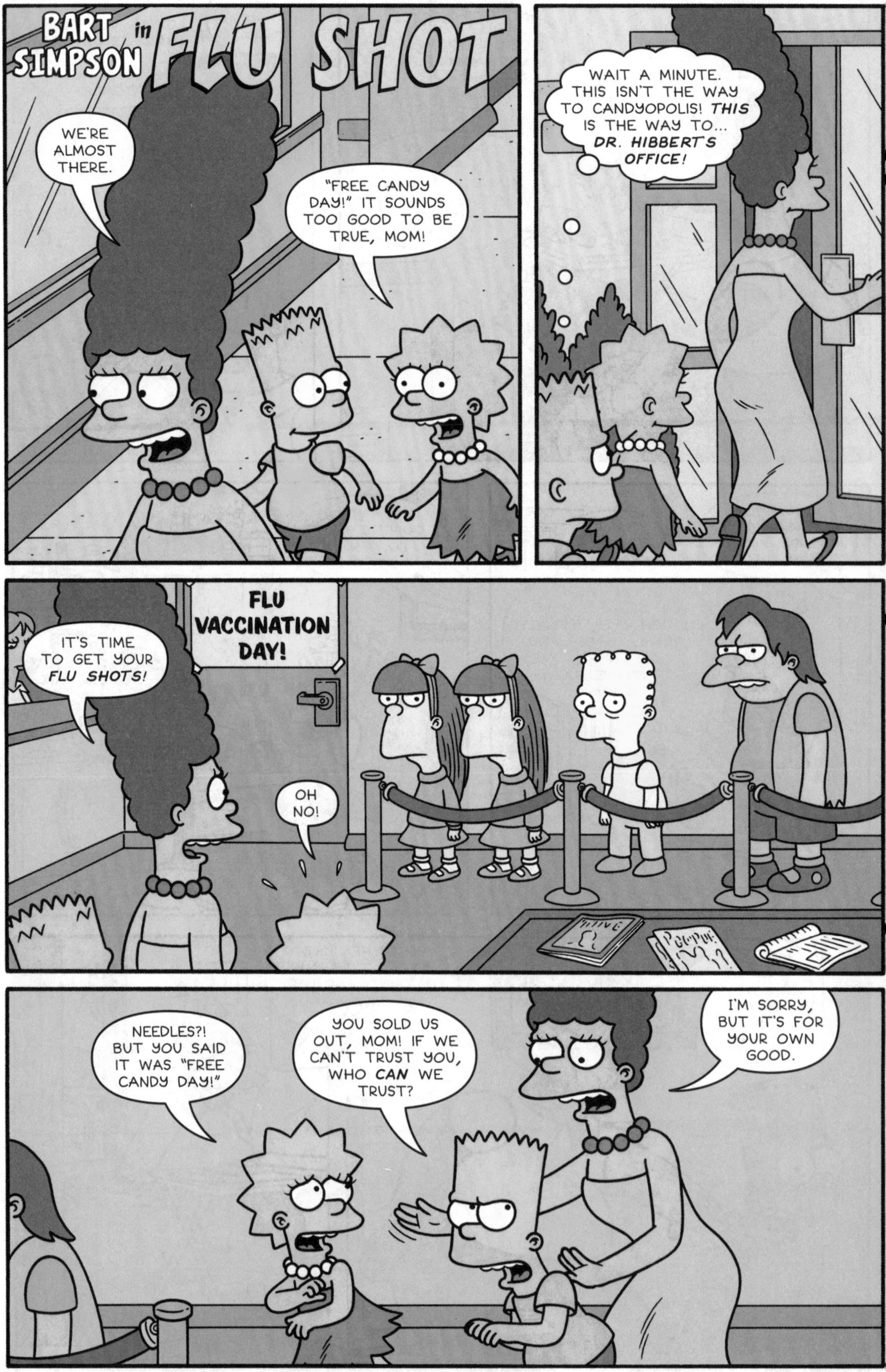
BART SIMPSON in FLU SHOT
WE'RE ALMOST THERE.
"FREE CANDY DAY!" IT SOUNDS TOO GOOD TO BE TRUE, MOM!
WAIT A MINUTE. THIS ISN'T THE WAY TO CANDYOPOLIS! THIS IS THE WAY TO... DR. HIBBERT'S OFFICE!
FLU VACCINATION DAY!
IT'S TIME TO GET YOUR FLU SHOTS!
OH NO!
NEEDLES?! BUT YOU SAID IT WAS "FREE CANDY DAY!"
YOU SOLD US OUT, MOM! IF WE CAN'T TRUST YOU, WHO CAN WE TRUST?
I'M SORRY, BUT IT'S FOR YOUR OWN GOOD.

JAMES BATES SCRIPT *JASON HO* PENCILS *MIKE ROTE* INKS *NATHAN HAMILL* COLORS *KAREN BATES* LETTERS *BILL MORRISON* EDITOR

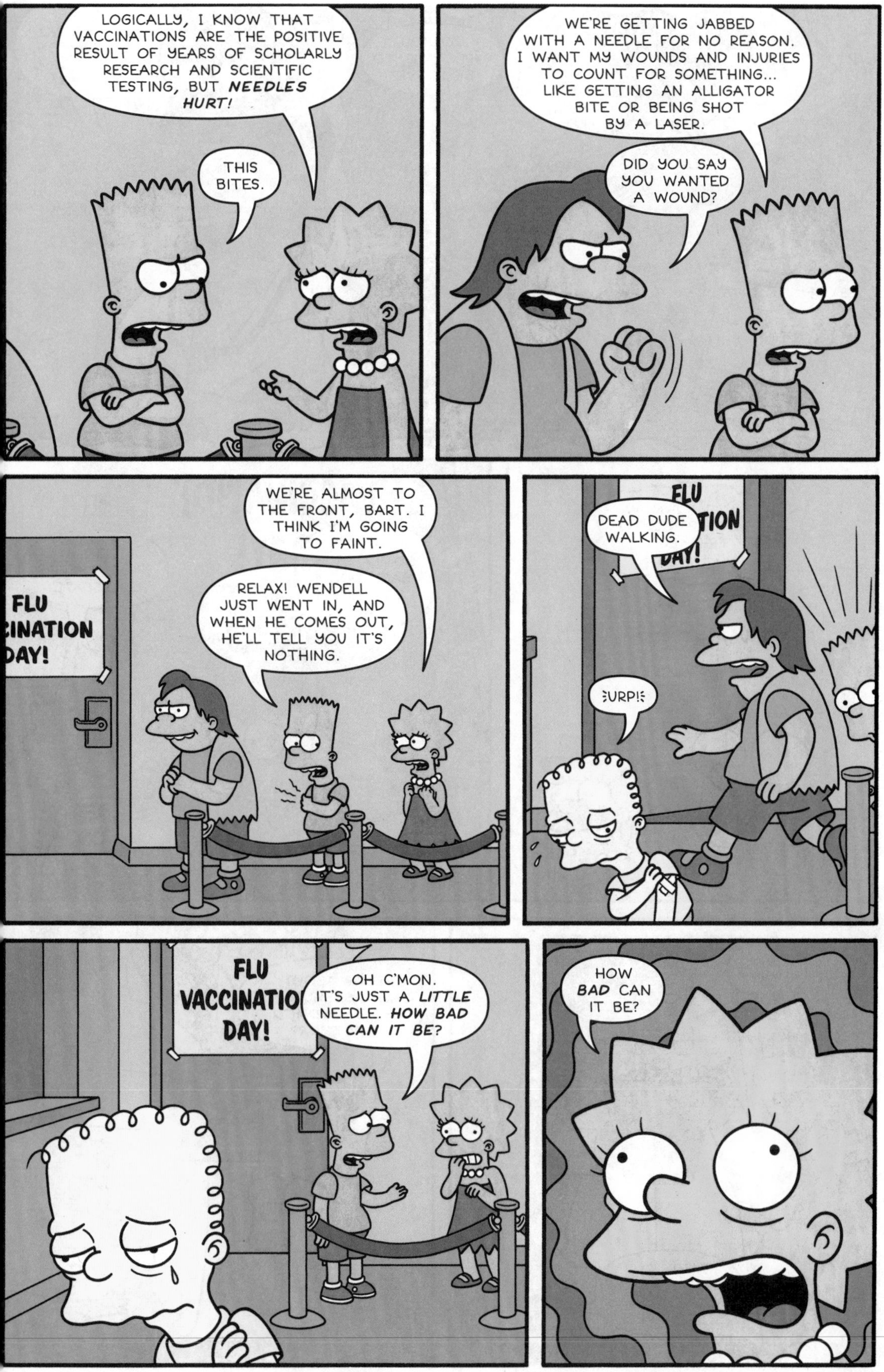
LOGICALLY, I KNOW THAT VACCINATIONS ARE THE POSITIVE RESULT OF YEARS OF SCHOLARLY RESEARCH AND SCIENTIFIC TESTING, BUT NEEDLES HURT!
THIS BITES.
WE'RE GETTING JABBED WITH A NEEDLE FOR NO REASON. I WANT MY WOUNDS AND INJURIES TO COUNT FOR SOMETHING... LIKE GETTING AN ALLIGATOR BITE OR BEING SHOT BY A LASER.
DID YOU SAY YOU WANTED A WOUND?
WE'RE ALMOST TO THE FRONT, BART. I THINK I'M GOING TO FAINT.
RELAX! WENDELL JUST WENT IN, AND WHEN HE COMES OUT, HE'LL TELL YOU IT'S NOTHING.
FLU
CINATION
DAY!
DEAD DUDE WALKING.
FLU
TION
DAY!
URP!
FLU
VACCINATIO
DAY!
OH C'MON. IT'S JUST A LITTLE NEEDLE. HOW BAD CAN IT BE?
HOW BAD CAN IT BE?

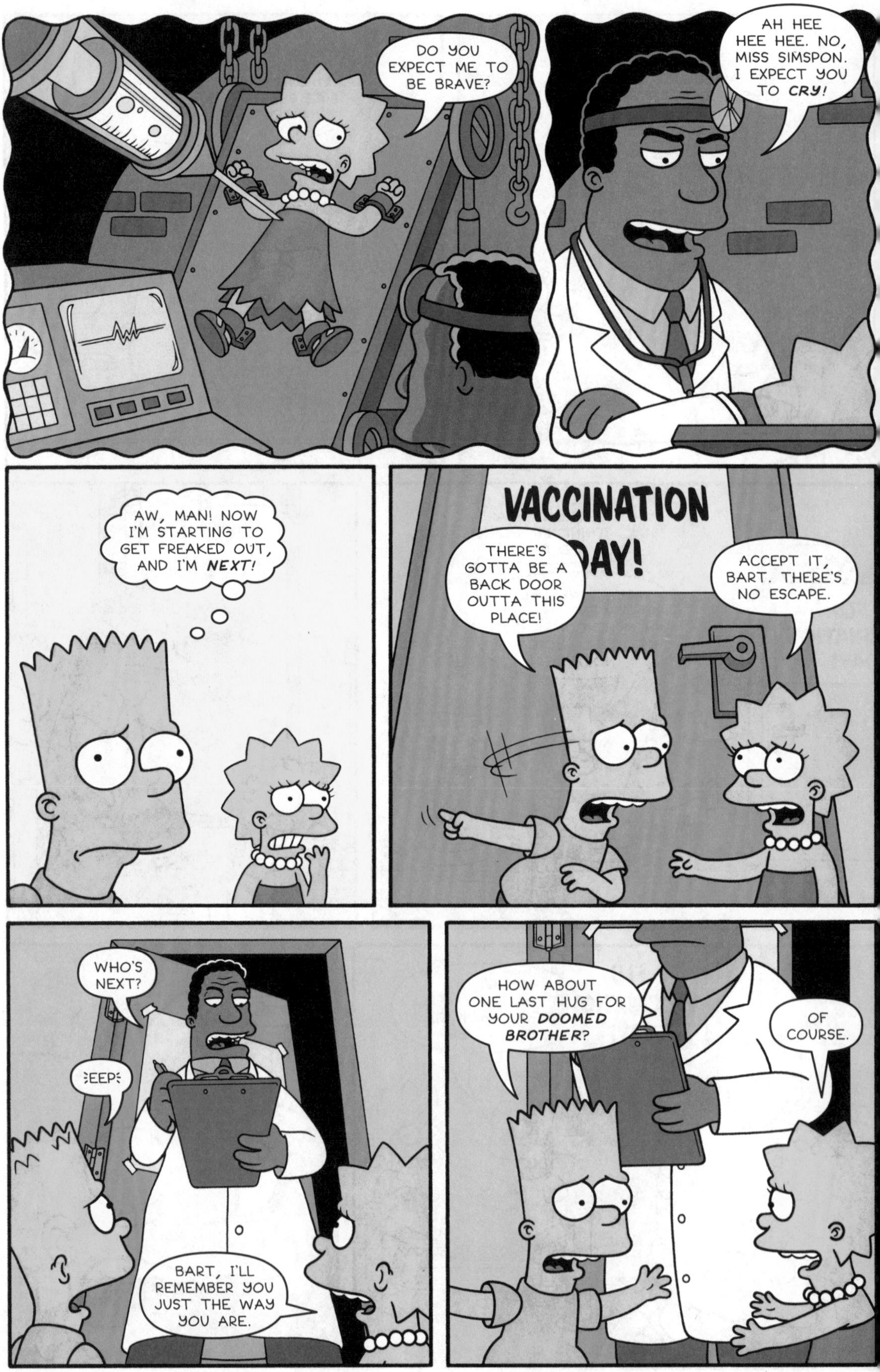
DO YOU EXPECT ME TO BE BRAVE?
AH HEE HEE HEE. NO, MISS SIMSPON. I EXPECT YOU TO CRY!
AW, MAN! NOW I'M STARTING TO GET FREAKED OUT, AND I'M NEXT!
VACCINATION DAY!
THERE'S GOTTA BE A BACK DOOR OUTTA THIS PLACE!
ACCEPT IT, BART. THERE'S NO ESCAPE.
WHO'S NEXT?
EEP
BART, I'LL REMEMBER YOU JUST THE WAY YOU ARE.
HOW ABOUT ONE LAST HUG FOR YOUR DOOMED BROTHER?
OF COURSE.

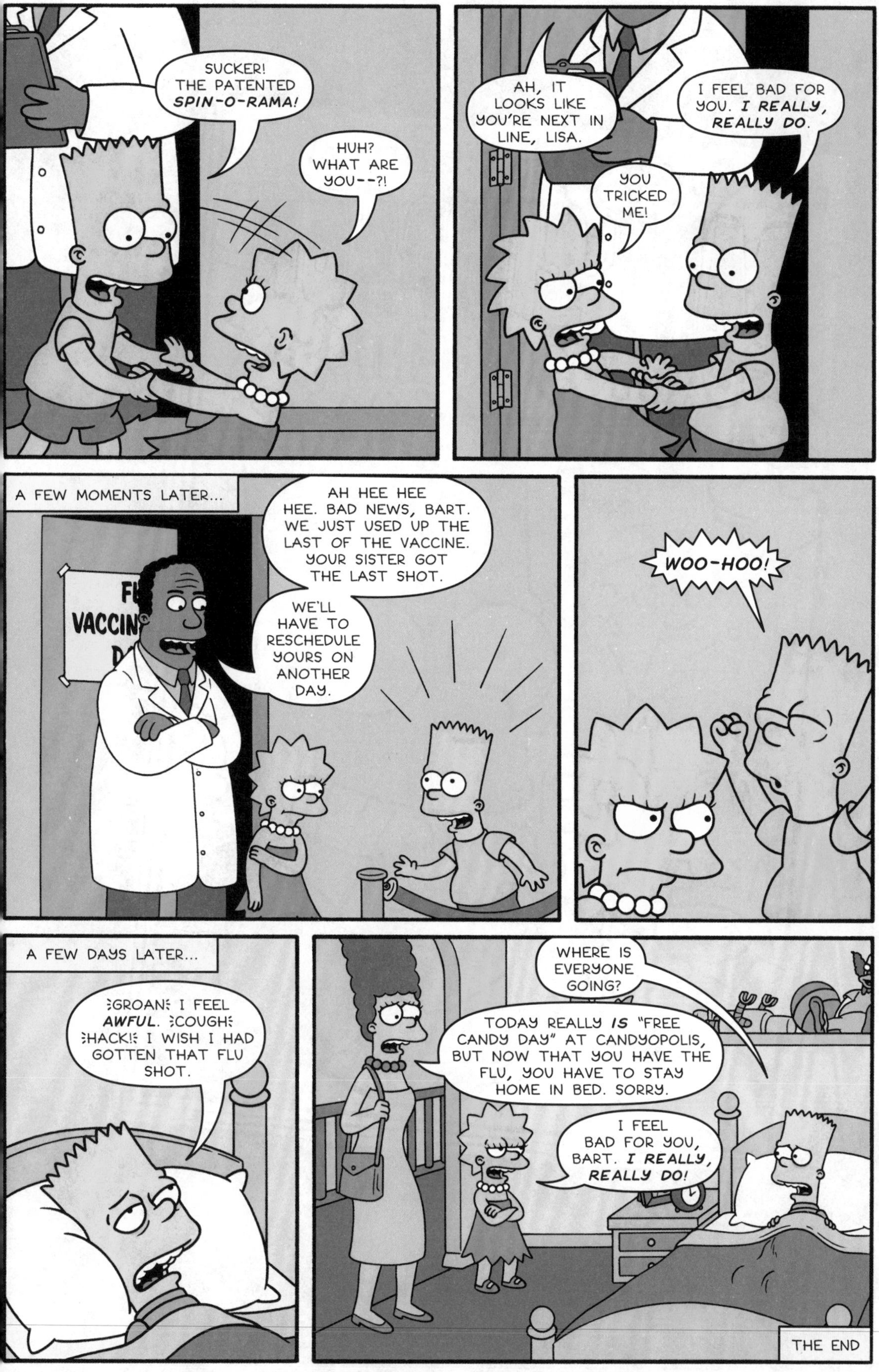
SUCKER! THE PATENTED *SPIN-O-RAMA!*
HUH? WHAT ARE YOU--?!
AH, IT LOOKS LIKE YOU'RE NEXT IN LINE, LISA.
I FEEL BAD FOR YOU. *I REALLY, REALLY DO*.
YOU TRICKED ME!
A FEW MOMENTS LATER...
AH HEE HEE HEE. BAD NEWS, BART. WE JUST USED UP THE LAST OF THE VACCINE. YOUR SISTER GOT THE LAST SHOT.
WE'LL HAVE TO RESCHEDULE YOURS ON ANOTHER DAY.
WOO-HOO!
A FEW DAYS LATER...
⁝GROAN⁝ I FEEL *AWFUL*. ⁝COUGH⁝ ⁝HACK!⁝ I WISH I HAD GOTTEN THAT FLU SHOT.
WHERE IS EVERYONE GOING?
TODAY REALLY *IS* "FREE CANDY DAY" AT CANDYOPOLIS, BUT NOW THAT YOU HAVE THE FLU, YOU HAVE TO STAY HOME IN BED. SORRY.
I FEEL BAD FOR YOU, BART. *I REALLY, REALLY DO!*
THE END

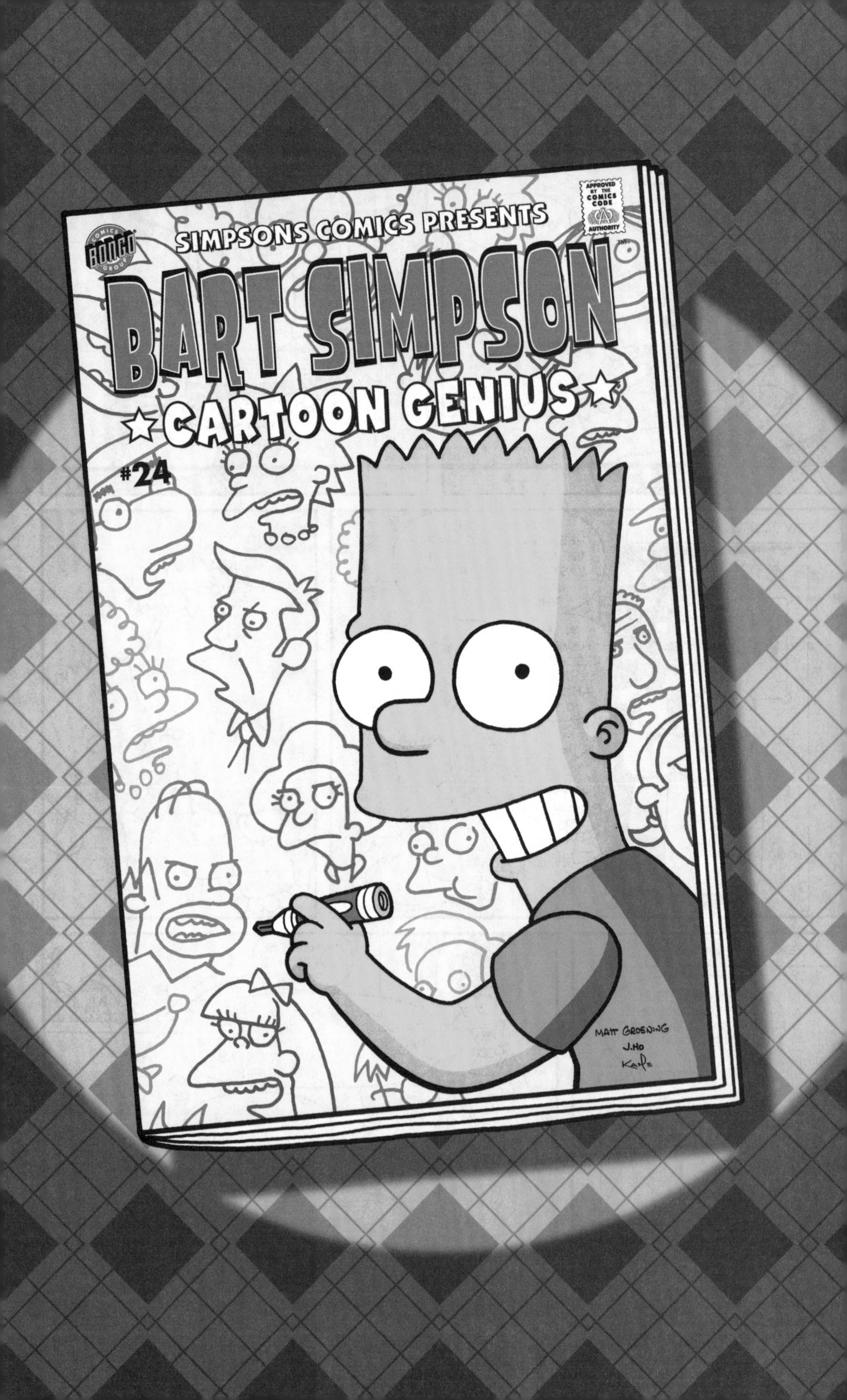

APPROVED BY THE COMICS CODE AUTHORITY
SIMPSONS COMICS PRESENTS
BART SIMPSON
CARTOON GENIUS
#24
MATT GROENING
J.HO

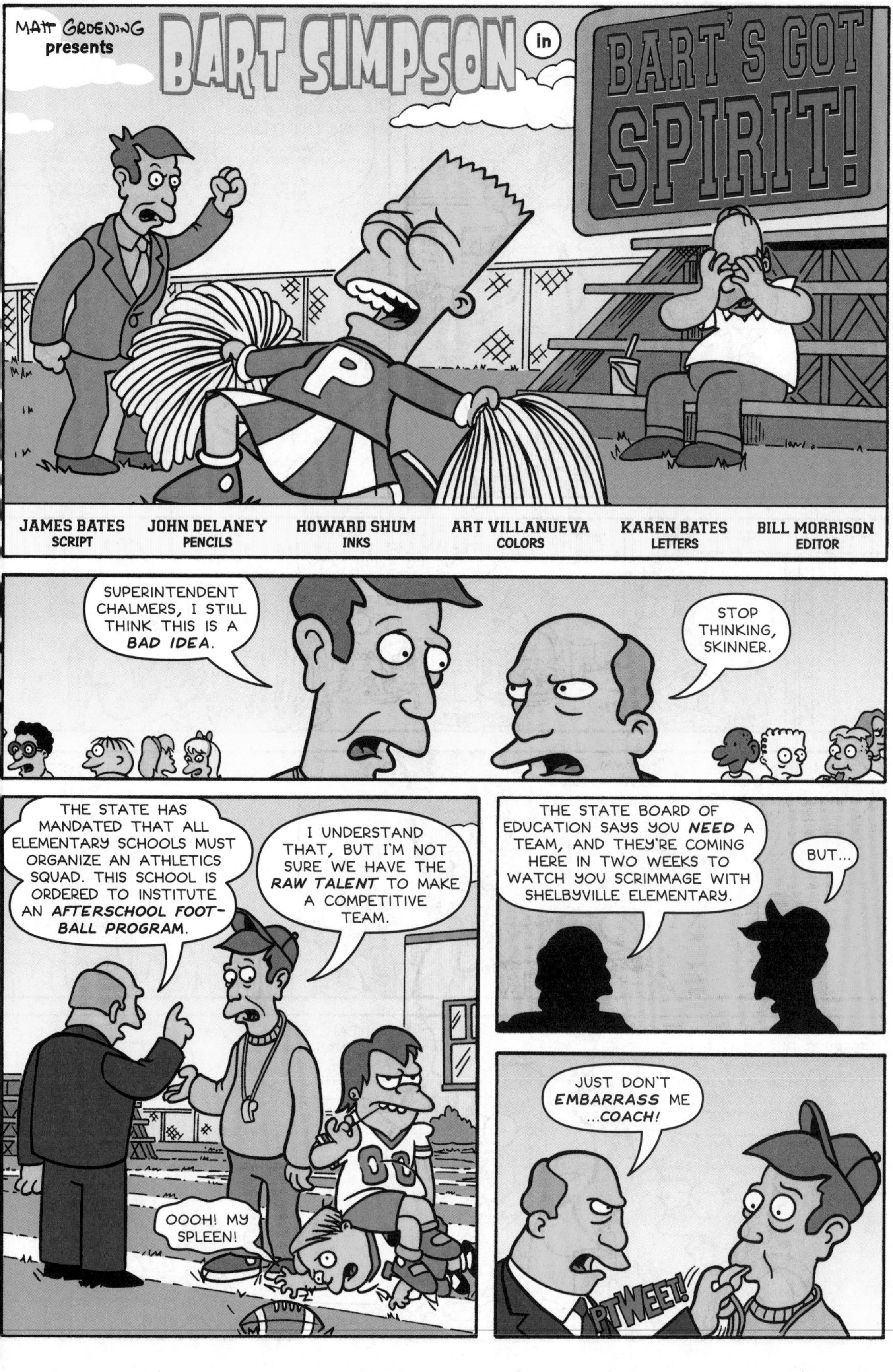
MATT GROENING presents
BART SIMPSON in
BART'S GOT SPIRIT!
JAMES BATES SCRIPT
JOHN DELANEY PENCILS
HOWARD SHUM INKS
ART VILLANUEVA COLORS
KAREN BATES LETTERS
BILL MORRISON EDITOR
SUPERINTENDENT CHALMERS, I STILL THINK THIS IS A *BAD IDEA*.
STOP THINKING, SKINNER.
THE STATE HAS MANDATED THAT ALL ELEMENTARY SCHOOLS MUST ORGANIZE AN ATHLETICS SQUAD. THIS SCHOOL IS ORDERED TO INSTITUTE AN ***AFTERSCHOOL FOOT-BALL PROGRAM***.
I UNDERSTAND THAT, BUT I'M NOT SURE WE HAVE THE ***RAW TALENT*** TO MAKE A COMPETITIVE TEAM.
OOOH! MY SPLEEN!
THE STATE BOARD OF EDUCATION SAYS YOU ***NEED*** A TEAM, AND THEY'RE COMING HERE IN TWO WEEKS TO WATCH YOU SCRIMMAGE WITH SHELBYVILLE ELEMENTARY.
BUT...
JUST DON'T ***EMBARRASS*** ME ...***COACH!***
PTWEET!

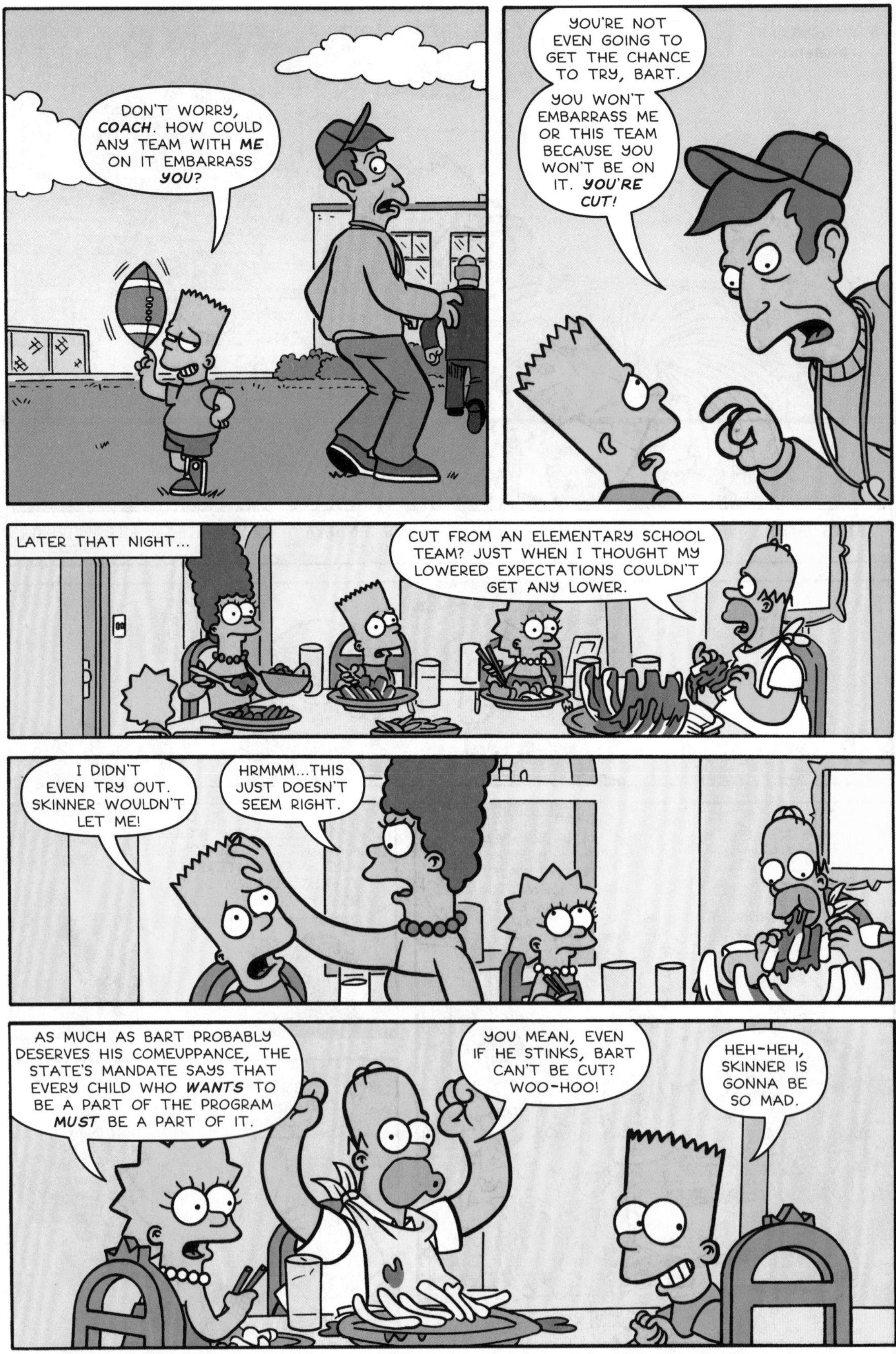
DON'T WORRY, **COACH**. HOW COULD ANY TEAM WITH **ME** ON IT EMBARRASS **YOU**?
YOU'RE NOT EVEN GOING TO GET THE CHANCE TO TRY, BART.
YOU WON'T EMBARRASS ME OR THIS TEAM BECAUSE YOU WON'T BE ON IT. **YOU'RE CUT**!
LATER THAT NIGHT...
CUT FROM AN ELEMENTARY SCHOOL TEAM? JUST WHEN I THOUGHT MY LOWERED EXPECTATIONS COULDN'T GET ANY LOWER.
I DIDN'T EVEN TRY OUT. SKINNER WOULDN'T LET ME!
HRMMM...THIS JUST DOESN'T SEEM RIGHT.
AS MUCH AS BART PROBABLY DESERVES HIS COMEUPPANCE, THE STATE'S MANDATE SAYS THAT EVERY CHILD WHO **WANTS** TO BE A PART OF THE PROGRAM **MUST** BE A PART OF IT.
YOU MEAN, EVEN IF HE STINKS, BART CAN'T BE CUT? WOO-HOO!
HEH-HEH, SKINNER IS GONNA BE SO MAD.

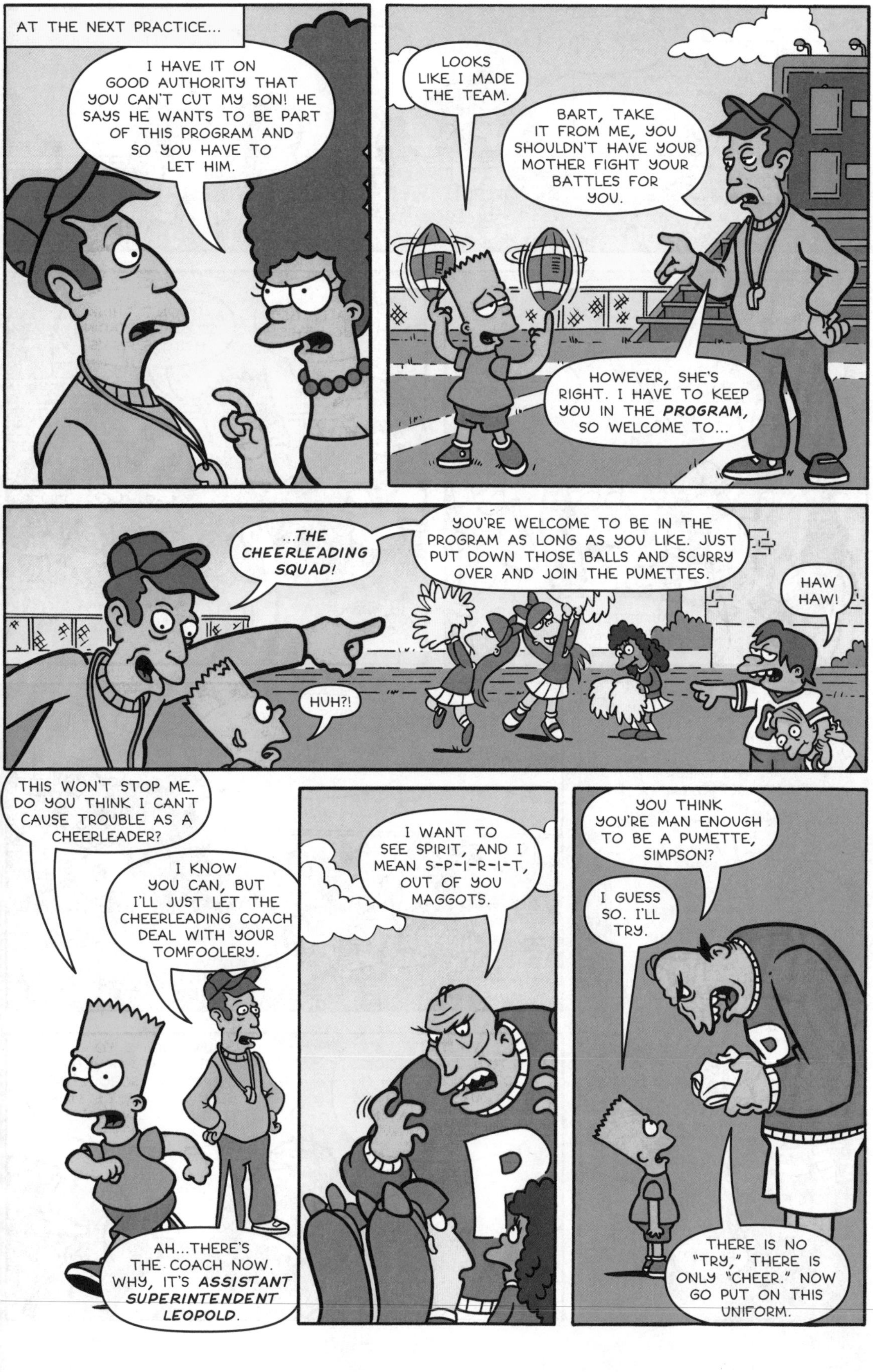
AT THE NEXT PRACTICE...
I HAVE IT ON GOOD AUTHORITY THAT YOU CAN'T CUT MY SON! HE SAYS HE WANTS TO BE PART OF THIS PROGRAM AND SO YOU HAVE TO LET HIM.
LOOKS LIKE I MADE THE TEAM.
BART, TAKE IT FROM ME, YOU SHOULDN'T HAVE YOUR MOTHER FIGHT YOUR BATTLES FOR YOU.
HOWEVER, SHE'S RIGHT. I HAVE TO KEEP YOU IN THE PROGRAM, SO WELCOME TO...
...THE CHEERLEADING SQUAD!
YOU'RE WELCOME TO BE IN THE PROGRAM AS LONG AS YOU LIKE. JUST PUT DOWN THOSE BALLS AND SCURRY OVER AND JOIN THE PUMETTES.
HUH?!
HAW HAW!
THIS WON'T STOP ME. DO YOU THINK I CAN'T CAUSE TROUBLE AS A CHEERLEADER?
I KNOW YOU CAN, BUT I'LL JUST LET THE CHEERLEADING COACH DEAL WITH YOUR TOMFOOLERY.
AH...THERE'S THE COACH NOW. WHY, IT'S ASSISTANT SUPERINTENDENT LEOPOLD.
I WANT TO SEE SPIRIT, AND I MEAN S-P-I-R-I-T, OUT OF YOU MAGGOTS.
YOU THINK YOU'RE MAN ENOUGH TO BE A PUMETTE, SIMPSON?
I GUESS SO. I'LL TRY.
THERE IS NO "TRY," THERE IS ONLY "CHEER." NOW GO PUT ON THIS UNIFORM.

MINUTES LATER...

SIMPSON, YOU LOOK...

...SO...

...COOL!

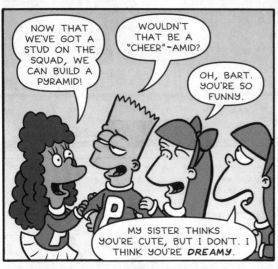

NOW THAT WE'VE GOT A STUD ON THE SQUAD, WE CAN BUILD A PYRAMID!

WOULDN'T THAT BE A "CHEER"-AMID?

OH, BART. YOU'RE SO FUNNY.

MY SISTER THINKS YOU'RE CUTE, BUT I DON'T. I THINK YOU'RE *DREAMY*.

SKINNER REALLY GOT YOU THIS TIME.

I DON'T THINK SO. CHEERLEADING HAS ITS PERKS.

SIMPSON! THIS IS NOT TALK TIME, IT'S CHEER TIME. GET OVER THERE!

YES, SIR!

PERKS?

CHINS UP! SUCK IN THOSE GUTS. I'VE NEVER SEEN A SORRIER GROUP OF RECRUITS IN MY LIFE!

WAIT...I'M SORRY. I MAY LOOK AND SOUND TOUGH ON THE OUTSIDE, BUT I'M REALLY JUST A BIG CHEERLEADER AT HEART.

YOU'RE GOING TO BE THE *BEST DARNED PEP SQUAD* THIS SCHOOL HAS EVER SEEN! C'MON, IT'S TIME TO SHOW ME WHAT YOU'VE GOT!

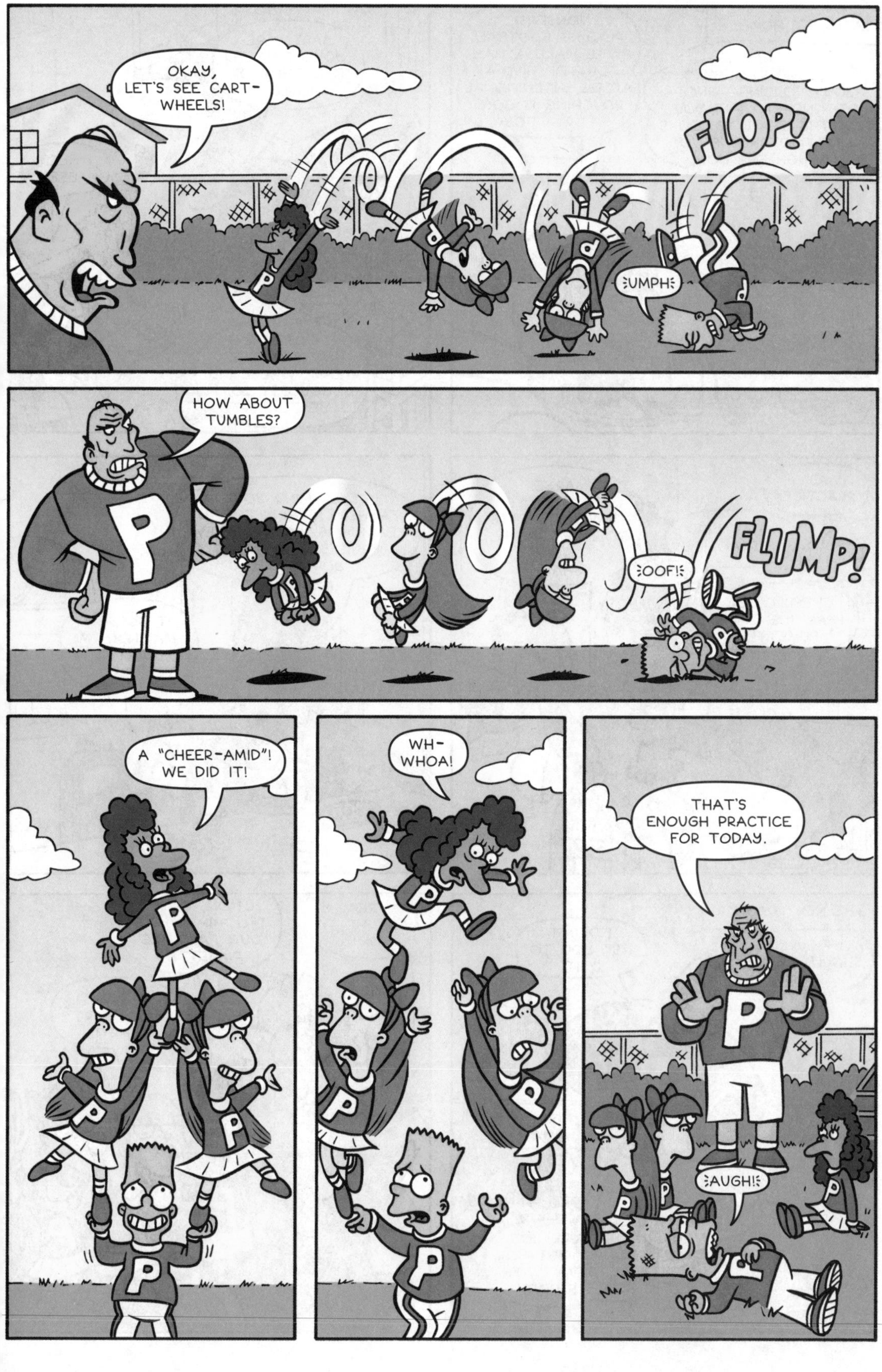

OKAY, LET'S SEE CART-WHEELS!
FLOP!
UMPH
HOW ABOUT TUMBLES?
FLUMP!
OOF!
A "CHEER-AMID"! WE DID IT!
WH- WHOA!
THAT'S ENOUGH PRACTICE FOR TODAY.
AUGH!

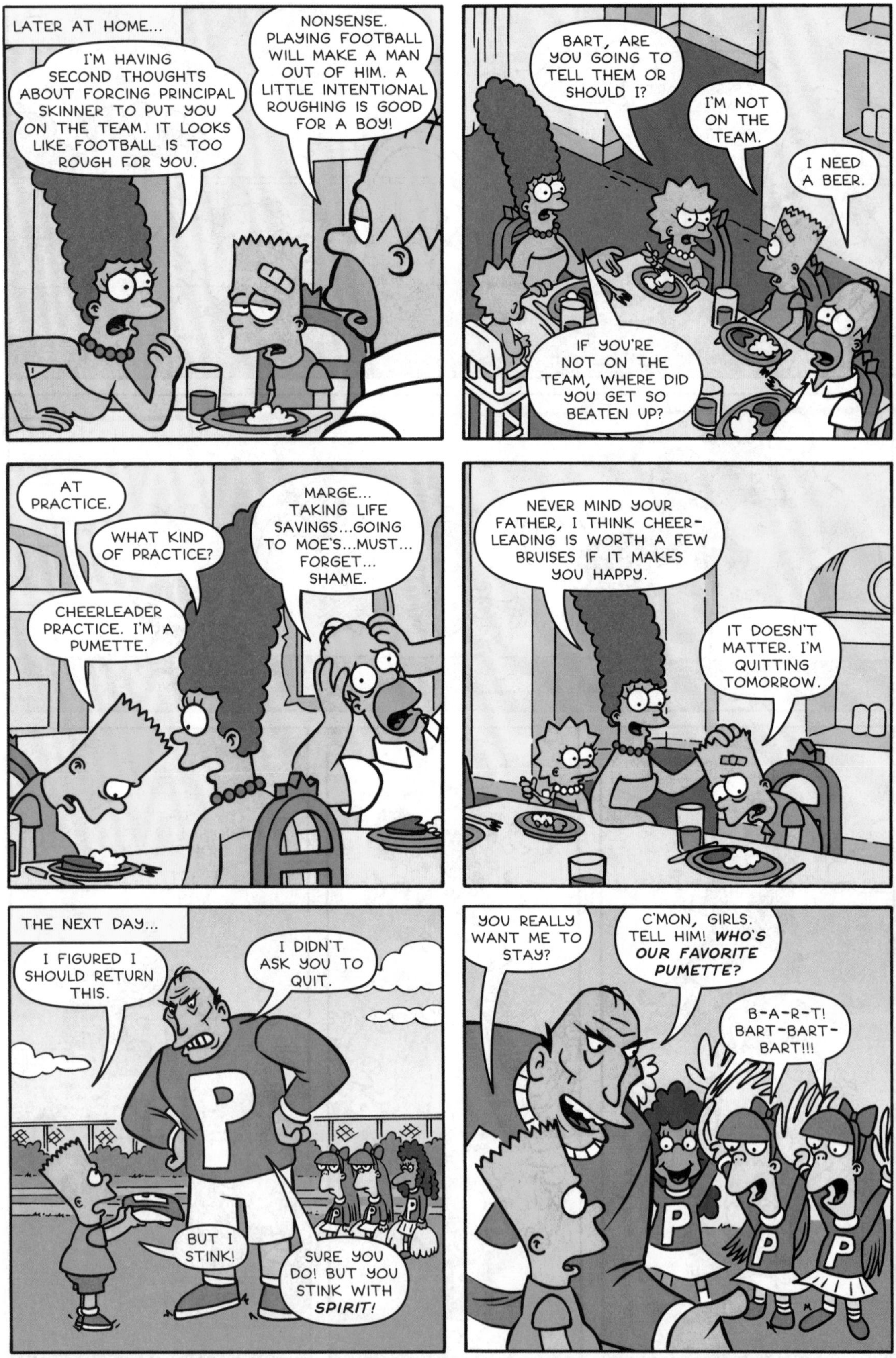
LATER AT HOME...
I'M HAVING SECOND THOUGHTS ABOUT FORCING PRINCIPAL SKINNER TO PUT YOU ON THE TEAM. IT LOOKS LIKE FOOTBALL IS TOO ROUGH FOR YOU.
NONSENSE. PLAYING FOOTBALL WILL MAKE A MAN OUT OF HIM. A LITTLE INTENTIONAL ROUGHING IS GOOD FOR A BOY!
BART, ARE YOU GOING TO TELL THEM OR SHOULD I?
I'M NOT ON THE TEAM.
I NEED A BEER.
IF YOU'RE NOT ON THE TEAM, WHERE DID YOU GET SO BEATEN UP?
AT PRACTICE.
WHAT KIND OF PRACTICE?
CHEERLEADER PRACTICE. I'M A PUMETTE.
MARGE... TAKING LIFE SAVINGS...GOING TO MOE'S...MUST... FORGET... SHAME.
NEVER MIND YOUR FATHER, I THINK CHEER-LEADING IS WORTH A FEW BRUISES IF IT MAKES YOU HAPPY.
IT DOESN'T MATTER. I'M QUITTING TOMORROW.
THE NEXT DAY...
I FIGURED I SHOULD RETURN THIS.
I DIDN'T ASK YOU TO QUIT.
BUT I STINK!
SURE YOU DO! BUT YOU STINK WITH *SPIRIT*!
YOU REALLY WANT ME TO STAY?
C'MON, GIRLS. TELL HIM! ***WHO'S OUR FAVORITE PUMETTE***?
B-A-R-T! BART-BART-BART!!!

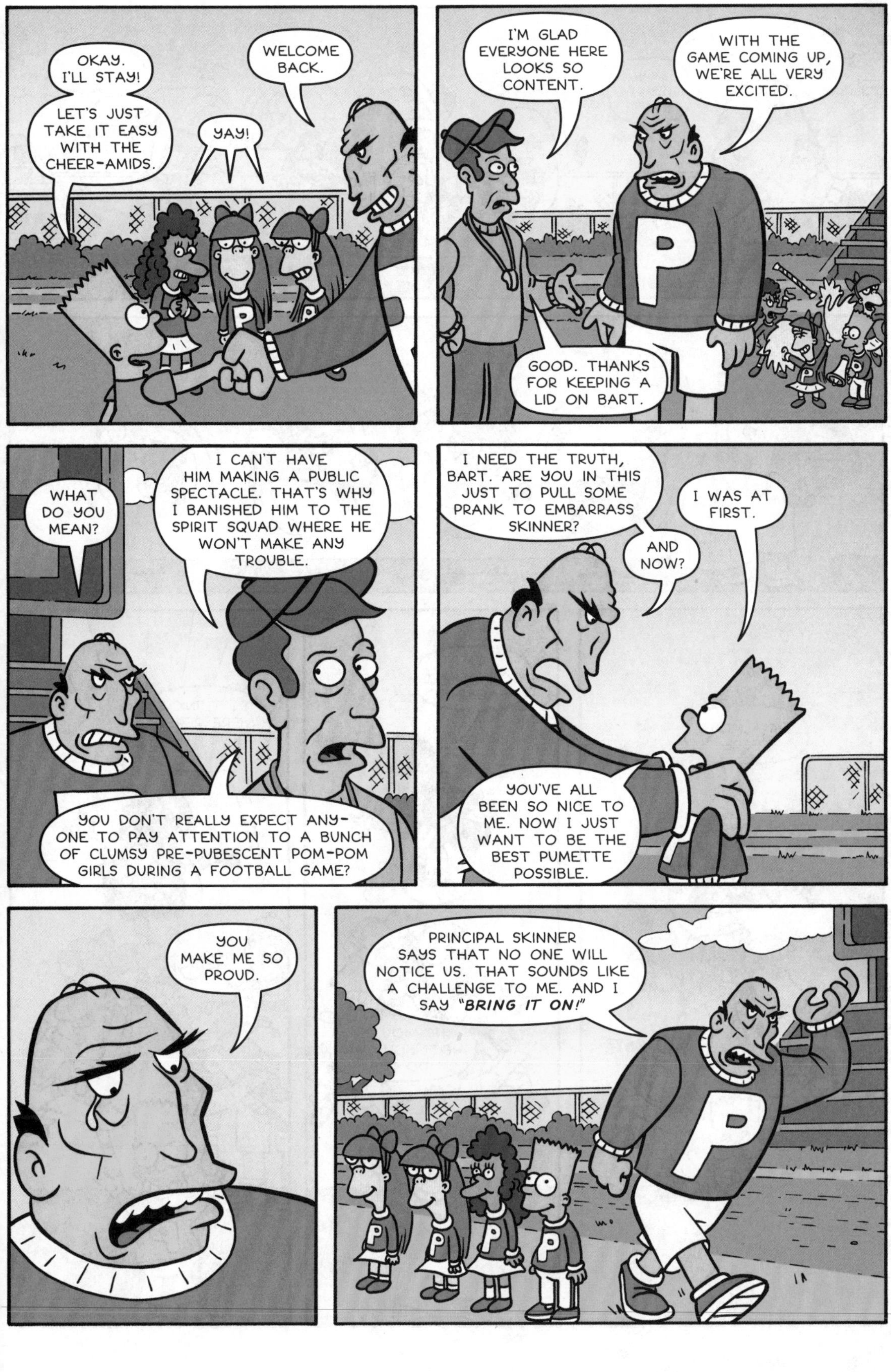
OKAY. I'LL STAY!
LET'S JUST TAKE IT EASY WITH THE CHEER-AMIDS.
WELCOME BACK.
YAY!
I'M GLAD EVERYONE HERE LOOKS SO CONTENT.
WITH THE GAME COMING UP, WE'RE ALL VERY EXCITED.
GOOD. THANKS FOR KEEPING A LID ON BART.
WHAT DO YOU MEAN?
I CAN'T HAVE HIM MAKING A PUBLIC SPECTACLE. THAT'S WHY I BANISHED HIM TO THE SPIRIT SQUAD WHERE HE WON'T MAKE ANY TROUBLE.
YOU DON'T REALLY EXPECT ANY-ONE TO PAY ATTENTION TO A BUNCH OF CLUMSY PRE-PUBESCENT POM-POM GIRLS DURING A FOOTBALL GAME?
I NEED THE TRUTH, BART. ARE YOU IN THIS JUST TO PULL SOME PRANK TO EMBARRASS SKINNER?
I WAS AT FIRST.
AND NOW?
YOU'VE ALL BEEN SO NICE TO ME. NOW I JUST WANT TO BE THE BEST PUMETTE POSSIBLE.
YOU MAKE ME SO PROUD.
PRINCIPAL SKINNER SAYS THAT NO ONE WILL NOTICE US. THAT SOUNDS LIKE A CHALLENGE TO ME. AND I SAY "BRING IT ON!"

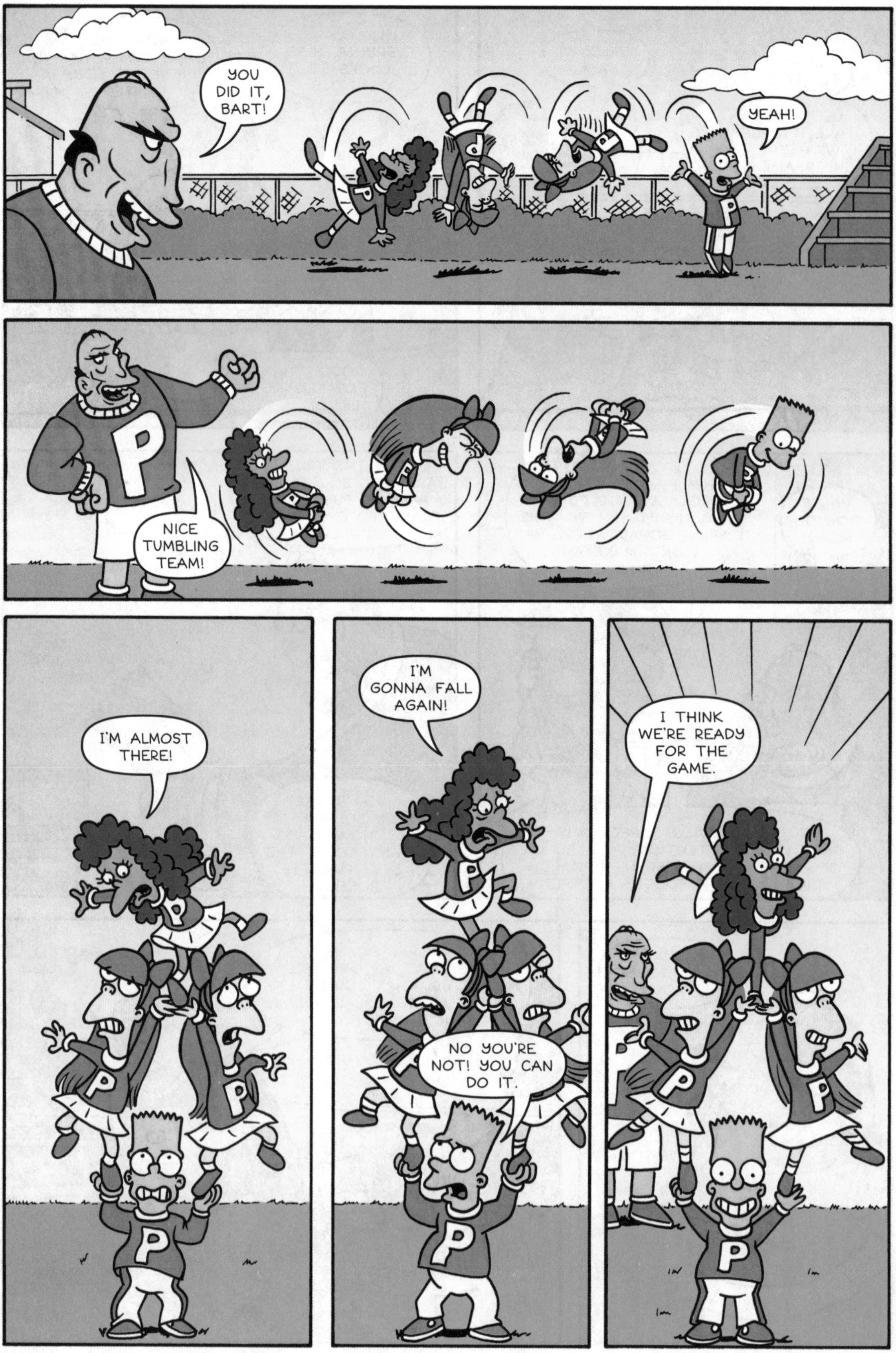
YOU DID IT, BART!
YEAH!
NICE TUMBLING TEAM!
I'M ALMOST THERE!
I'M GONNA FALL AGAIN!
NO YOU'RE NOT! YOU CAN DO IT.
I THINK WE'RE READY FOR THE GAME.

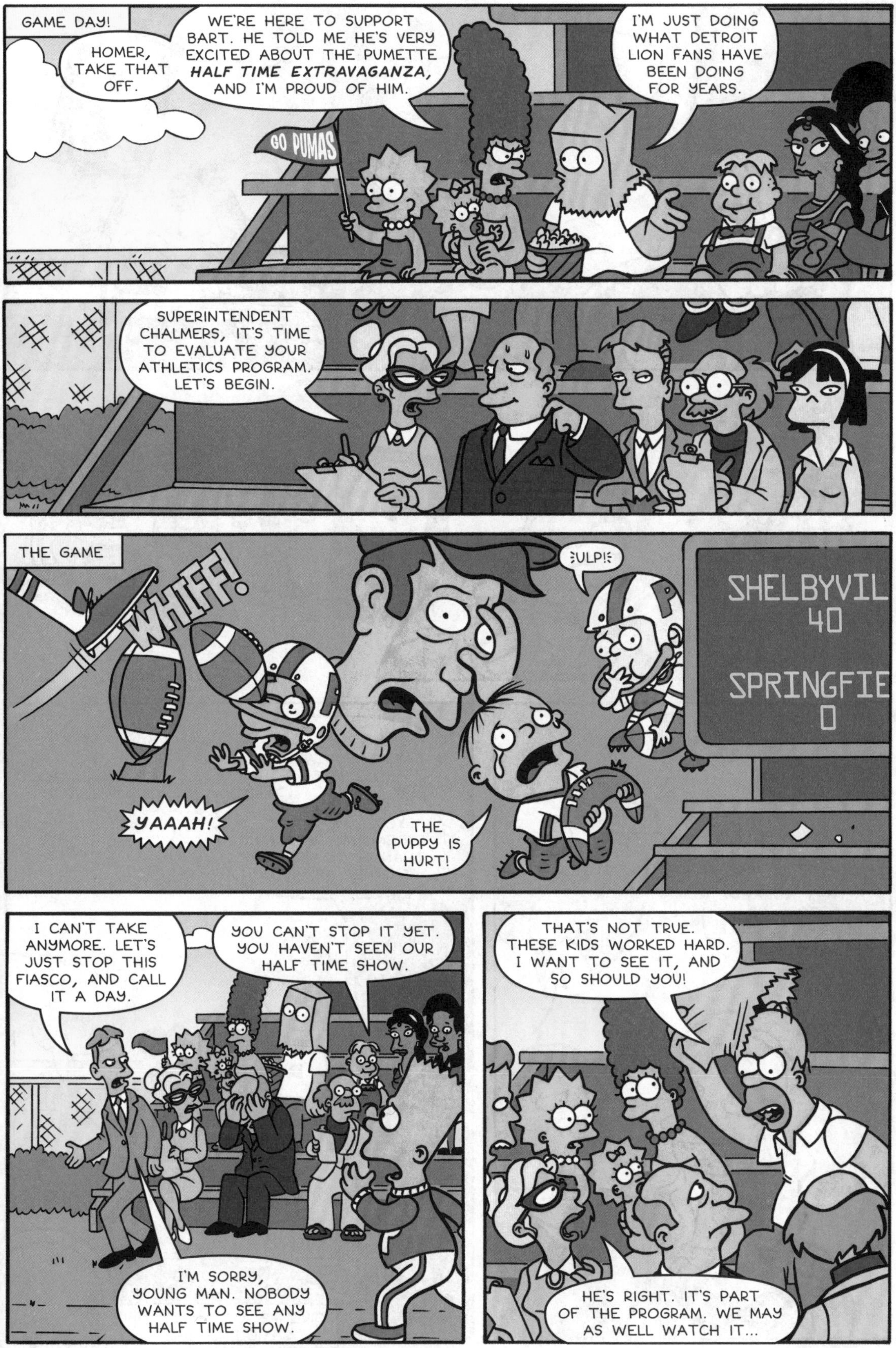

GAME DAY!
HOMER, TAKE THAT OFF.
WE'RE HERE TO SUPPORT BART. HE TOLD ME HE'S VERY EXCITED ABOUT THE PUMETTE HALF TIME EXTRAVAGANZA, AND I'M PROUD OF HIM.
GO PUMAS
I'M JUST DOING WHAT DETROIT LION FANS HAVE BEEN DOING FOR YEARS.
SUPERINTENDENT CHALMERS, IT'S TIME TO EVALUATE YOUR ATHLETICS PROGRAM. LET'S BEGIN.
THE GAME
WHIFF!
ULP!
SHELBYVIL 40
SPRINGFIE 0
YAAAH!
THE PUPPY IS HURT!
I CAN'T TAKE ANYMORE. LET'S JUST STOP THIS FIASCO, AND CALL IT A DAY.
YOU CAN'T STOP IT YET. YOU HAVEN'T SEEN OUR HALF TIME SHOW.
I'M SORRY, YOUNG MAN. NOBODY WANTS TO SEE ANY HALF TIME SHOW.
THAT'S NOT TRUE. THESE KIDS WORKED HARD. I WANT TO SEE IT, AND SO SHOULD YOU!
HE'S RIGHT. IT'S PART OF THE PROGRAM. WE MAY AS WELL WATCH IT...

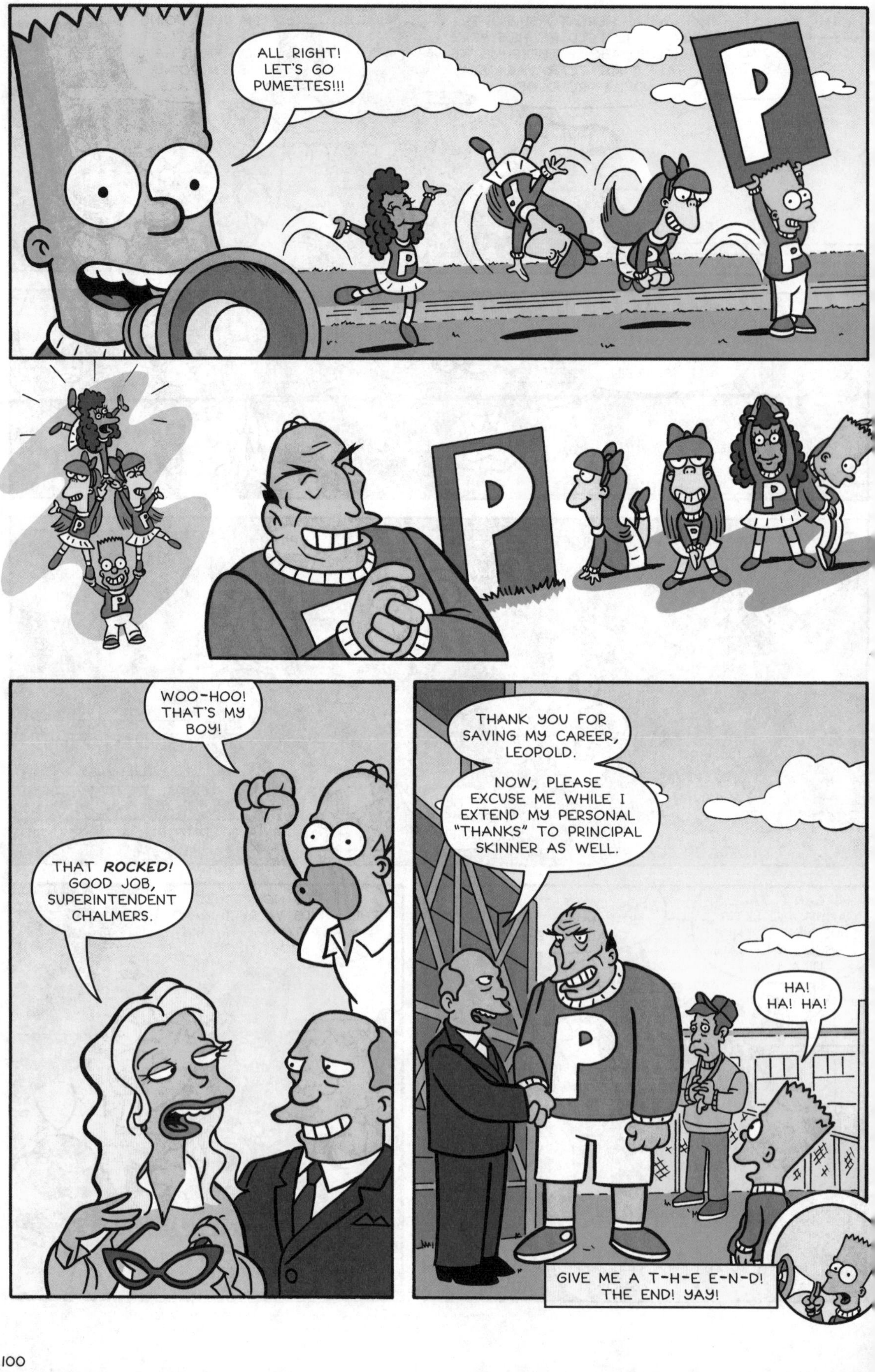
ALL RIGHT! LET'S GO PUMETTES!!!
P
P
WOO-HOO! THAT'S MY BOY!
THAT ROCKED! GOOD JOB, SUPERINTENDENT CHALMERS.
THANK YOU FOR SAVING MY CAREER, LEOPOLD.
NOW, PLEASE EXCUSE ME WHILE I EXTEND MY PERSONAL "THANKS" TO PRINCIPAL SKINNER AS WELL.
HA! HA! HA!
GIVE ME A T-H-E E-N-D! THE END! YAY!

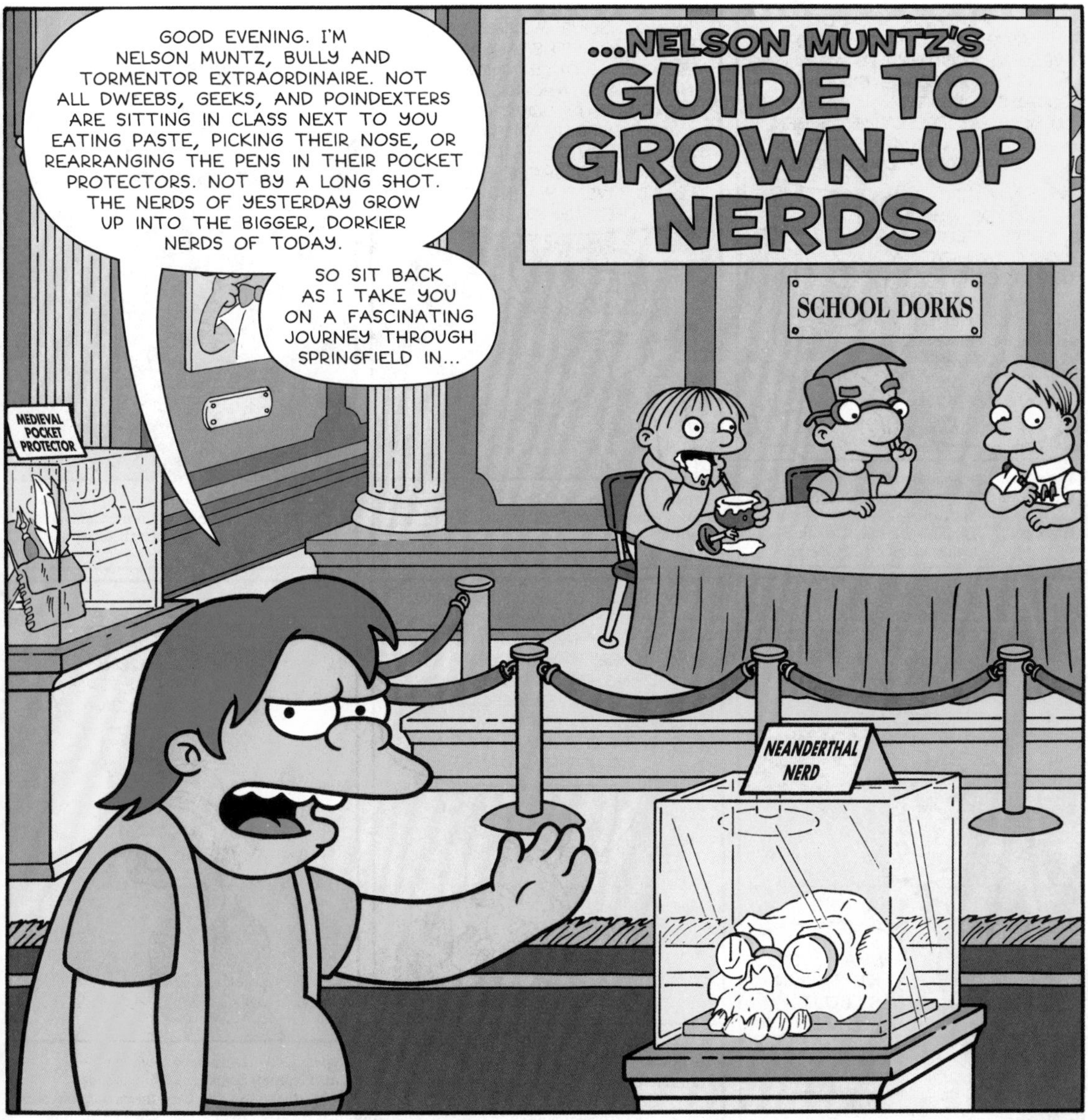
GOOD EVENING. I'M NELSON MUNTZ, BULLY AND TORMENTOR EXTRAORDINAIRE. NOT ALL DWEEBS, GEEKS, AND POINDEXTERS ARE SITTING IN CLASS NEXT TO YOU EATING PASTE, PICKING THEIR NOSE, OR REARRANGING THE PENS IN THEIR POCKET PROTECTORS. NOT BY A LONG SHOT. THE NERDS OF YESTERDAY GROW UP INTO THE BIGGER, DORKIER NERDS OF TODAY.
SO SIT BACK AS I TAKE YOU ON A FASCINATING JOURNEY THROUGH SPRINGFIELD IN...
...NELSON MUNTZ'S GUIDE TO GROWN-UP NERDS
SCHOOL DORKS
MEDIEVAL POCKET PROTECTOR
NEANDERTHAL NERD

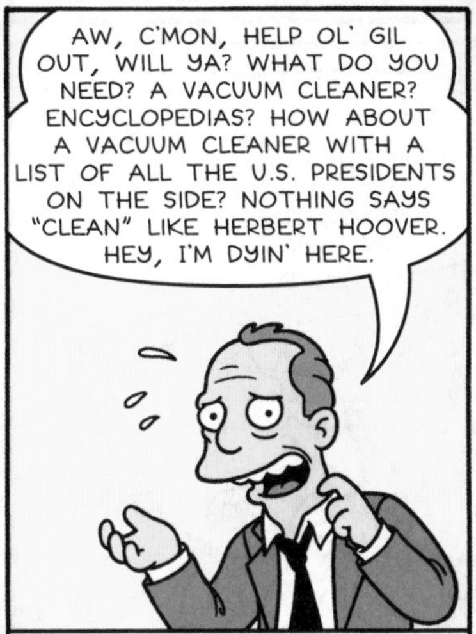
AW, C'MON, HELP OL' GIL OUT, WILL YA? WHAT DO YOU NEED? A VACUUM CLEANER? ENCYCLOPEDIAS? HOW ABOUT A VACUUM CLEANER WITH A LIST OF ALL THE U.S. PRESIDENTS ON THE SIDE? NOTHING SAYS "CLEAN" LIKE HERBERT HOOVER. HEY, I'M DYIN' HERE.

Type: Door-to-door Dweeb
Latin Name: Homo Saleus Desperaticus
Habitat: Flophouses, cheap motels, your porch

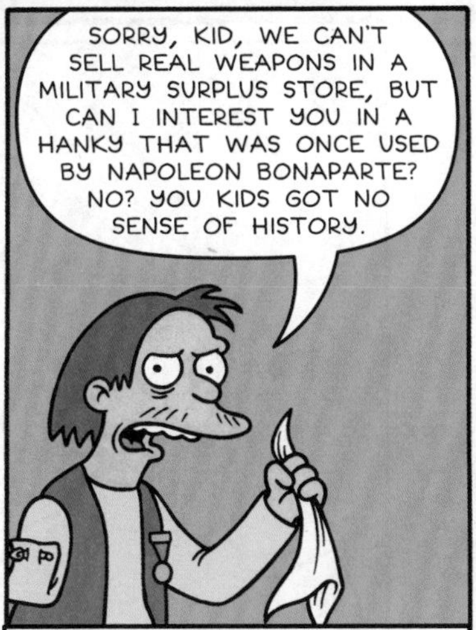
SORRY, KID, WE CAN'T SELL REAL WEAPONS IN A MILITARY SURPLUS STORE, BUT CAN I INTEREST YOU IN A HANKY THAT WAS ONCE USED BY NAPOLEON BONAPARTE? NO? YOU KIDS GOT NO SENSE OF HISTORY.

Type: Warmongering Nerd
Latin Name: Militantus Extremeus
Habitat: Army surplus stores, gun shows, militia meetings

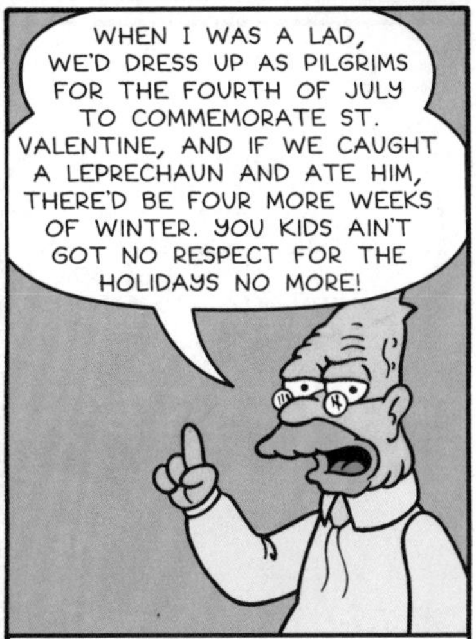
WHEN I WAS A LAD, WE'D DRESS UP AS PILGRIMS FOR THE FOURTH OF JULY TO COMMEMORATE ST. VALENTINE, AND IF WE CAUGHT A LEPRECHAUN AND ATE HIM, THERE'D BE FOUR MORE WEEKS OF WINTER. YOU KIDS AIN'T GOT NO RESPECT FOR THE HOLIDAYS NO MORE!

Type: Ancient Dork
Latin Name: Ramblon Andonicus
Habitat: Nursing home, voting booths, Florida

TONY DIGEROLAMO SCRIPT | *JASON HO* PENCILS | *PHYLLIS NOVIN* INKS | *ART VILLANUEVA* COLORS | *KAREN BATES* LETTERS | *BILL MORRISON* EDITOR

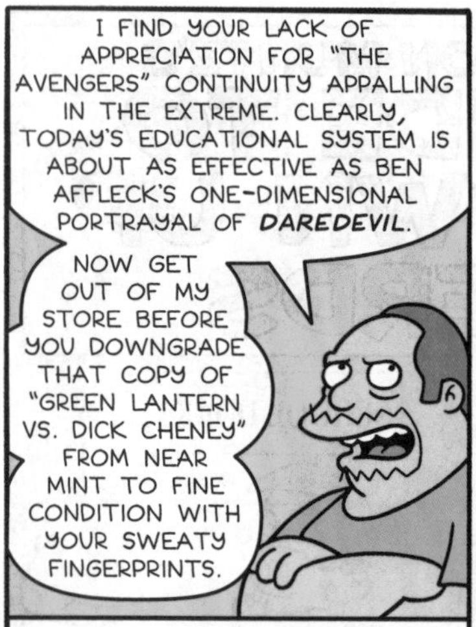
I FIND YOUR LACK OF APPRECIATION FOR "THE AVENGERS" CONTINUITY APPALLING IN THE EXTREME. CLEARLY, TODAY'S EDUCATIONAL SYSTEM IS ABOUT AS EFFECTIVE AS BEN AFFLECK'S ONE-DIMENSIONAL PORTRAYAL OF ***DAREDEVIL***.
NOW GET OUT OF MY STORE BEFORE YOU DOWNGRADE THAT COPY OF "GREEN LANTERN VS. DICK CHENEY" FROM NEAR MINT TO FINE CONDITION WITH YOUR SWEATY FINGERPRINTS.

Type: Comic Book Nerd
Latin Name: Sequentialartum Connoisseurius Sarcasticus
Habitat: Comic book stores, comic book conventions, Krusty Burger

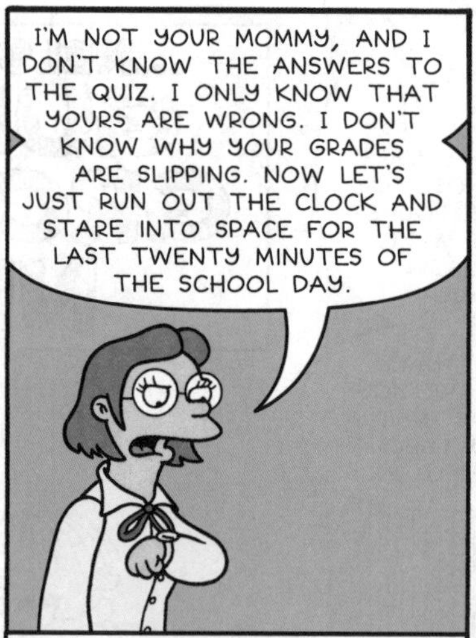
I'M NOT YOUR MOMMY, AND I DON'T KNOW THE ANSWERS TO THE QUIZ. I ONLY KNOW THAT YOURS ARE WRONG. I DON'T KNOW WHY YOUR GRADES ARE SLIPPING. NOW LET'S JUST RUN OUT THE CLOCK AND STARE INTO SPACE FOR THE LAST TWENTY MINUTES OF THE SCHOOL DAY.

Type: Teacher Dingus
Latin Name: Eyerollum Fedupicus
Habitat: Classrooms, faculty lounges, therapist couch

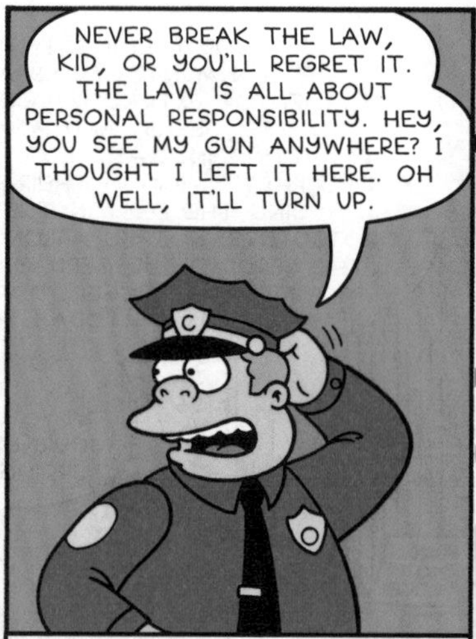
NEVER BREAK THE LAW, KID, OR YOU'LL REGRET IT. THE LAW IS ALL ABOUT PERSONAL RESPONSIBILITY. HEY, YOU SEE MY GUN ANYWHERE? I THOUGHT I LEFT IT HERE. OH WELL, IT'LL TURN UP.

Type: Police Dork
Latin Name: Lazias Protectorum Corruptus
Habitat: Donut Shops, police stations, on his butt

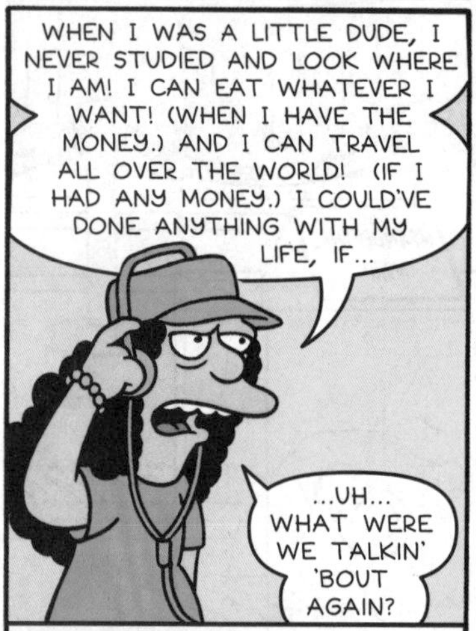
WHEN I WAS A LITTLE DUDE, I NEVER STUDIED AND LOOK WHERE I AM! I CAN EAT WHATEVER I WANT! (WHEN I HAVE THE MONEY.) AND I CAN TRAVEL ALL OVER THE WORLD! (IF I HAD ANY MONEY.) I COULD'VE DONE ANYTHING WITH MY LIFE, IF...
...UH... WHAT WERE WE TALKIN' 'BOUT AGAIN?

Type: Bus Schmoe
Latin Name: Vehicularum Operatus Cannabis
Habitat: Beanbag chairs, dumpsters, his parents' basement

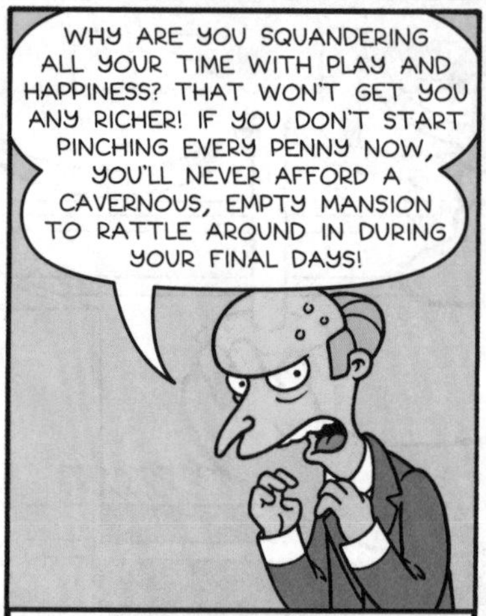
WHY ARE YOU SQUANDERING ALL YOUR TIME WITH PLAY AND HAPPINESS? THAT WON'T GET YOU ANY RICHER! IF YOU DON'T START PINCHING EVERY PENNY NOW, YOU'LL NEVER AFFORD A CAVERNOUS, EMPTY MANSION TO RATTLE AROUND IN DURING YOUR FINAL DAYS!

Type: Millionaire Doofus
Latin Name: Greedae Consumicus
Habitat: Country clubs, manor houses, mausoleums that resemble manor houses

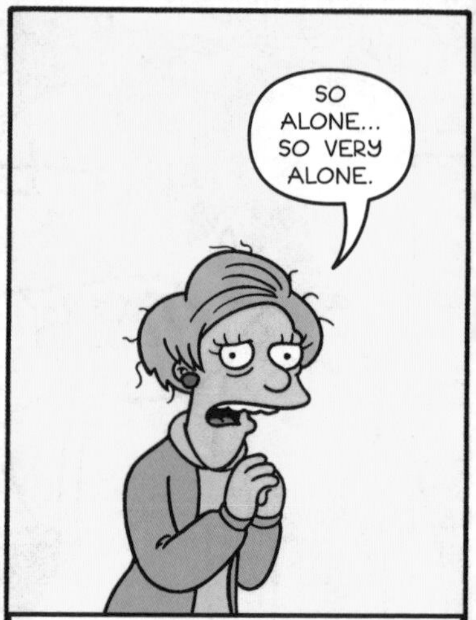
SO ALONE... SO VERY ALONE.

Type: Ding-dong Divorcée
Latin Name: Spinsterus Oldmaidicus
Habitat: Singles bars, internet dating chat rooms, one bedroom apartments

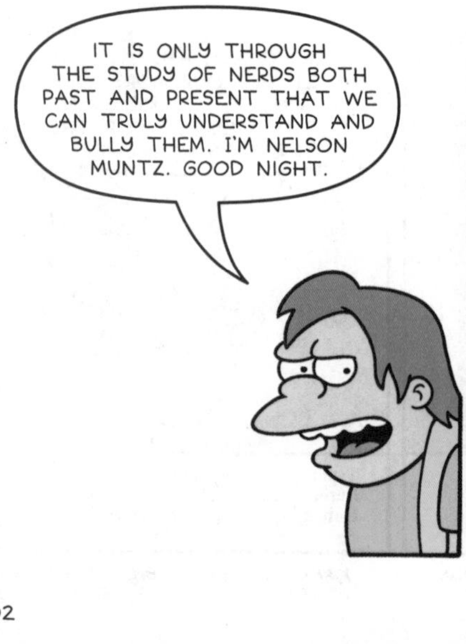
IT IS ONLY THROUGH THE STUDY OF NERDS BOTH PAST AND PRESENT THAT WE CAN TRULY UNDERSTAND AND BULLY THEM. I'M NELSON MUNTZ. GOOD NIGHT.

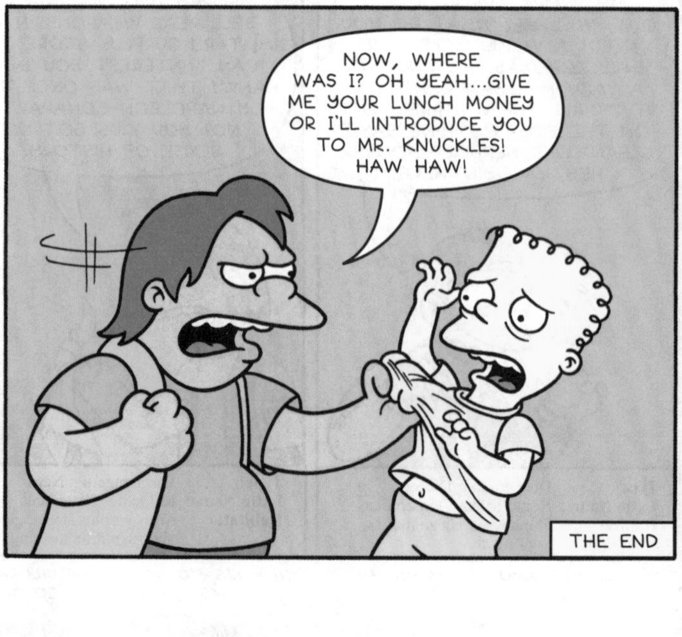
NOW, WHERE WAS I? OH YEAH...GIVE ME YOUR LUNCH MONEY OR I'LL INTRODUCE YOU TO MR. KNUCKLES! HAW HAW!
THE END

SHERRI & TERRI
in
THE KISS OF BLECCH!

MILHOUSE! YOU GOTTA HIDE ME!

WHAT'S WRONG? DID YOU FILL SKINNER'S CAR WITH OATMEAL AGAIN? THAT WAS A CLASSIC!

LISTEN TO ME! YOU'VE GOT TO HELP ME HIDE! IT'S A MATTER OF LIFE AND DEATH!

WHY? WHAT HAPPENED? ARE ZOMBIES ATTACKING US?

WORSE!

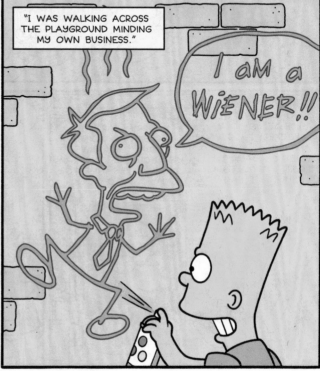

"I WAS WALKING ACROSS THE PLAYGROUND MINDING MY OWN BUSINESS."

I am a WIENER!!

TONY DIGEROLAMO
SCRIPT

JASON HO
PENCILS

MIKE ROTE
INKS

ART VILLANUEVA
COLORS

KAREN BATES
LETTERS

BILL MORRISON
EDITOR

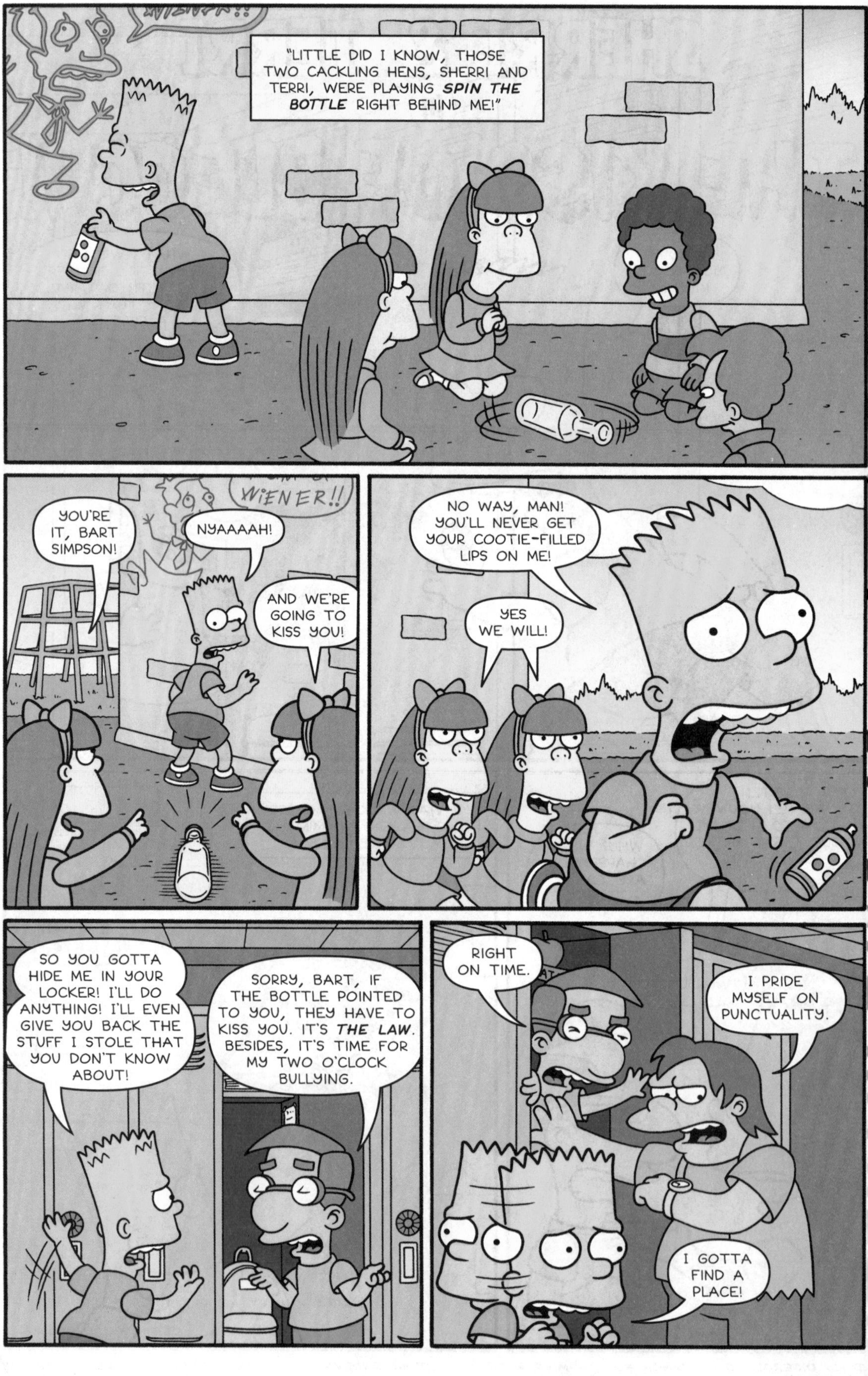
"LITTLE DID I KNOW, THOSE TWO CACKLING HENS, SHERRI AND TERRI, WERE PLAYING SPIN THE BOTTLE RIGHT BEHIND ME!"
YOU'RE IT, BART SIMPSON!
NYAAAAH!
AND WE'RE GOING TO KISS YOU!
WIENER!!
NO WAY, MAN! YOU'LL NEVER GET YOUR COOTIE-FILLED LIPS ON ME!
YES WE WILL!
SO YOU GOTTA HIDE ME IN YOUR LOCKER! I'LL DO ANYTHING! I'LL EVEN GIVE YOU BACK THE STUFF I STOLE THAT YOU DON'T KNOW ABOUT!
SORRY, BART, IF THE BOTTLE POINTED TO YOU, THEY HAVE TO KISS YOU. IT'S THE LAW. BESIDES, IT'S TIME FOR MY TWO O'CLOCK BULLYING.
RIGHT ON TIME.
I PRIDE MYSELF ON PUNCTUALITY.
I GOTTA FIND A PLACE!

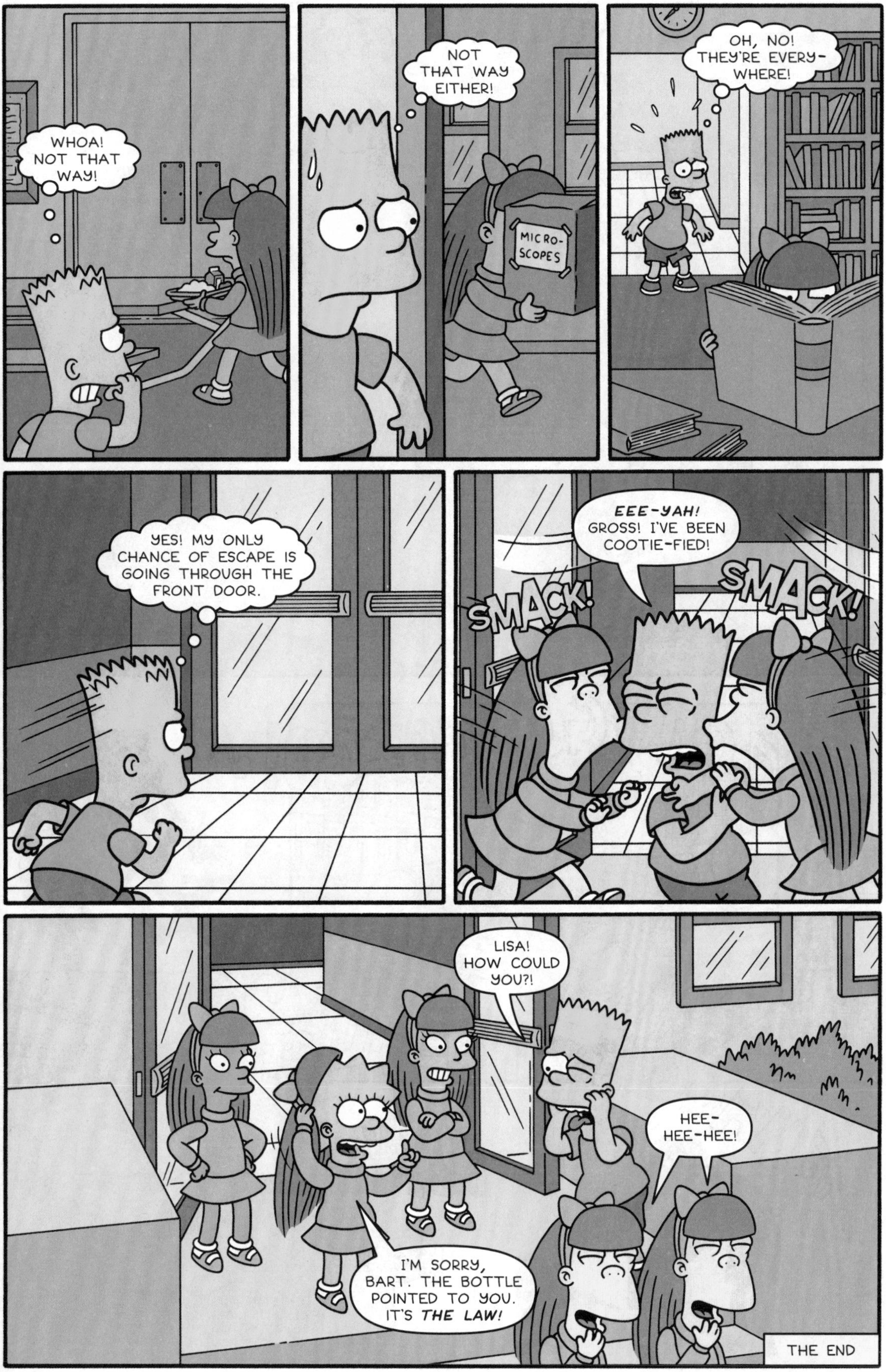
WHOA! NOT THAT WAY!
NOT THAT WAY EITHER!
MICRO-SCOPES
OH, NO! THEY'RE EVERY-WHERE!
YES! MY ONLY CHANCE OF ESCAPE IS GOING THROUGH THE FRONT DOOR.
SMACK!
EEE-YAH! GROSS! I'VE BEEN COOTIE-FIED!
SMACK!
LISA! HOW COULD YOU?!
HEE-HEE-HEE!
I'M SORRY, BART. THE BOTTLE POINTED TO YOU. IT'S THE LAW!
THE END

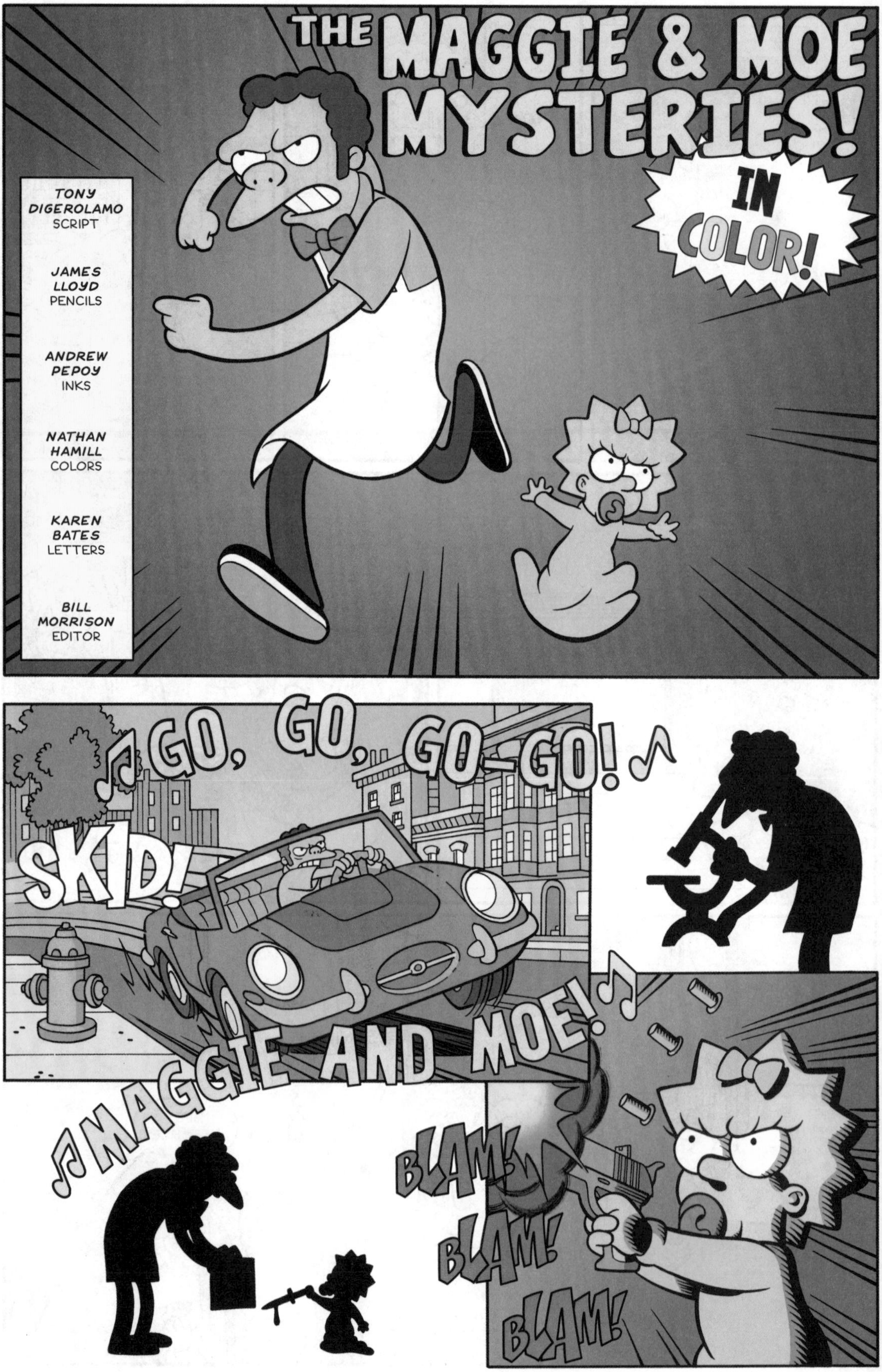
THE MAGGIE & MOE MYSTERIES!
IN COLOR!
TONY DIGEROLAMO SCRIPT
JAMES LLOYD PENCILS
ANDREW PEPOY INKS
NATHAN HAMILL COLORS
KAREN BATES LETTERS
BILL MORRISON EDITOR
GO, GO, GO-GO!
SKID!
MAGGIE AND MOE!
BLAM!
BLAM!
BLAM!

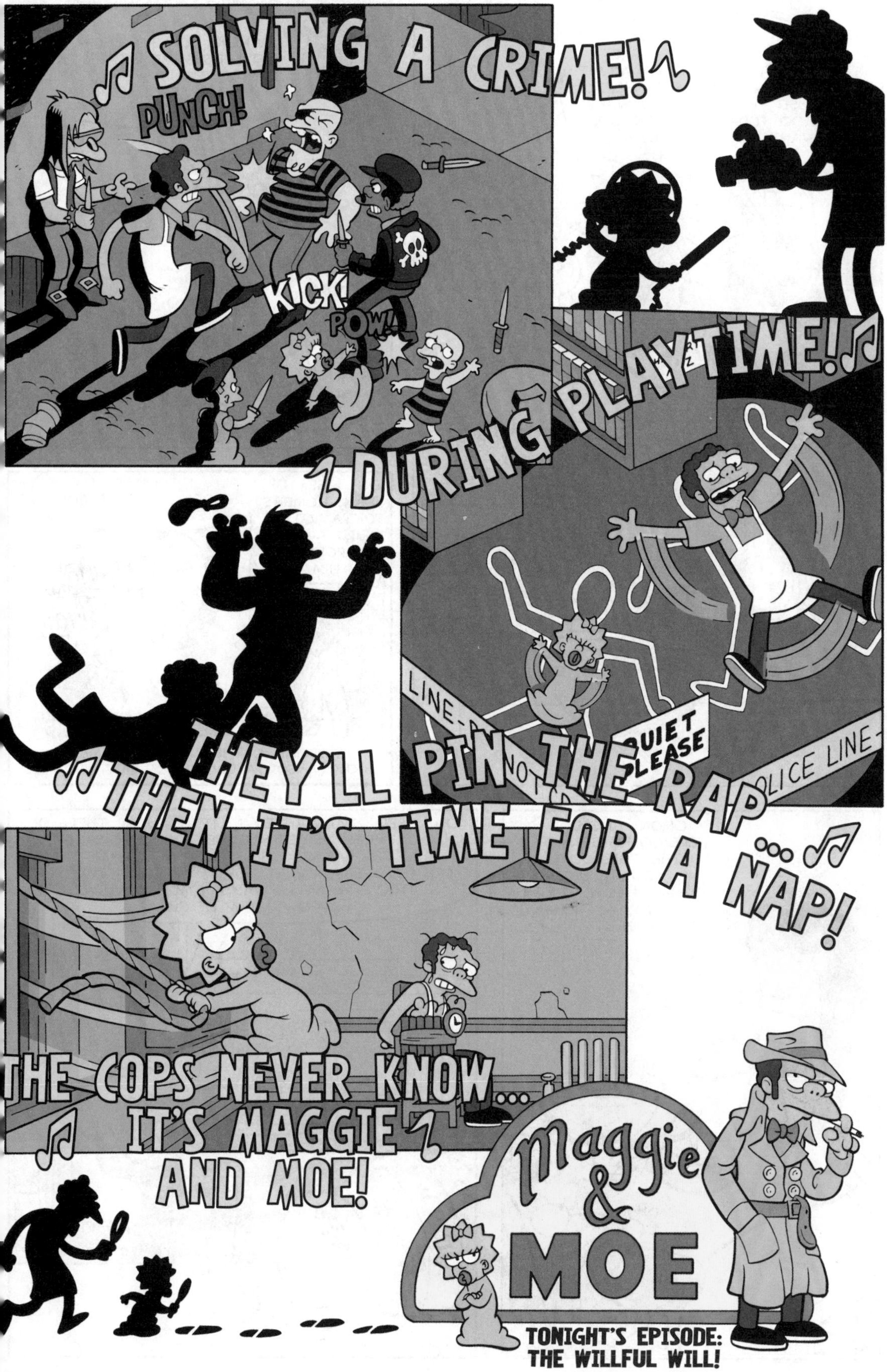

SOLVING A CRIME!
PUNCH!
KICK!
POW!
DURING PLAYTIME!
THEY'LL PIN THE RAP
THEN IT'S TIME FOR A NAP!
QUIET PLEASE
POLICE LINE
LINE
THE COPS NEVER KNOW...
IT'S MAGGIE
AND MOE!
Maggie & MOE
TONIGHT'S EPISODE:
THE WILLFUL WILL!

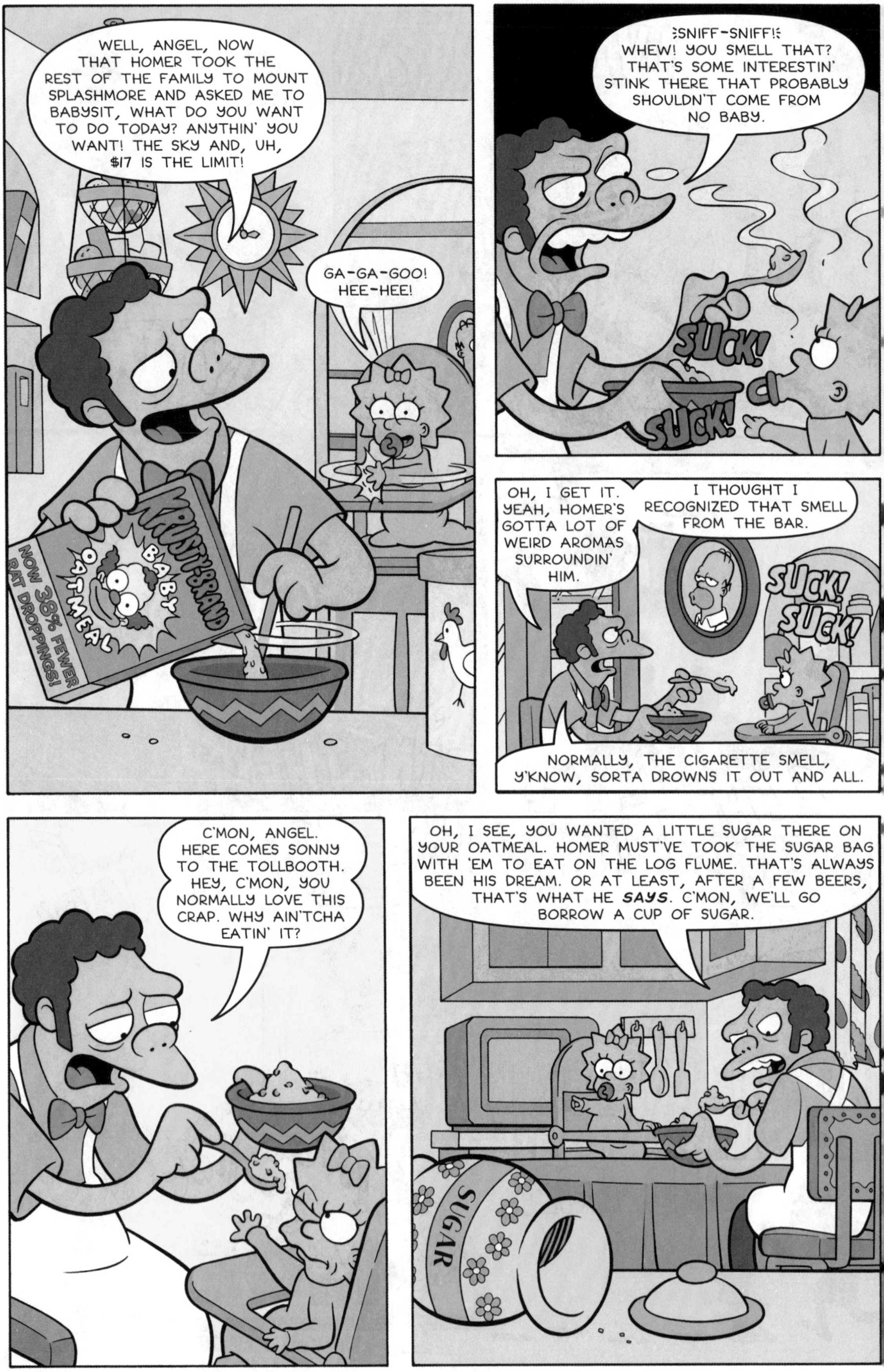

WELL, ANGEL, NOW THAT HOMER TOOK THE REST OF THE FAMILY TO MOUNT SPLASHMORE AND ASKED ME TO BABYSIT, WHAT DO YOU WANT TO DO TODAY? ANYTHIN' YOU WANT! THE SKY AND, UH, $17 IS THE LIMIT!
GA-GA-GOO! HEE-HEE!
KRUSTY-BRAND BABY OATMEAL
NOW 38% FEWER RAT DROPPINGS!
SNIFF-SNIFF! WHEW! YOU SMELL THAT? THAT'S SOME INTERESTIN' STINK THERE THAT PROBABLY SHOULDN'T COME FROM NO BABY.
SUCK!
SUCK!
OH, I GET IT. YEAH, HOMER'S GOTTA LOT OF WEIRD AROMAS SURROUNDIN' HIM.
I THOUGHT I RECOGNIZED THAT SMELL FROM THE BAR.
SUCK! SUCK!
NORMALLY, THE CIGARETTE SMELL, Y'KNOW, SORTA DROWNS IT OUT AND ALL.
C'MON, ANGEL. HERE COMES SONNY TO THE TOLLBOOTH. HEY, C'MON, YOU NORMALLY LOVE THIS CRAP. WHY AIN'TCHA EATIN' IT?
OH, I SEE, YOU WANTED A LITTLE SUGAR THERE ON YOUR OATMEAL. HOMER MUST'VE TOOK THE SUGAR BAG WITH 'EM TO EAT ON THE LOG FLUME. THAT'S ALWAYS BEEN HIS DREAM. OR AT LEAST, AFTER A FEW BEERS, THAT'S WHAT HE SAYS. C'MON, WE'LL GO BORROW A CUP OF SUGAR.
SUGAR

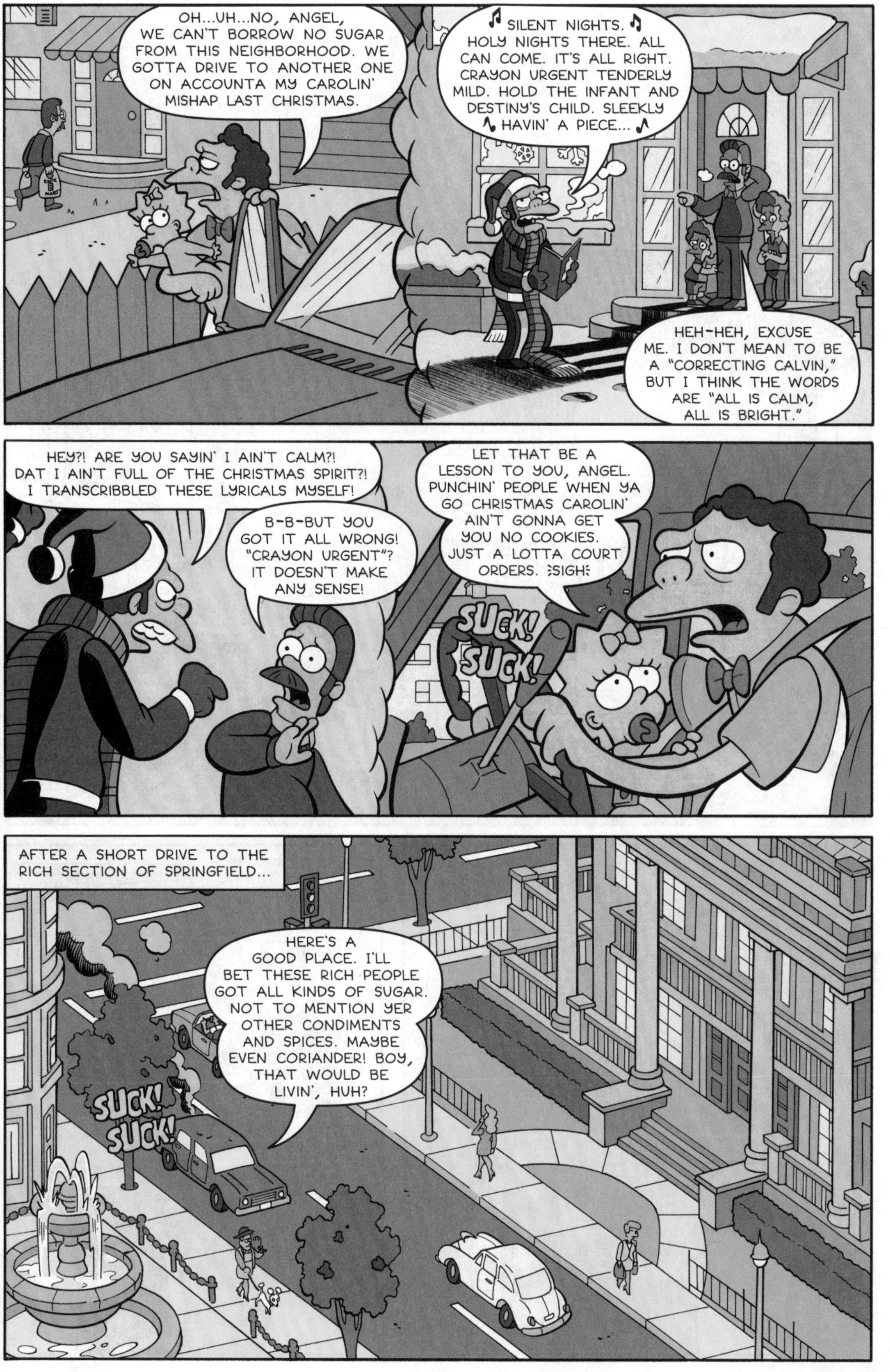

OH...UH...NO, ANGEL, WE CAN'T BORROW NO SUGAR FROM THIS NEIGHBORHOOD. WE GOTTA DRIVE TO ANOTHER ONE ON ACCOUNTA MY CAROLIN' MISHAP LAST CHRISTMAS.
♪ SILENT NIGHTS. ♪ HOLY NIGHTS THERE. ALL CAN COME. IT'S ALL RIGHT. CRAYON URGENT TENDERLY MILD. HOLD THE INFANT AND DESTINY'S CHILD. SLEEKLY ♪ HAVIN' A PIECE... ♪
HEH-HEH, EXCUSE ME. I DON'T MEAN TO BE A "CORRECTING CALVIN," BUT I THINK THE WORDS ARE "ALL IS CALM, ALL IS BRIGHT."
HEY?! ARE YOU SAYIN' I AIN'T CALM?! DAT I AIN'T FULL OF THE CHRISTMAS SPIRIT?! I TRANSCRIBBLED THESE LYRICALS MYSELF!
B-B-BUT YOU GOT IT ALL WRONG! "CRAYON URGENT"? IT DOESN'T MAKE ANY SENSE!
LET THAT BE A LESSON TO YOU, ANGEL. PUNCHIN' PEOPLE WHEN YA GO CHRISTMAS CAROLIN' AIN'T GONNA GET YOU NO COOKIES. JUST A LOTTA COURT ORDERS. ≷SIGH≶
SUCK! SUCK!
AFTER A SHORT DRIVE TO THE RICH SECTION OF SPRINGFIELD...
HERE'S A GOOD PLACE. I'LL BET THESE RICH PEOPLE GOT ALL KINDS OF SUGAR. NOT TO MENTION YER OTHER CONDIMENTS AND SPICES. MAYBE EVEN CORIANDER! BOY, THAT WOULD BE LIVIN', HUH?
SUCK! SUCK!

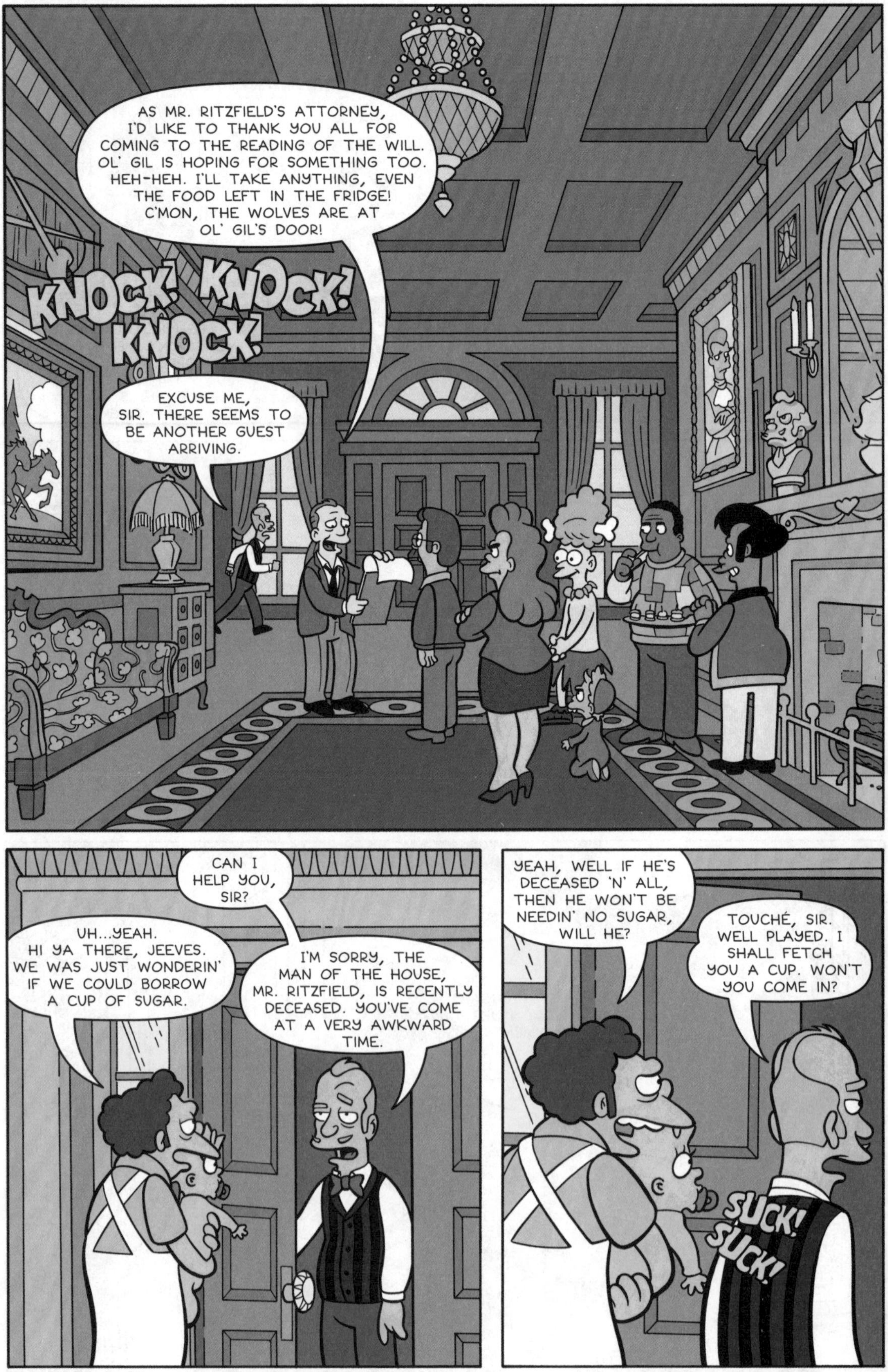
AS MR. RITZFIELD'S ATTORNEY, I'D LIKE TO THANK YOU ALL FOR COMING TO THE READING OF THE WILL. OL' GIL IS HOPING FOR SOMETHING TOO. HEH-HEH. I'LL TAKE ANYTHING, EVEN THE FOOD LEFT IN THE FRIDGE! C'MON, THE WOLVES ARE AT OL' GIL'S DOOR!
KNOCK! KNOCK! KNOCK!
EXCUSE ME, SIR. THERE SEEMS TO BE ANOTHER GUEST ARRIVING.
CAN I HELP YOU, SIR?
UH...YEAH. HI YA THERE, JEEVES. WE WAS JUST WONDERIN' IF WE COULD BORROW A CUP OF SUGAR.
I'M SORRY, THE MAN OF THE HOUSE, MR. RITZFIELD, IS RECENTLY DECEASED. YOU'VE COME AT A VERY AWKWARD TIME.
YEAH, WELL IF HE'S DECEASED 'N' ALL, THEN HE WON'T BE NEEDIN' NO SUGAR, WILL HE?
TOUCHÉ, SIR. WELL PLAYED. I SHALL FETCH YOU A CUP. WON'T YOU COME IN?
SUCK! SUCK!

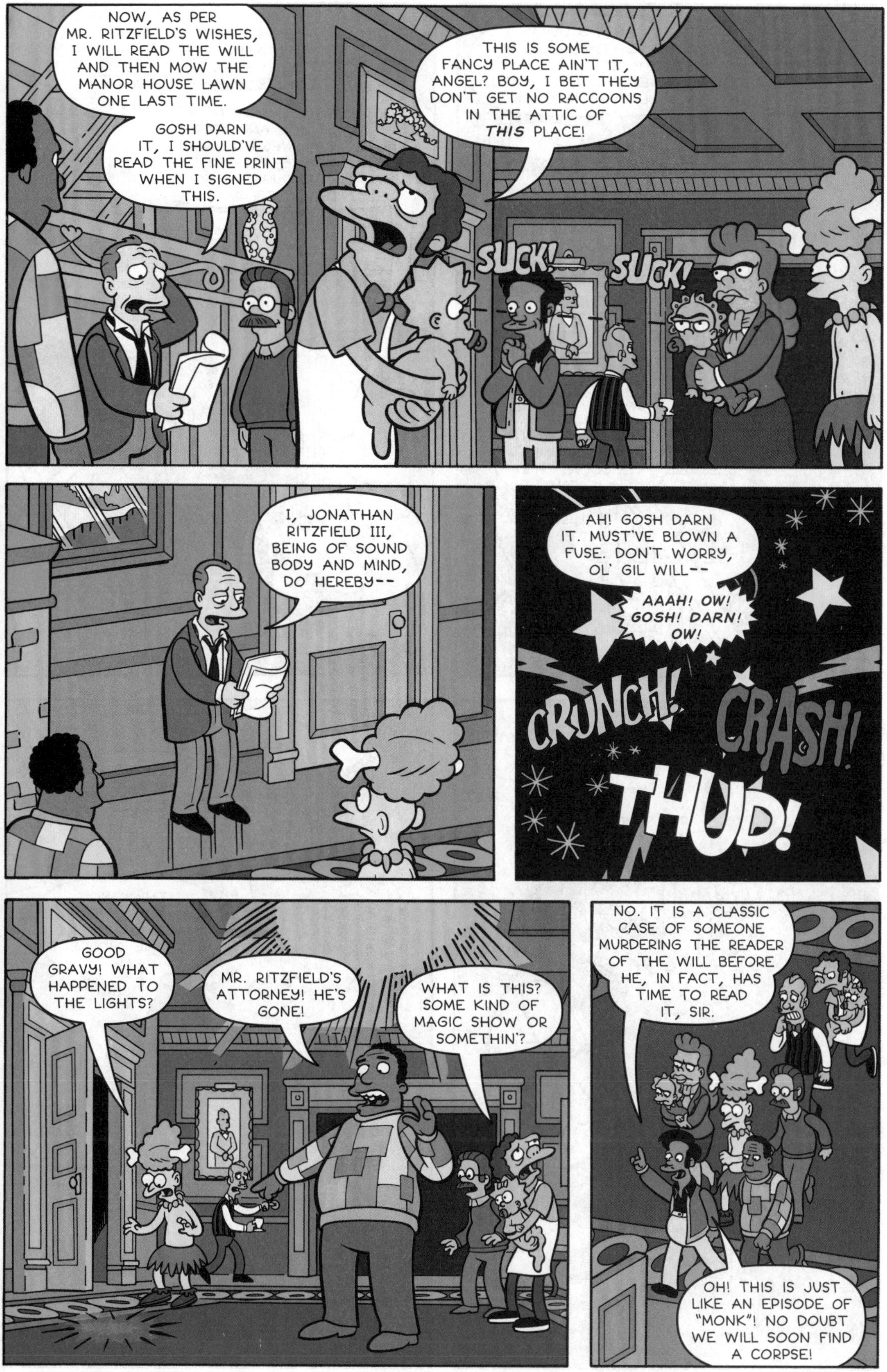
NOW, AS PER MR. RITZFIELD'S WISHES, I WILL READ THE WILL AND THEN MOW THE MANOR HOUSE LAWN ONE LAST TIME.
GOSH DARN IT, I SHOULD'VE READ THE FINE PRINT WHEN I SIGNED THIS.
THIS IS SOME FANCY PLACE AIN'T IT, ANGEL? BOY, I BET THEY DON'T GET NO RACCOONS IN THE ATTIC OF *THIS* PLACE!
SUCK!
SUCK!
I, JONATHAN RITZFIELD III, BEING OF SOUND BODY AND MIND, DO HEREBY--
AH! GOSH DARN IT. MUST'VE BLOWN A FUSE. DON'T WORRY, OL' GIL WILL--
AAAH! OW! GOSH! DARN! OW!
CRUNCH!
CRASH!
THUD!
GOOD GRAVY! WHAT HAPPENED TO THE LIGHTS?
MR. RITZFIELD'S ATTORNEY! HE'S GONE!
WHAT IS THIS? SOME KIND OF MAGIC SHOW OR SOMETHIN'?
NO. IT IS A CLASSIC CASE OF SOMEONE MURDERING THE READER OF THE WILL BEFORE HE, IN FACT, HAS TIME TO READ IT, SIR.
OH! THIS IS JUST LIKE AN EPISODE OF "MONK"! NO DOUBT WE WILL SOON FIND A CORPSE!

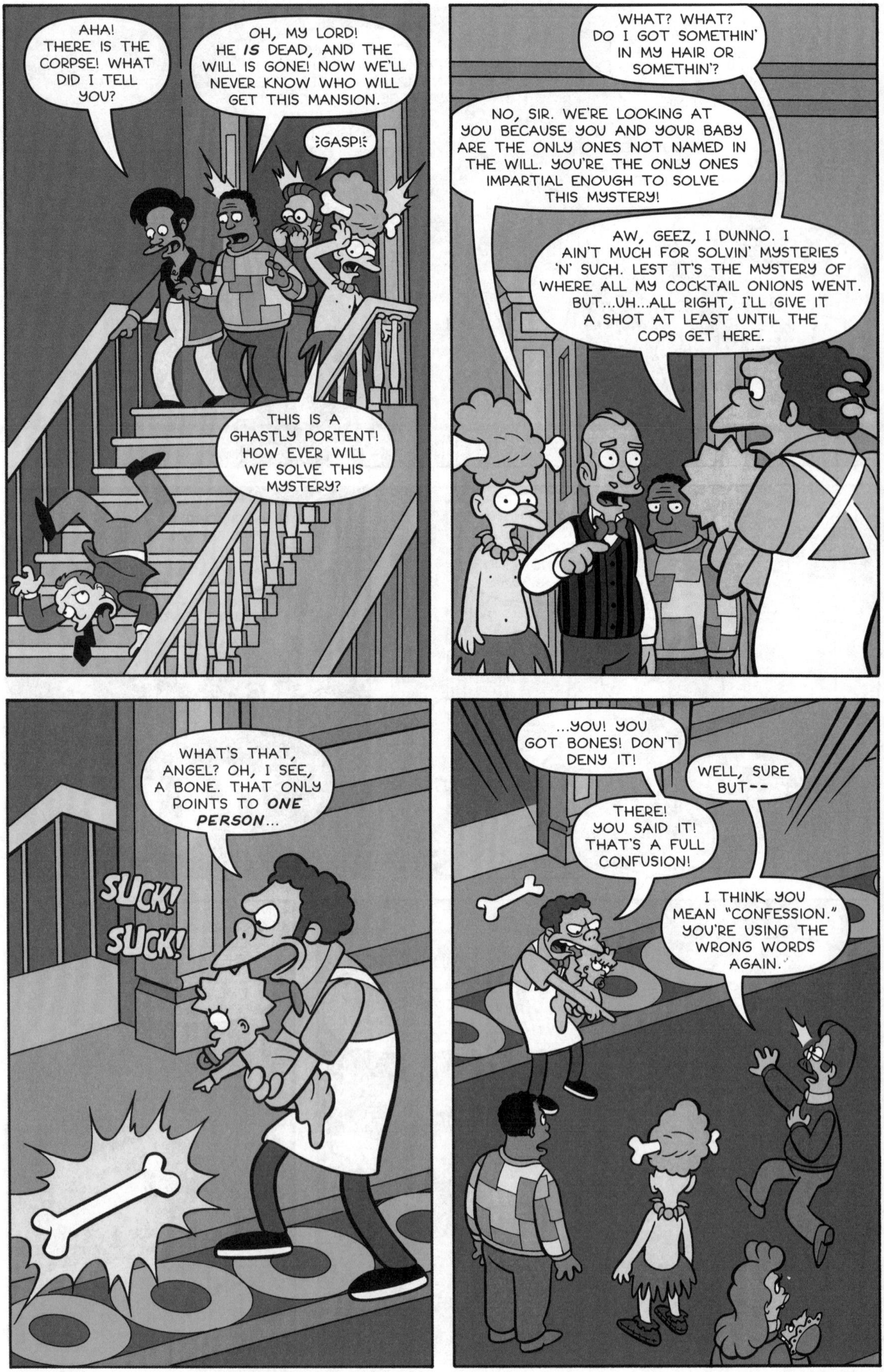
AHA! THERE IS THE CORPSE! WHAT DID I TELL YOU?
OH, MY LORD! HE *IS* DEAD, AND THE WILL IS GONE! NOW WE'LL NEVER KNOW WHO WILL GET THIS MANSION.
GASP!
THIS IS A GHASTLY PORTENT! HOW EVER WILL WE SOLVE THIS MYSTERY?
WHAT? WHAT? DO I GOT SOMETHIN' IN MY HAIR OR SOMETHIN'?
NO, SIR. WE'RE LOOKING AT YOU BECAUSE YOU AND YOUR BABY ARE THE ONLY ONES NOT NAMED IN THE WILL. YOU'RE THE ONLY ONES IMPARTIAL ENOUGH TO SOLVE THIS MYSTERY!
AW, GEEZ, I DUNNO. I AIN'T MUCH FOR SOLVIN' MYSTERIES 'N' SUCH. LEST IT'S THE MYSTERY OF WHERE ALL MY COCKTAIL ONIONS WENT. BUT...UH...ALL RIGHT, I'LL GIVE IT A SHOT AT LEAST UNTIL THE COPS GET HERE.
WHAT'S THAT, ANGEL? OH, I SEE, A BONE. THAT ONLY POINTS TO ***ONE PERSON***...
SUCK! SUCK!
...YOU! YOU GOT BONES! DON'T DENY IT!
WELL, SURE BUT--
THERE! YOU SAID IT! THAT'S A FULL CONFUSION!
I THINK YOU MEAN "CONFESSION." YOU'RE USING THE WRONG WORDS AGAIN.

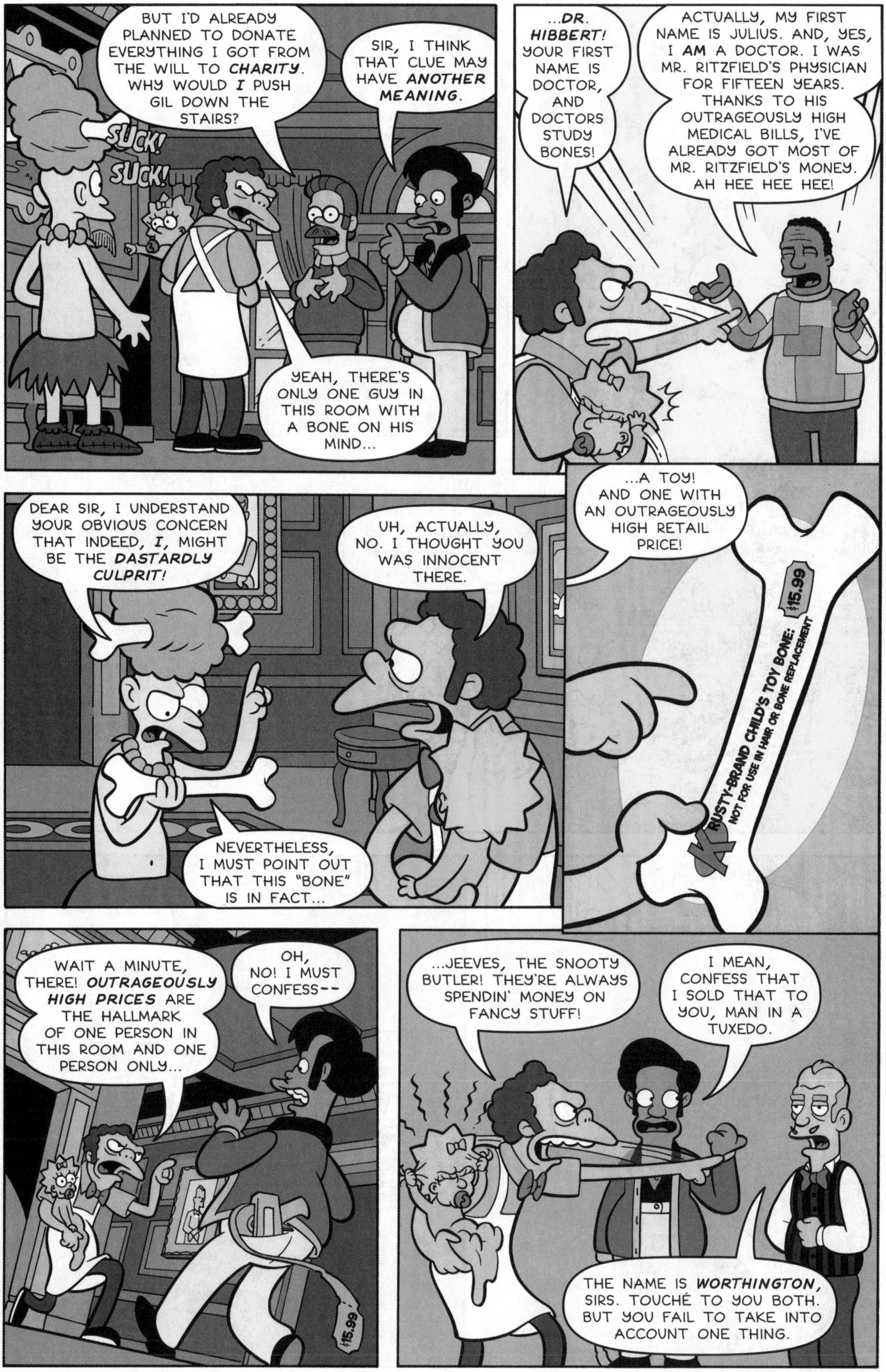

BUT I'D ALREADY PLANNED TO DONATE EVERYTHING I GOT FROM THE WILL TO CHARITY. WHY WOULD I PUSH GIL DOWN THE STAIRS?
SUCK! SUCK!
SIR, I THINK THAT CLUE MAY HAVE ANOTHER MEANING.
YEAH, THERE'S ONLY ONE GUY IN THIS ROOM WITH A BONE ON HIS MIND...
...DR. HIBBERT! YOUR FIRST NAME IS DOCTOR, AND DOCTORS STUDY BONES!
ACTUALLY, MY FIRST NAME IS JULIUS. AND, YES, I AM A DOCTOR. I WAS MR. RITZFIELD'S PHYSICIAN FOR FIFTEEN YEARS. THANKS TO HIS OUTRAGEOUSLY HIGH MEDICAL BILLS, I'VE ALREADY GOT MOST OF MR. RITZFIELD'S MONEY. AH HEE HEE HEE!
DEAR SIR, I UNDERSTAND YOUR OBVIOUS CONCERN THAT INDEED, I, MIGHT BE THE DASTARDLY CULPRIT!
UH, ACTUALLY, NO. I THOUGHT YOU WAS INNOCENT THERE.
NEVERTHELESS, I MUST POINT OUT THAT THIS "BONE" IS IN FACT...
...A TOY! AND ONE WITH AN OUTRAGEOUSLY HIGH RETAIL PRICE!
$15.99
KRUSTY-BRAND CHILD'S TOY BONE:
NOT FOR USE IN HAIR OR BONE REPLACEMENT
WAIT A MINUTE, THERE! OUTRAGEOUSLY HIGH PRICES ARE THE HALLMARK OF ONE PERSON IN THIS ROOM AND ONE PERSON ONLY...
OH, NO! I MUST CONFESS--
$15.99
...JEEVES, THE SNOOTY BUTLER! THEY'RE ALWAYS SPENDIN' MONEY ON FANCY STUFF!
I MEAN, CONFESS THAT I SOLD THAT TO YOU, MAN IN A TUXEDO.
THE NAME IS WORTHINGTON, SIRS. TOUCHÉ TO YOU BOTH. BUT YOU FAIL TO TAKE INTO ACCOUNT ONE THING.

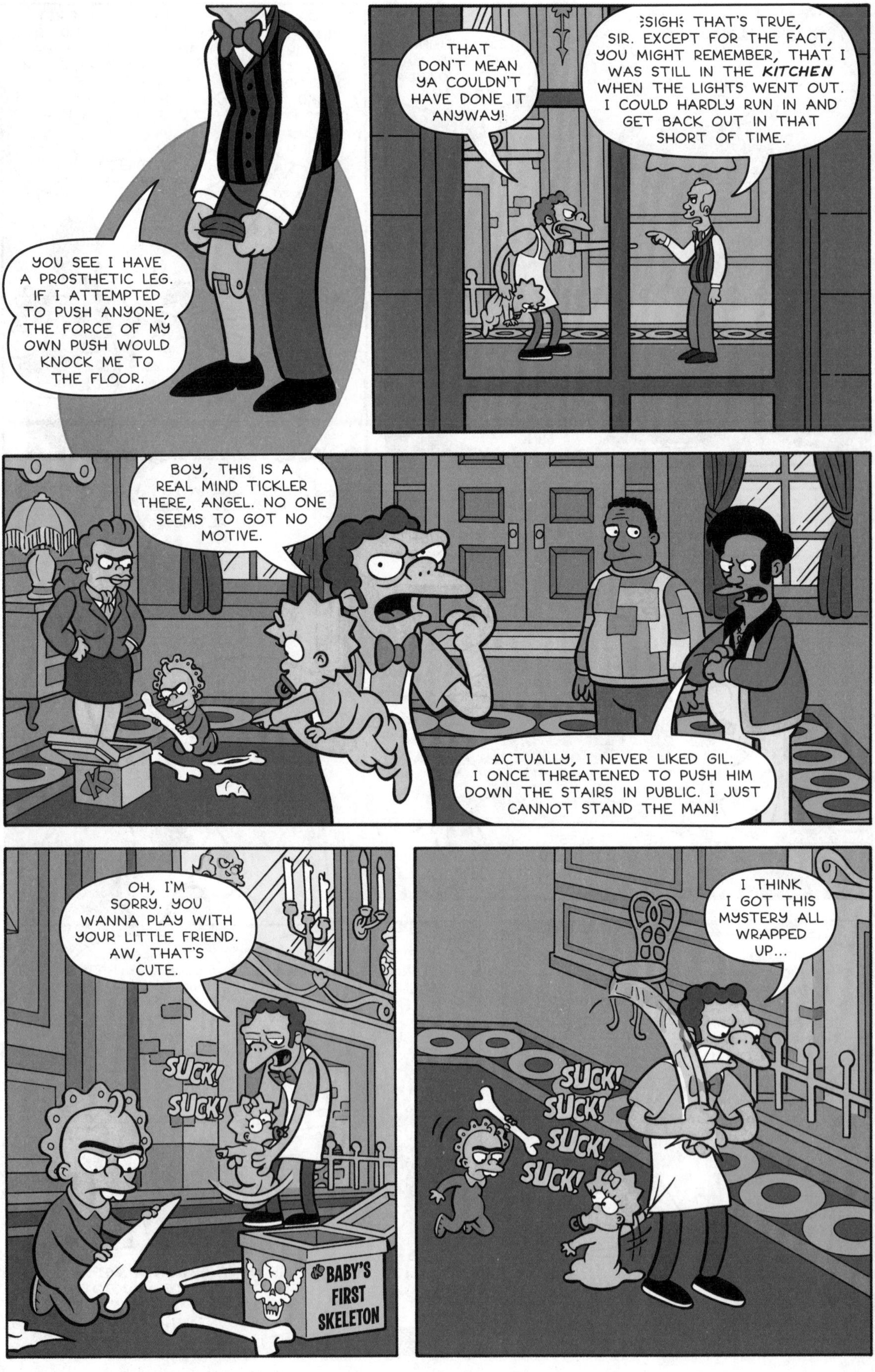
THAT DON'T MEAN YA COULDN'T HAVE DONE IT ANYWAY!
:SIGH: THAT'S TRUE, SIR. EXCEPT FOR THE FACT, YOU MIGHT REMEMBER, THAT I WAS STILL IN THE **KITCHEN** WHEN THE LIGHTS WENT OUT. I COULD HARDLY RUN IN AND GET BACK OUT IN THAT SHORT OF TIME.
YOU SEE I HAVE A PROSTHETIC LEG. IF I ATTEMPTED TO PUSH ANYONE, THE FORCE OF MY OWN PUSH WOULD KNOCK ME TO THE FLOOR.
BOY, THIS IS A REAL MIND TICKLER THERE, ANGEL. NO ONE SEEMS TO GOT NO MOTIVE.
ACTUALLY, I NEVER LIKED GIL. I ONCE THREATENED TO PUSH HIM DOWN THE STAIRS IN PUBLIC. I JUST CANNOT STAND THE MAN!
OH, I'M SORRY. YOU WANNA PLAY WITH YOUR LITTLE FRIEND. AW, THAT'S CUTE.
SUCK! SUCK!
BABY'S FIRST SKELETON
I THINK I GOT THIS MYSTERY ALL WRAPPED UP...
SUCK! SUCK! SUCK! SUCK!

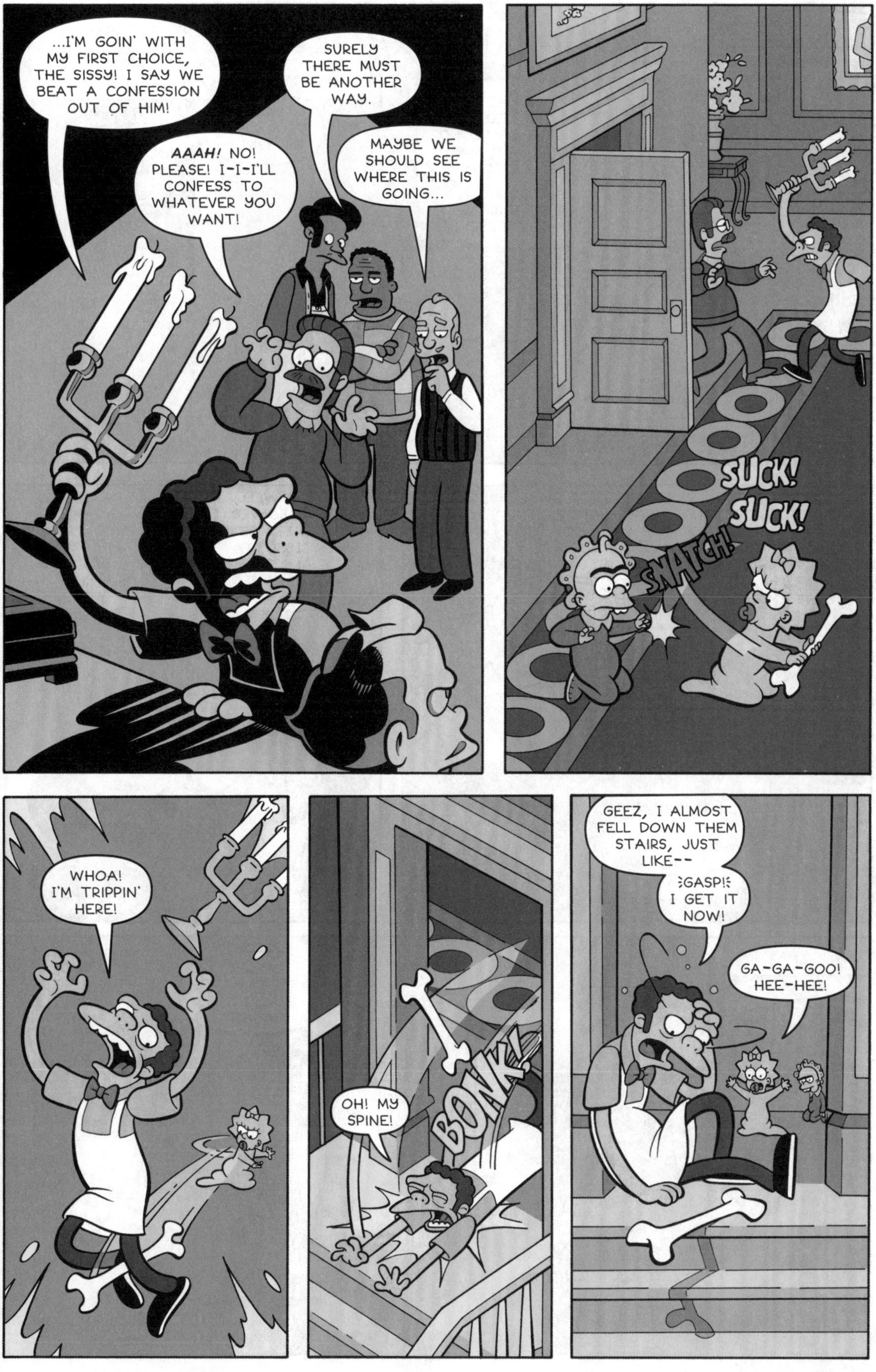
...I'M GOIN' WITH MY FIRST CHOICE, THE SISSY! I SAY WE BEAT A CONFESSION OUT OF HIM!
SURELY THERE MUST BE ANOTHER WAY.
AAAH! NO! PLEASE! I-I-I'LL CONFESS TO WHATEVER YOU WANT!
MAYBE WE SHOULD SEE WHERE THIS IS GOING...
SUCK!
SUCK!
SNATCH!
WHOA! I'M TRIPPIN' HERE!
BONK!
OH! MY SPINE!
GEEZ, I ALMOST FELL DOWN THEM STAIRS, JUST LIKE--
GASP! I GET IT NOW!
GA-GA-GOO! HEE-HEE!

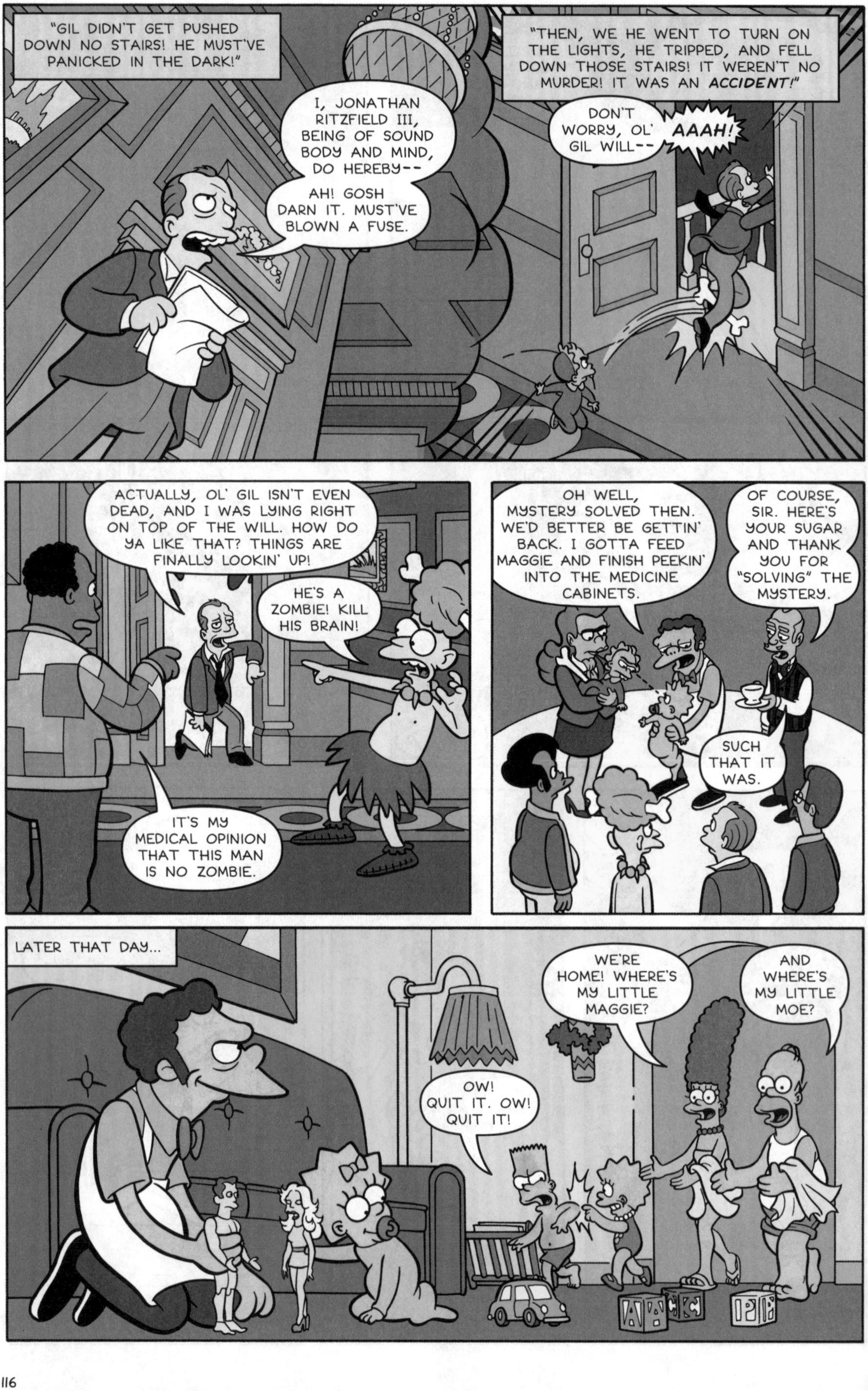
"GIL DIDN'T GET PUSHED DOWN NO STAIRS! HE MUST'VE PANICKED IN THE DARK!"
I, JONATHAN RITZFIELD III, BEING OF SOUND BODY AND MIND, DO HEREBY--
AH! GOSH DARN IT. MUST'VE BLOWN A FUSE.
"THEN, WE HE WENT TO TURN ON THE LIGHTS, HE TRIPPED, AND FELL DOWN THOSE STAIRS! IT WEREN'T NO MURDER! IT WAS AN ACCIDENT!"
DON'T WORRY, OL' GIL WILL--
AAAH!
ACTUALLY, OL' GIL ISN'T EVEN DEAD, AND I WAS LYING RIGHT ON TOP OF THE WILL. HOW DO YA LIKE THAT? THINGS ARE FINALLY LOOKIN' UP!
HE'S A ZOMBIE! KILL HIS BRAIN!
IT'S MY MEDICAL OPINION THAT THIS MAN IS NO ZOMBIE.
OH WELL, MYSTERY SOLVED THEN. WE'D BETTER BE GETTIN' BACK. I GOTTA FEED MAGGIE AND FINISH PEEKIN' INTO THE MEDICINE CABINETS.
OF COURSE, SIR. HERE'S YOUR SUGAR AND THANK YOU FOR "SOLVING" THE MYSTERY.
SUCH THAT IT WAS.
LATER THAT DAY...
WE'RE HOME! WHERE'S MY LITTLE MAGGIE?
AND WHERE'S MY LITTLE MOE?
OW! QUIT IT. OW! QUIT IT!

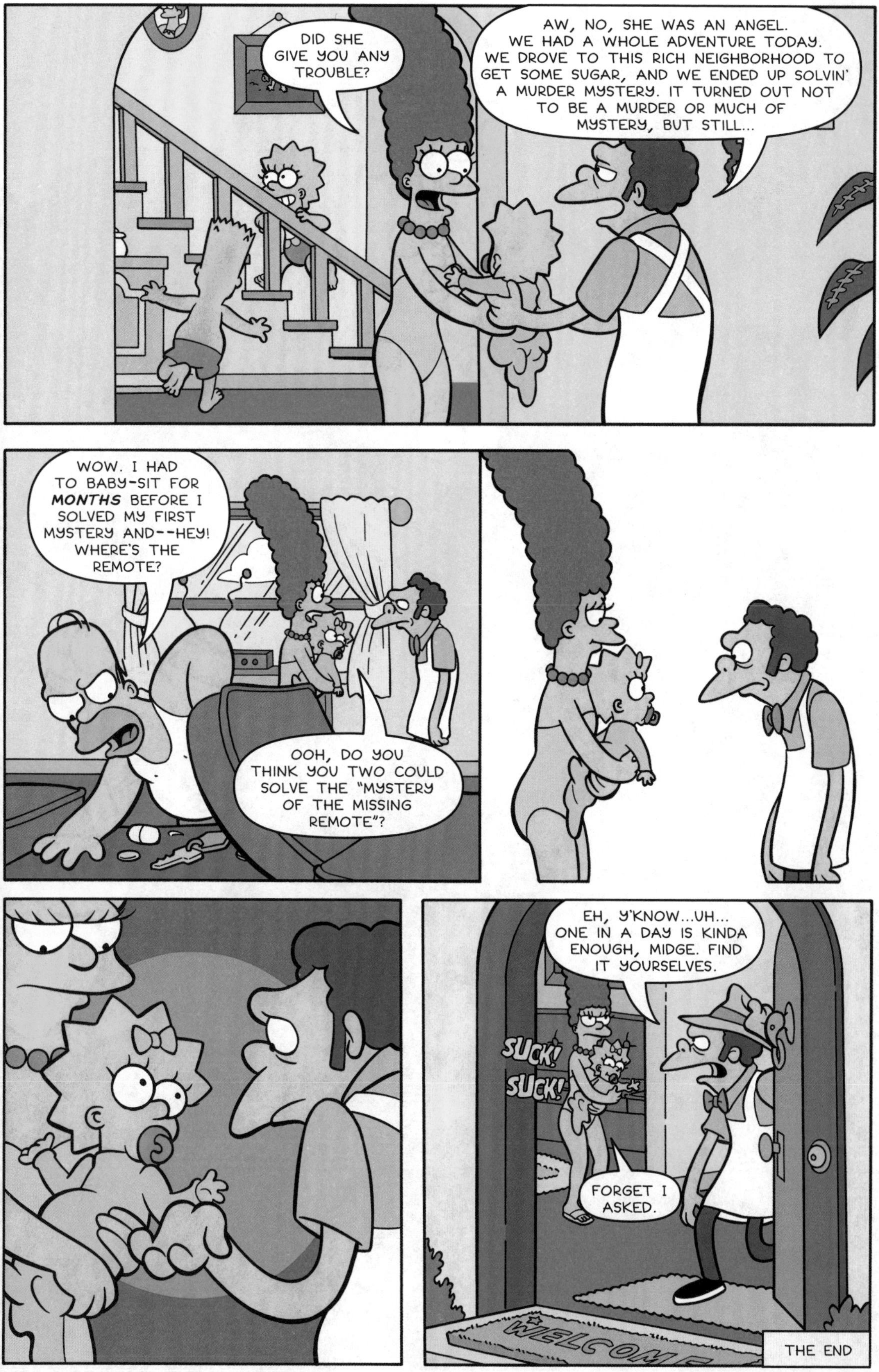
DID SHE GIVE YOU ANY TROUBLE?
AW, NO, SHE WAS AN ANGEL. WE HAD A WHOLE ADVENTURE TODAY. WE DROVE TO THIS RICH NEIGHBORHOOD TO GET SOME SUGAR, AND WE ENDED UP SOLVIN' A MURDER MYSTERY. IT TURNED OUT NOT TO BE A MURDER OR MUCH OF MYSTERY, BUT STILL...
WOW. I HAD TO BABY-SIT FOR **MONTHS** BEFORE I SOLVED MY FIRST MYSTERY AND--HEY! WHERE'S THE REMOTE?
OOH, DO YOU THINK YOU TWO COULD SOLVE THE "MYSTERY OF THE MISSING REMOTE"?
EH, Y'KNOW...UH... ONE IN A DAY IS KINDA ENOUGH, MIDGE. FIND IT YOURSELVES.
SUCK! SUCK!
FORGET I ASKED.
WELCOME
THE END

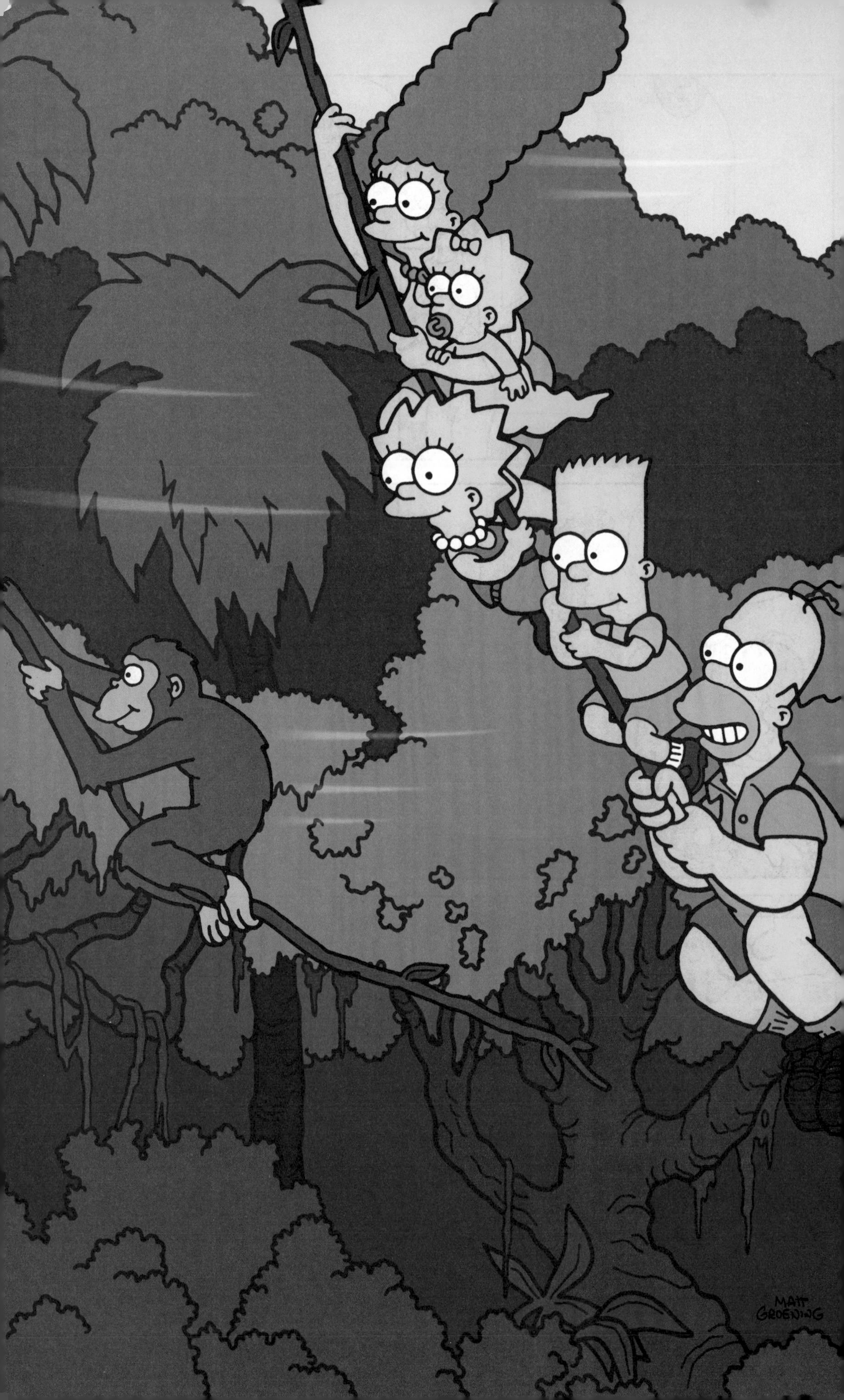
MATT GROENING

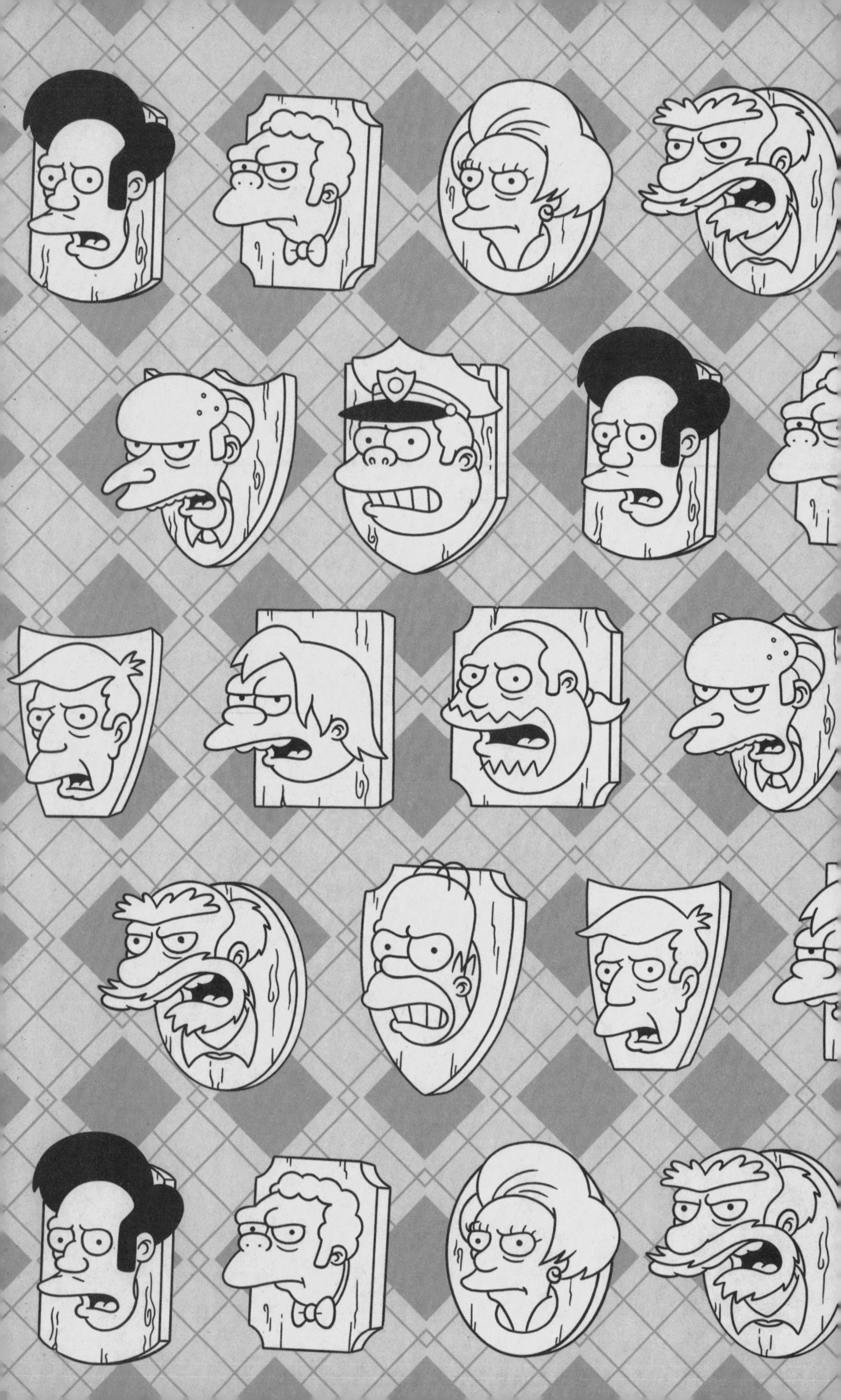